Mastering Android Game Development

Master game development with the Android SDK
to develop highly interactive and amazing games

Raul Portales

[PACKT] open source
PUBLISHING
community experience distilled

BIRMINGHAM - MUMBAI

Mastering Android Game Development

First published: June 2015

Production reference: 1250615

Published by Packt Publishing Ltd.
Livery Place
35 Livery Street
Birmingham B3 2PB, UK.

ISBN 978-1-78355-177-4

www.packtpub.com

Credits

Author
Raul Portales

Reviewers
Sergio Viudes Carbonell
Antonio Hernández Niñirola

Commissioning Editor
Nadeem N. Bagban

Acquisition Editor
Harsha Bharwani

Content Development Editor
Arun Nadar

Technical Editor
Ruchi Desai

Copy Editors
Stephen Copestake
Akshata Lobo

Project Coordinator
Nikhil Nair

Proofreader
Safis Editing

Indexer
Monica Ajmera Mehta

Graphics
Abhinash Sahu

Production Coordinator
Conidon Miranda

Cover Work
Conidon Miranda

About the Author

Raul Portales is a software engineer who works as a contract consultant with Platty Soft. He cofounded the game studio The Pill Tree, which ran for a year and produced several titles that were featured by Google Play, including Chalk Ball and SpaceCat.

He has been a Google Developer Expert for Android since the start of 2015, and he loves public speaking. He has presented at several DroidCons and Game Developers conferences, talking about how to survive as an indie game developer.

At the moment, Raul lives in Dublin and you can easily find him collaborating with the local community on different meetups, especially the ones organized by GDG Dublin.

About the Reviewers

Sergio Viudes Carbonell is a 32-year-old developer from Elche (Spain). He has loved to play video games since his childhood days (since the ZX Spectrum was around). Also, he has drawn and composed electronic music as a hobby. Then, he started coding and studied computer engineering at the University of Alicante.

He started working as a software and web developer. But he always wanted to create video games. So, he founded Baviux and now Sergio, designing and developing mobile apps and games. He has reviewed the following books for Packt Publishing in the past:

- *AndEngine for Android Game Development Cookbook*
- *Learning AndEngine*
- *Mobile Game Design Essentials*
- *Mastering AndEngine Game Development*
- *Javascript Security*

I would like to thank Raul Portales for writing this book. Special thanks go to my wife, Estefanía, who encourages and supports me every day.

Antonio Hernández Niñirola is a European PhD candidate in software engineering in the last phase of his doctorate program. He has a BSc in computer science and a masters degree by the University of Murcia in Spain.

Currently located in San Francisco since May 2015, he is working as part of the Android development team at Yelp.

In the academic year 2013-14, he worked with the Department of Software Engineering in the Université Mohammed V in Rabat. This was a great opportunity to focus on his research on mobile usability and resulted in several academic papers for both JCR journals and CORE conferences.

He has also collaborated with Packt Publishing in the past as both author and reviewer. If you want to learn more advanced techniques on testing and security for Android, check out his book *Testing and Securing Android Studio Applications*, also published by Packt Publishing. If you are new to Android development, you can check these books he has reviewed: *Android Studio Application Development* and *Android Studio Essentials*.

For more information on him, visit his website (`http://www.ninirola.es`) and follow him on Twitter at `@hdezninirola`.

www.PacktPub.com

Support files, eBooks, discount offers, and more

For support files and downloads related to your book, please visit www.PacktPub.com.

Did you know that Packt offers eBook versions of every book published, with PDF and ePub files available? You can upgrade to the eBook version at www.PacktPub.com and as a print book customer, you are entitled to a discount on the eBook copy. Get in touch with us at service@packtpub.com for more details.

At www.PacktPub.com, you can also read a collection of free technical articles, sign up for a range of free newsletters and receive exclusive discounts and offers on Packt books and eBooks.

https://www2.packtpub.com/books/subscription/packtlib

Do you need instant solutions to your IT questions? PacktLib is Packt's online digital book library. Here, you can search, access, and read Packt's entire library of books.

Why subscribe?

- Fully searchable across every book published by Packt
- Copy and paste, print, and bookmark content
- On demand and accessible via a web browser

Free access for Packt account holders

If you have an account with Packt at www.PacktPub.com, you can use this to access PacktLib today and view 9 entirely free books. Simply use your login credentials for immediate access.

All your android are belong to us.

Table of Contents

Preface

Android is the most widespread Operating System and games are what people spend most time using on their phones. Video games have never been easier to make and distribute. Who would not want to make games for Android?

And on top of this, making games is fun!

You will build a real-time game from scratch using the Android SDK. Starting with the creation of a game engine and moving into handling user input, doing efficient drawing, implementing collision detection, playing sound effects, using animations, and so on. You will learn all the aspects of developing a game using a space shooter game as the example that will evolve with you throughout the chapters.

What this book covers

Chapter 1, Setting Up the Project, allows you to set up the project and will describe in which cases it makes sense to use the Android SDK for a game and in which cases it is best to use an external engine. We will create the top-level architecture of a game engine and study how it is different from the one of a typical app, explaining why there is an update thread and why it is separated from the input thread and also from the draw thread.

Chapter 2, Managing User Input, discusses how to read and process user input and how to make controls for our game, from making a virtual gamepad to evolving it as a virtual joystick to adding support for physical controllers. Finally, we'll introduce how to use sensors as input.

Chapter 3, Into the Draw Thread, explores how drawing on a canvas provides better performance. We will discuss the pros and cons of using a normal view versus a SurfaceView.

Chapter 4, Collision Detection, explains how to run and add a basic collision detection system to our game and shows how it fits inside the game engine.

Chapter 5, Particle Systems, helps us learn several uses of particle systems and we'll build one based on the Leonids library wherein a particle system is a big part of a game.

Chapter 6, Sound FX and Music, explores the different options to play sound effects and music in Android and we'll build a SoundManager to handle them since a game feels incomplete without sounds.

Chapter 7, Menus and Dialogs, explains techniques to use the same layouts across phones and tablets and learn how to make them work on both because a compelling UI requires nice menus and dialogs. Finally, since the dialogs available in the Android framework are quite limited, we'll see how we can create more complex dialogs.

Chapter 8, The Animation Framework, dives into the different ways Android offers to animate views and objects and what they can be used for, from frame-by-frame animations to view animations and property animators.

Chapter 9, Integrating Google Play Services, covers the tools that Google Play Services offers for game developers. We'll see the integration of achievements and leaderboards in detail, take an overview of events and quests, save games, and use turn-based and real-time multiplaying.

Chapter 10, To the Big Screen, explores the extra restrictions that games have when going to Android TV, mainly screen overcast and controller-based navigation and also extra options in the Manifest that are specific for Android TV.

Appendix, API Levels for Android Versions, lists all 22 API levels, from Base to Lollipop_MR1, along with the version code.

What you need for this book

For this book, you will need the latest version of Android Studio and the Android SDK for Lollipop or newer (API level 22) versions, which you can download using Android Studio.

Android Studio is a free tool that you can download from `https://developer.android.com/sdk/index.html` and it runs on Windows, Mac, and Linux.

It is advisable to have several Android devices for testing, but is not necessary. It is also advisable to have a Bluetooth game controller (which will become useful for any mobile game developer anyway), but it is not required.

Who this book is for

If you are an Android developer who wants to make games and doesn't want to learn a new third-party tool or engine, this book is for you. Make the journey of building a game from scratch to get insights into all the aspects of game development, from implementing your own engine to getting a game ready for Android TV, always with a hands-on approach.

Conventions

In this book, you will find a number of text styles that distinguish between different kinds of information. Here are some examples of these styles and an explanation of their meaning.

Code words in text, database table names, folder names, filenames, file extensions, pathnames, dummy URLs, user input, and Twitter handles are shown as follows: "It will be used intensively during onUpdate and onDraw."

A block of code is set as follows:

```
public void removeGameObject(final GameObject gameObject) {
  mObjectsToRemove.add(gameObject);
  mActivity.runOnUiThread(gameObject.mOnRemovedRunnable);
}
```

When we wish to draw your attention to a particular part of a code block, the relevant lines or items are set in bold:

```
<style name="iconButton" >
  <item name="android:background">@drawable/icon_button_bg</item>
  <item name="android:layout_width">@dimen/btn_round_size</item>
  <item name="android:layout_height">@dimen/btn_round_size</item>
  <item name="android:padding">@dimen/round_button_padding</item>
  <item name="android:focusable">true</item>
</style>
```

New terms and **important words** are shown in bold. Words that you see on the screen, for example, in menus or dialog boxes, appear in the text like this: "We have a link at the bottom named **Get resources** that pops up a dialog with the string resources we need."

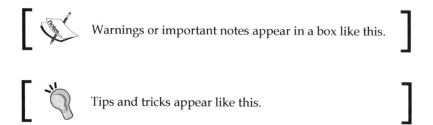

[Warnings or important notes appear in a box like this.   ]

[Tips and tricks appear like this.   ]

Reader feedback

Feedback from our readers is always welcome. Let us know what you think about this book—what you liked or disliked. Reader feedback is important for us as it helps us develop titles that you will really get the most out of.

To send us general feedback, simply e-mail feedback@packtpub.com and mention the book's title in the subject of your message.

If there is a topic that you have expertise in and you are interested in either writing or contributing to a book, see our author guide at www.packtpub.com/authors.

Customer support

Now that you are the proud owner of a Packt book, we have a number of things to help you to get the most from your purchase.

Downloading the example code

You can download the example code files from your account at http://www.packtpub.com for all the Packt Publishing books you have purchased. If you purchased this book elsewhere, you can visit http://www.packtpub.com/support and register to have the files e-mailed directly to you.

Downloading the color images of this book

We also provide you with a PDF file that has color images of the screenshots/diagrams used in this book. The color images will help you better understand the changes in the output. You can download this file from `https://www.packtpub.com/sites/default/files/downloads/1774OS_ImageBundle.pdf`.

Errata

Although we have taken every care to ensure the accuracy of our content, mistakes do happen. If you find a mistake in one of our books—maybe a mistake in the text or the code—we would be grateful if you could report this to us. By doing so, you can save other readers from frustration and help us improve subsequent versions of this book. If you find any errata, please report them by visiting `http://www.packtpub.com/submit-errata`, selecting your book, clicking on the **Errata Submission Form** link, and entering the details of your errata. Once your errata are verified, your submission will be accepted and the errata will be uploaded to our website or added to any list of existing errata under the Errata section of that title.

To view the previously submitted errata, go to `https://www.packtpub.com/books/content/support` and enter the name of the book in the search field. The required information will appear under the **Errata** section.

Piracy

Piracy of copyrighted material on the Internet is an ongoing problem across all media. At Packt, we take the protection of our copyright and licenses very seriously. If you come across any illegal copies of our works in any form on the Internet, please provide us with the location address or website name immediately so that we can pursue a remedy.

Please contact us at `copyright@packtpub.com` with a link to the suspected pirated material.

We appreciate your help in protecting our authors and our ability to bring you valuable content.

Questions

If you have a problem with any aspect of this book, you can contact us at `questions@packtpub.com`, and we will do our best to address the problem.

1

Setting Up the Project

In this chapter, we will describe the situations in which it makes sense to use the Android SDK for a game and those where it is best to use an external engine, explaining the pros and cons of each case.

We will create a simple project that we will be improving throughout the book, until it becomes a complete game. The particular game we are going to build is a Space Shooter.

A few top-level decisions will be made and explained, such as which orientation to use and how are we going to use activities and fragments.

We will describe the top-level architecture of a game engine, study how it is different from a typical app's, explaining why there is an `UpdateThread` and how it interacts with the user input and why it is separated from the `DrawThread`; we will include those elements in our project.

Once the game engine is completed, we will expand the project to show a pause dialog, handle the Android back key properly, be consistent with the `Activity` lifecycle, and make it fullscreen.

Finally, we will summarize some best practices in writing code for games.

Topics that will be covered in this chapter are as follows:

- The right tool for the right game
- Setting up the project with Android Studio
- Game architecture
- Alert dialogs
- Handling the back key
- Dealing with the fullscreen mode
- Good practices for game developers

The right tool for the right game

Before we begin entering the details about making games with the Android SDK, let's first take a step back and consider why are we doing this and what the other alternatives are for making a game that runs on Android.

People tend to reinvent the wheel quite often and developers use to do it ever more, especially in the case of video games. While creating a complete engine from scratch is a great learning experience, it also takes a lot of time. So, if you want to just make a game, it may be more cost-efficient for you to use one of the existing engines instead.

We are in a golden age of tools for creating video games. Not only are there lots of them, but most of them are free as well. This makes choosing the right one a little bit more complicated.

Let's take a look at several questions to help us decide which tool to use to suit the needs of a specific game. Since you are already reading this book, I consider that multiplatform is not high on your list of priorities and that reusing your existing Java and Android knowledge is a plus.

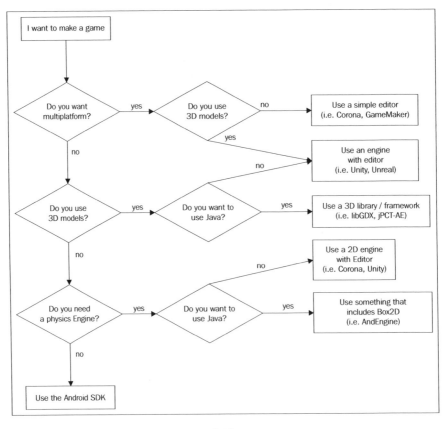

Do you want to use 3D?

If the answer is yes; I would definitely recommend you to use an already existing engine. There are some well-known tasks you'll need to implement to build even the simplest 3D engine such as loading models, loading and applying textures, handling transformations, and dealing with cameras. On top of this, you'd need to be writing OpenGL. All this is a lot of work.

Writing an OpenGL engine is the very definition of reinventing the wheel. It is fine if what you want is to learn the internals of a 3D engine, but if you go this road you'll spend a few months before you can even start with the game. If you want to go straight into making the game, you'd better start with an existing 3D engine.

The second question on this road is: do you prefer to work with code or are you more comfortable with a complete editor? For code, you can use jPCT-AE and libGDX, while, on the editor side, the most common alternative is Unity.

Do you want to use physics?

An affirmative answer to this question should point you straight to an existing engine.

Physics simulation is a very well-known area where there is a lot of documentation, and you should be able to implement your own physics engine. Again, this is a great learning experience, but if you want to go straight into making the game it is much more convenient to use an existing engine that supports physics. The most used physics engine around is Box2D, which is written in C++ and it has been ported to Android using the NDK.

While we are going to talk about collision detection later in the book, physics is out beyond the scope of this book. Anything more complex than two spheres colliding can become quite complex to handle.

Once again, it depends whether you prefer to work with code or if you want a complete editor. To work with code, AndEngine should be your weapon of choice. In the case of an editor, Corona and Unity are among the most popular choices.

Do you want to use Java?

Most of the feature-rich environments we are mentioning have their own environment, including a specific IDE. It takes effort to learn them and some of them use a different language (for example Unity has its own environment and uses JavaScript or C#).

On the other hand, the frameworks are simpler. You just have to include them and you'll still be writing an Android game. This is an interesting middle ground, where you still can reuse your Android and Java knowledge and make use of features such as physics or 3D models. In this section, we can mention AndEngine for 2D and physics and jPCT-AE for 3D as good options.

Pros of building games with the Android SDK

There are several advantages to building games using the Android SDK:

- It is faster to build a prototype
- You have full control over the engine
- It has a smaller learning curve (you already know Android, Java, and Android Studio)
- Most of your knowledge can be applied to apps
- You can use Google Play services and other libraries natively

Cons of building games with the Android SDK

Of course, not everything is awesome. There are some serious disadvantages, most of them already mentioned, such as:

- The code is not portable to other platforms (namely iOS).
- Performance can be an issue. If the game gets to a certain complexity, you may need to use OpenGL.
- It lacks a physics engine; you'd need to write it yourself.
- The support for OpenGL is just primitives; you need to build everything (or use a library).

I want the Android SDK!

Are you still here? Congratulations, you have chosen the right book!

If you want to explore other options, there are books available for Unity, AndEngine, and libGDX, and published by Packt.

Now that we are all on the same page, let's get down to business.

The project – YASS (Yet Another Space Shooter)

Along the book, we will be building a game as a demo of the concepts we will be studying in each chapter. The game is going to be a classic Space Shooter arcade game. We'll call it YASS—Yet Another Space Shooter.

This means some decisions will be taken for this particular type of game, but other options will also be commented since the book is meant for generic video game development.

Activities and Fragments

We are going to create a project with a single `Activity` and we will add fragments when necessary.

In the versions prior to Android 5.0 Lollipop, the transitions between activities could be modified, but only in a very limited way. The user can even disable them in a setting. All in all, this will make your game look clunky while transitioning from one `Activity` to another. You will need to save the state of the `Activity` in case it gets destroyed. Since each `Activity` is a separate instance, you will need to take care of communication among them, if required.

On the other hand, when you work with fragments, you never exit the `Activity` and you have complete control over the transition animations. In addition to these, you still have the code and layout of each section separated, so modularity and encapsulation are not compromised.

Finally, when it comes to handling third-party libraries such as In-App Billing or Google Play services, you have to take care if initialization and configuration only once, since those are linked at the `Activity` level.

[For games, it is more efficient to use only one Activity with multiple Fragments.]

One good practice is to have a base `Fragment` for our game (`YassBaseFragment`) from which all the other fragments will inherit. One good use of this fragment is to have a method to replace `getActivity` that returns our specific `Activity`, but there are other cases in which having a common base fragment is handy.

Project setup

We are going to use Android Studio as the IDE. We are going to create the project with minSDK 15 (Ice Cream Sandwich — ICS). As a good practice, we don't want to move the minimum SDK, unless we are using some features that were not available before. By keeping the minSDK low, you make your game available to as many devices as possible.

The two main features we are going to use from ICS are Fragments, ValueAnimators, and ViewPropertyAnimators. All of these were already available in Honeycomb, but 3.x is considered little more than a test for ICS; it was not mature and has been replaced by ICS in almost all devices.

In the unlikely case that you want to support older versions such as Gingerbread, you can make use of the compatibility library and NineOldAndroids to add backwards-compatibility for the features we are using.

Creating the stub project

Let's go on and navigate to **File > New Project**. We are going to use YASS as the **Application name** and example.com as the **Company Domain**.

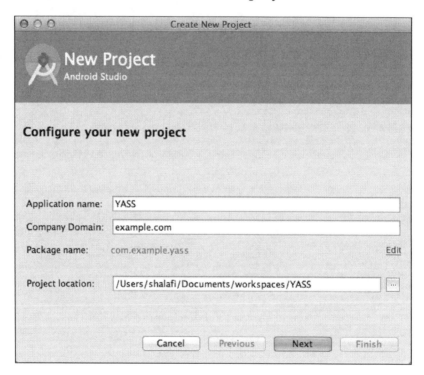

We include support for Android TV, since we want to be able to run our game on the big screen. This will create an extra module that we can compile for, but we are not going to touch this until the last chapter.

As explained before, we will use **Minimum SDK** version 15 for phones and 21 for Android TV, since this is when it was made available.

For the **Package name** of the application, we are going to use com.example.yass.

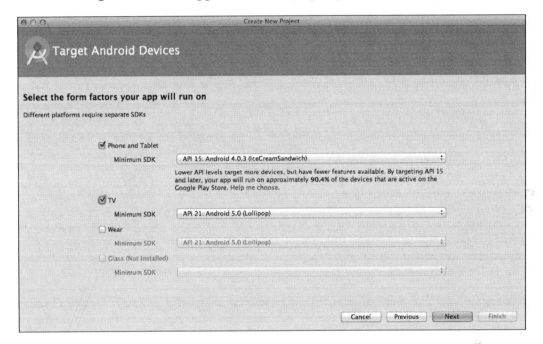

We are not going to use any of the default wizards, since all of them include the action bar/toolbar that is great for apps, but of no use for games. So, we'll go with the empty project options:

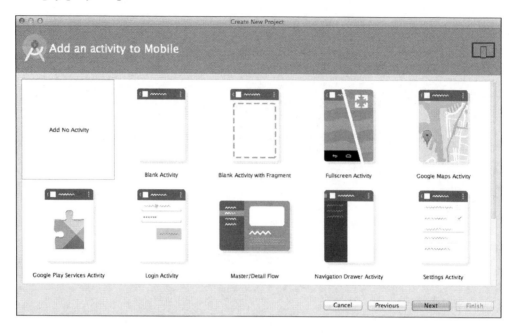

Similarly, we are not going to create any Activity for TV:

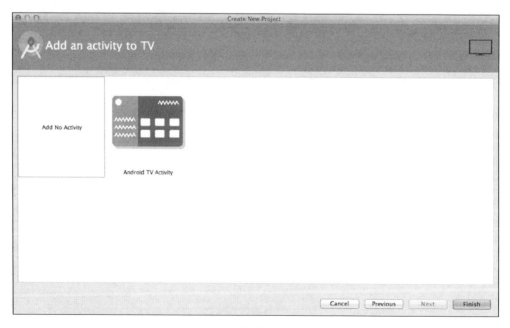

Once the project is created, we will create a single `Activity` with one `Fragment`. This is done via the menu option **New > Activity > Blank Activity with Fragment**.

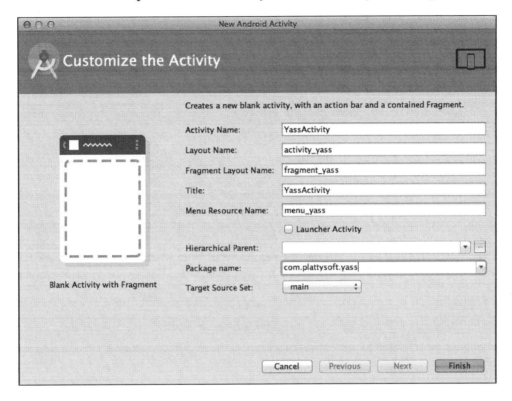

We are going to customize the `Activity` by filling the dialog as follows:

- **Activity Name**: `YassActivity`
- **Layout Name**: `activity_yass` (will be the default as soon as we change the Activity name)
- **Fragment Layout Name**: `fragment_yass` (will be the default as soon as we change the Activity name)
- **Title**: `YassActivity`

This will create the following files:

- `YassActivity.java` with the code for `YassActivity` and `PlaceholderFragment`
- `activity_main.xml`: A `FrameLayout` with `@+id/container`, which will be used to load the fragments into
- `fragment_main.xml`: A placeholder layout with the text `Hello World!`

Since we did not tell Android Studio that this activity is going to be our launch activity, we need to edit the `AndroidManifest.xml` to configure it as such, by adding the proper intent filter:

```
<intent-filter>
  <action android:name="android.intent.action.MAIN" />
  <category android:name="android.intent.category.LAUNCHER" />
</intent-filter>
```

Cleaning up

We are not going to use menus at all, so there are a few methods and files we will not need and we can delete them. You can leave all those methods there if you want, but it is better to have a clean environment, free of unused code.

So, we can remove the `menu` folder under `resources` and the files in it, which are meant to be the menu for the `YassActivity`.

The methods that handle menu-creation and menu-item-selection are also useless, so we can remove the following methods from `YassActivity`:

- `onCreateOptionsMenu`: Invoked when the menu is created
- `OnOptionsItemSelected`: Invoked when an option from the menu is selected

Choosing an orientation

Deciding the orientation of a game is a very important point. Given the diversity of Android phones, the resolution and aspect ratio are a couple of things we have to deal with.

Gaming is traditionally done in landscape orientation: computers have monitors in landscape mode, and so do TV screens when you play with your gaming console. Almost all handheld consoles are designed with landscape orientation as well. Even more, most tablets consider landscape to be the default orientation.

Landscape is the traditional orientation for gaming.

YASS is going to be a landscape game. The key reason why we are doing it is to be able to port the game to Android consoles later on, both on Android TV and OUYA. This does not mean that the portrait mode is not a valid orientation for games, but it is a less familiar one for players.

We are going to use `sensorLandscape` instead of just `landscape`, so the device can rotate 180 degrees to adjust to whatever side is down. We have to update the `AndroidManifest.xml` to look like this:

```
<application
  android:icon="@mipmap/ic_launcher"
  android:label="@string/app_name"
  android:theme="@style/AppTheme" >
  <activity
    android:screenOrientation="sensorLandscape"
    android:name=".YassActivity"
    android:label="@string/title_activity_yass" >
    <intent-filter>
      <action android:name="android.intent.action.MAIN" />
      <category android:name="android.intent.category.LAUNCHER" />
    </intent-filter>
  </activity>
</application>
```

As you probably know, when an `Activity` changes orientation on Android, it is destroyed and recreated and so are all the fragments inside it. This means that, unless you explicitly save and restore information, the fragments will not remember the previous state.

 The `sensorLandscape` and `sensorPortrait` modes do not destroy activities on rotation.

Some good news here: while using `sensorLandscape`, the rotation does not kill the Activity, so no extra work is required. This happens because the layout is exactly the same and nothing needs to be recreated.

If you plan to make a game that can rotate, you must pay extra attention to saving and restoring the status of the game when the orientation changes. This in itself is another good reason to keep the game locked to a particular orientation, be it landscape or portrait.

Dealing with aspect ratios

Android devices come in a lot of different aspect ratios, form 4:3 to 16:9 at least. This is not counting the number of pixels.

While designing a game for multiple aspect ratios, there are basically two ways of doing it. For each of them, we design for the most extreme aspect ratio. We will be using the extra space for "smart letterboxes," which means that we can have more game view.

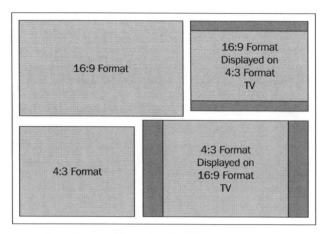

Several ways of designing for different aspect ratios

The most common option is to make the camera centered and fix the smallest size (the height for the landscape orientation). This allows for more view space on the sides, while making sure that the smallest screen will have enough display space. This is the equivalent of viewing 4:3 images on a 16:9 screen.

You can also fix the bigger size if the game design makes sense. This will add extra space on the top and bottom if the screen is square. This is the equivalent of viewing 16:9 images on a 4:3 screen.

There is an alternative approach: simply having "more camera space." We can, as well, make the game view a certain size and use the extra space for other controls such as scores, levels, and so on.

If you take this approach to the extreme, you can design the game area completely square and put the extra information in "smart letterboxes" for both landscape and portrait. One very good example of this approach is done by Candy Crush Saga. This is the best approach for versatility, but it is also the one that requires the most work.

For our game, we are going to use a "more camera space" approach with fixed size letterboxes to display scores and lives.

For the difference in resolution and pixel density, we will be designing for a low density screen. We will read the resolution of the device programmatically and apply a conversion factor. Some in-depth details of this approach are given in the chapters dedicated to low-level drawing, menus, and dialogs.

Game architecture

Games have a different architecture and control flow than apps. Both seem to respond to user input instantly, but while an app does this by setting listeners and reacting to events with method calls (most commonly the `onClick` method calls the `OnClickListener`), this approach is not valid for a real-time game (although it is valid for non-real-time games).

Once a game is running, it must evaluate and update everything as fast as possible. This is the reason why it cannot be interrupted by user events. Those events or states should be recorded instead and then read by the game objects during its update.

The game engine should be created inside the fragment that runs the game, because we only need the game engine running while we are playing. This has the advantage that we can use our existing Android knowledge to create and handle the rest of the screens of the game.

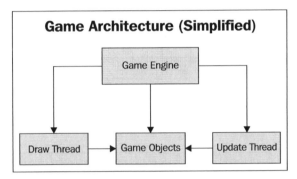

Simplified architecture of a game engine

The basic **Game Engine** architecture is composed of an **Update Thread**, a **Draw Thread**, and a series of **Game Objects** that belong to the **Game Engine**.

The **Game Engine** is the component through which the rest of the program interacts with the game. Its mission is also to encapsulate the existence of the update and draw threads as well as to handle the game objects.

A game is composed of **Game Objects** that are both updated and drawn. These objects are held inside the **Game Engine**.

The **Update Thread** is responsible for updating the state of the game objects as fast as it can. It will run through all the game objects calling an update method.

The UI has to also be constantly updating and be independent of the update thread. It will draw all the game objects by calling a draw method on them.

Let's analyze each component in detail.

GameEngine and GameObjects

The GameEngine contains the three elements already mentioned.

GameObject is an abstract class that all game objects in our game must extend from. This interface connects them with the Update and Draw threads.

```
public abstract class GameObject {
  public abstract void startGame();
  public abstract void onUpdate(long elapsedMillis,
    GameEngine gameEngine);
  public abstract void onDraw();
  public final Runnable mOnAddedRunnable = new Runnable() {
    @Override
    public void run() {
      onAddedToGameUiThread();
    }
  };

  public final Runnable mOnRemovedRunnable = new Runnable() {
    @Override
    public void run() {
      onRemovedFromGameUiThread();
    }
  };

  public void onRemovedFromGameUiThread(){
  }

  public void onAddedToGameUiThread(){
  }
}
```

- startGame is used for the initialization of the object before a game can start.

- onUpdate is called by the game engine as fast as possible, providing the number of milliseconds that have passed since the previous call and a reference to the GameEngine itself for future uses such as accessing user input.

- onDraw makes the component render itself. We are not using any parameters just yet, but later we will pass a Canvas to draw on.

- onRemovedFromGameUiThread contains code that must be run on the UIThread when the object is removed from the game.

- onAddedToGameUiThread contains code that must be run on the UIThread when the object is added to the game.

- The two Runnable objects are used to call onRemovedFromGameUiThread and onAddedToGameUiThread inside the UIThread.

The GameEngine will provide us with easy methods to start, stop, pause, and resume the game, so we don't have to worry about the threads or the game objects from the outside.

The game engine is composed of three items: the list of game objects, the UpdateThread, and the DrawThread.

```
private List<GameObject> mGameObjects =
  new ArrayList<GameObject>();

private UpdateThread mUpdateThread;
private DrawThread mDrawThread;
```

Let's take a look at the different methods of the engine to handle a game.

Starting a game

The code to start a game from the GameEngine is as follows:

```
public void startGame() {
  // Stop a game if it is running
  stopGame();

  // Setup the game objects
  int numGameObjects = mGameObjects.size();
  for (int i=0; i<numGameObjects; i++) {
    mGameObjects.get(i).startGame();
  }

  // Start the update thread
  mUpdateThread = new UpdateThread(this);
  mUpdateThread.start();

  // Start the drawing thread
  mDrawThread = new DrawThread(this);
  mDrawThread.start();
}
```

First of all, we have to make sure that no game is running, so we call stopGame at the beginning to stop a game if there is one in progress.

Secondly, we reset all the game objects that are linked to the engine. It is important to do this before we start the threads, so everything starts from the initial position.

Finally, we create and start the UpdateThread and the DrawThread.

Stopping a game

Stopping a game is even simpler. We just have to stop the `Update` and `Draw` threads if they exist:

```
public void stopGame() {
  if (mUpdateThread != null) {
    mUpdateThread.stopGame();
  }
  if (mDrawThread != null) {
    mDrawThread.stopGame();
  }
}
```

We also have methods for `pauseGame` and `resumeGame` that are functionally equivalent to this one. In these methods, the logic of the action belongs to each thread. We are not including the code of these methods here, because they are redundant.

Managing game objects

The engine has to manage the addition and removal of game objects. We cannot just handle the list directly, since it will be used intensively during `onUpdate` and `onDraw`.

```
public void addGameObject(final GameObject gameObject) {
  if (isRunning()){
    mObjectsToAdd.add(gameObject);
  }
  else {
    mGameObjects.add(gameObject);
  }
  mActivity.runOnUiThread(gameObject.mOnAddedRunnable);
}

public void removeGameObject(final GameObject gameObject) {
  mObjectsToRemove.add(gameObject);
  mActivity.runOnUiThread(gameObject.mOnRemovedRunnable);
}
```

We use the lists `mObjectsToAdd` and `mObjectsToRemove` to keep track of the objects that must be added or removed. We will do both as the last step of the `onUpdate` method with the exception of when the game engine is not running, in which case it is safe to add and remove them directly.

We are also running the corresponding `Runnable` object from the `GameObject` on the `UIThread`.

To update the game objects from the engine, we just call `onUpdate` on all of them. Once the update loop has finished, we take care of the objects that must be removed or added to `mGameObjects`. This part is done using a `synchronized` section that is also important for the `onDraw` method.

```
public void onUpdate(long elapsedMillis) {
   int numGameObjects = mGameObjects.size();
   for (int i=0; i<numGameObjects; i++) {
     mGameObjects.get(i).onUpdate(elapsedMillis, this);
   }
   synchronized (mGameObjects) {
     while (!mObjectsToRemove.isEmpty()) {
       mGameObjects.remove(mObjectsToRemove.remove(0));
     }
     while (!mObjectsToAdd.isEmpty()) {
        mGameObjects.add(mObjectsToAdd.remove(0));
     }
   }
}
```

We do the same for drawing, except that the drawing must be done on the `UIThread`. So, we create a `Runnable` object that we pass to the `runOnUIThread` method of the activity.

```
private Runnable mDrawRunnable = new Runnable() {
   @Override
   public void run() {
     synchronized (mGameObjects) {
       int numGameObjects = mGameObjects.size();
       for (int i = 0; i < numGameObjects; i++) {
         mGameObjects.get(i).onDraw();
       }
     }
   }
};

public void onDraw(Canvas canvas) {
   mActivity.runOnUiThread(mDrawRunnable);
}
```

Note that we synchronize the run method using `mGameObjects`. We do it so we are sure that the list is not modified while we iterate it.

It is also important that only the last part of the onUpdate is synchronized. If no objects are added or removed, the threads are independent. If we synchronize the complete onUpdate method, we will be losing all the advantages of having the Update and Draw threads separated.

UpdateThread

UpdateThread is a thread that continuously runs updates on the game engine. For each call to onUpdate, it provides the number of milliseconds since the previous execution.

The basic run method of the update thread is as follows:

```
@Override
public void run() {
  long previousTimeMillis;
  long currentTimeMillis;
  long elapsedMillis;
  previousTimeMillis = System.currentTimeMillis();

  while (mGameIsRunning) {
    currentTimeMillis = System.currentTimeMillis();
    elapsedMillis = currentTimeMillis - previousTimeMillis;
    mGameEngine.onUpdate(elapsedMillis);
    previousTimeMillis = currentTimeMillis;
  }
}
```

The thread stays in a loop for as long as the game is running. On each iteration, it will get the current time, calculate the elapsed milliseconds since the previous run, and call onUpdate on the GameEngine object.

While this first version works and is very simple to follow, it can only start and stop a game. We want to be able to pause and resume it as well.

To pause and resume the game, we need a variable that we read inside the loop to check when to pause the execution. We'll need to keep track of the elapsed milliseconds and discount the time spent paused. A simple way to do it is like this:

```
while (mGameIsRunning) {
  currentTimeMillis = System.currentTimeMillis();
  elapsedMillis = currentTimeMillis - previousTimeMillis;
  if (mPauseGame) {
    while (mPauseGame) {
```

```
   try {
     Thread.sleep(20);
   } catch (InterruptedException e) {
     // We stay on the loop
   }
 }
 currentTimeMillis = System.currentTimeMillis();
}
mGameEngine.onUpdate(elapsedMillis);
previousTimeMillis = currentTimeMillis;
}
```

The code for the `pauseGame` and `resumeGame` methods is just setting the variable `mPauseGame` to true or false.

If the game is paused, we enter a while loop in which we will remain until the game is resumed. To avoid having an empty loop that runs continuously, we can put the thread to sleep for a short amount of time (20 milliseconds). Note that `Thread.sleep` can trigger an `InterruptedException`. If that happens we can just continue since it is going to be run in 20 milliseconds again. Besides, we are going to improve it right now.

This approach works, but there is still a lot of idle processing being done. For threads, there are mechanisms to pause and resume in a much more efficient way. We are going to improve this using `wait`/`notify`.

The code can be updated to be like this:

```
while (mGameIsRunning) {
  currentTimeMillis = System.currentTimeMillis();
  elapsedMillis = currentTimeMillis - previousTimeMillis;
  if (mPauseGame) {
    while (mPauseGame) {
      try {
        synchronized (mLock) {
          mLock.wait();
        }
      } catch (InterruptedException e) {
        // We stay on the loop
      }
    }
    currentTimeMillis = System.currentTimeMillis();
  }
  mGameEngine.onUpdate(elapsedMillis);
  previousTimeMillis = currentTimeMillis;
}
```

The `pauseGame` method is the same as before, but we need to update `resumeGame` to be at the place from where the lock is notified and released:

```
public void resumeGame() {
  if (mPauseGame == true) {
    mPauseGame = false;
    synchronized (mLock) {
      mLock.notify();
    }
  }
}
```

With the use of `wait`/`notify`, we ensure that the thread will not do any work while it is idle and we also know that it will be woken up as soon as we notify it. It is important to first set `mPauseGame` to `false` and then awake the thread, otherwise the main loop could stop again.

Finally, to start and stop the game, we just need to change the values of the variables:

```
public void start() {
  mGameIsRunning = true;
  mPauseGame = false;
  super.start();
}

public void stopGame() {
  mGameIsRunning = false;
  resumeGame();
}
```

The game never starts in a paused state. To stop a game, we just need to set the `mGameIsRunning` value to `false` and the loop inside the `run` method will end.

It is important to call `resumeGame` as a part of the `stopGame` method. If we call stop while the game is paused, the thread will be waiting, so nothing will happen unless we resume the game. If the game is not paused, nothing is done inside `resumeGame`, so it does not matter if we called it.

DrawThread

There are several ways to implement `DrawThread`. It could be done in a similar way to the update thread, but we are going to use a much simpler approach that does not use a `Thread`.

We are going to use the `Timer` and `TimerTask` classes to send the `onDraw` callback to the game engine with a high-enough frequency to render at 30 frames per second:

```
private static int EXPECTED_FPS = 30;
private static final long TIME_BETWEEN_DRAWS = 1000 / EXPECTED_FPS;

public void start() {
  stopGame();
  mTimer = new Timer();
  mTimer.schedule(new TimerTask() {
    @Override
    public void run() {
      mGameEngine.onDraw();
    }
  }, 0, TIME_BETWEEN_DRAWS);
}
```

We have this method called every 33 milliseconds. In simple implementations, this method will just call `invalidate` in the `GameView`, which will cause a call to the `onDraw` method of the `View`.

This implementation relies on one feature of the Android UI. To redisplay views, Android has a contingency system that is built in to avoid recurrent invalidates. If an invalidation is requested while the view is being drawn, it will be queued. If more than one invalidations are queued, they will be discarded as they won't have any effect.

With this, if the view takes longer than `TIME_BETWEEN_DRAWS` to be drawn, the system will fall back to fewer frames per second automatically.

Later in the book, we will revisit this thread for more complex implementations but, for now, let's keep it simple.

Stopping, pausing, and resuming the `DrawThread` is also simple:

```
public void stopGame() {
  if (mTimer != null) {
    mTimer.cancel();
    mTimer.purge();
  }
}

public void pauseGame() {
  stopGame();
}

public void resumeGame() {
  start();
}
```

To stop the game, we only need to `cancel` and `purge` the timer. The `cancel` method will cancel the timer and all scheduled tasks, while `purge` will remove all the canceled tasks from the queue.

Since we do not need to keep track of any state, we can just make the `pauseGame` and `resumeGame` equivalents to `stopGame` and start.

Note that, if we want to have a smooth game at 30fps, the drawing of all the items on the screen must be performed in less than 33 milliseconds. This implies that the code of these methods usually needs to be optimized.

User input

As we mentioned, user input is to be processed by some input controller and then read by the objects that need it, when they need it. We will go into the details of such an input controller in the next chapter. For now, we just want to check whether the game engine works as expected and handles the start, stop, pause, and resume calls properly.

Pause, resume, and start are different from the other user inputs, because they affect the state of the engine and threads themselves instead of modifying the state of the game objects. For this reason, we are going to use standard event-oriented programming to trigger these functions.

Putting everything together

Let's pick up our stub project, add all the classes we need to have a working game engine, and then modify the code so it allows us to start, stop, pause, and resume the game engine and display the number of milliseconds since the game was started.

We will put our current implementation of `GameEngine`, `UpdateThread`, `DrawThread`, and `GameObject` inside the `com.example.yass.engine` package.

Next, we will create another package named `com.example.yass.counter`, which we will use for the code of this example.

Inside `YassActivity`, we have an inner class named `PlaceholderFragment`. We are going to rename it to `GameFragment`, refactor it to a separate file, and put it under the `com.example.yass.counter` package.

We are going to add a `TextView` that will show the number of milliseconds and two buttons: one to start and stop the game engine and another one to pause and resume it.

We are going to add them to the layout of `fragment_yass_main.xml`, which will look like this:

```
<LinearLayout xmlns:android="http://schemas.android.com/apk/res/
android"
  xmlns:tools="http://schemas.android.com/tools"
  android:layout_width="match_parent"
  android:layout_height="match_parent"
  android:orientation="vertical"
  android:padding="@dimen/activity_horizontal_margin"
  android:paddingLeft="@dimen/activity_horizontal_margin"
  tools:context="com.example.yass.counter.PlaceholderFragment">

  <TextView
    android:id="@+id/txt_score"
   android:layout_width="wrap_content"
    android:layout_height="wrap_content"
    android:text="@string/hello_world" />

  <Button
    android:id="@+id/btn_start_stop"
    android:layout_width="wrap_content"
    android:layout_height="wrap_content"
    android:text="@string/start" />

  <Button
    android:id="@+id/btn_play_pause"
    android:layout_width="wrap_content"
    android:layout_height="wrap_content"
    android:text="@string/pause" />
</LinearLayout>
```

For the game fragment, we need to add the following code inside `onViewCreated`:

```
@Override
public void onViewCreated(View view, Bundle savedInstanceState) {
  super.onViewCreated(view, savedInstanceState);
  mGameEngine = new GameEngine(getActivity());
  mGameEngine.addGameObject(
    new ScoreGameObject(view, R.id.txt_score));
  view.findViewById(R.id.btn_start_stop)
    .setOnClickListener(this);
  view.findViewById(R.id.btn_play_pause)
    .setOnClickListener(this);
}
```

Once the view is created, we create the game engine and add a new `ScoreGameObject` to it. Then we set the current fragment as the listener for the two buttons we have added.

The code for `onClick` is very simple; just decide which method to call for each button:

```
@Override
public void onClick(View v) {
  if (v.getId() == R.id.btn_play_pause) {
    playOrPause();
  }
  if (v.getId() == R.id.btn_start_stop) {
    startOrStop();
  }
}
```

Deciding whether the game should be paused or resumed is as simple as this:

```
private void playOrPause() {
  Button button = (Button)
  getView().findViewById(R.id.btn_play_pause);
  if (mGameEngine.isPaused()) {
    mGameEngine.resumeGame();
    button.setText(R.string.pause);
  }
  else {
    mGameEngine.pauseGame();
    button.setText(R.string.resume);
  }
}
```

We also handle a name change on the button to make sure the UI is consistent. In the code, we are making use of the `isPaused` method from `GameEngine`. This method just returns the status of the `UpdateThread` object as long as it is not null:

```
public boolean isPaused() {
  return mUpdateThread != null && mUpdateThread.isGamePaused();
}
```

Similarly, to play/pause the game and keep the state of the buttons, we will add this method:

```
private void startOrStop() {
  Button button = (Button)
    getView().findViewById(R.id.btn_start_stop);
  Button playPauseButton = (Button)
    getView().findViewById(R.id.btn_play_pause);
```

```
if (mGameEngine.isRunning()) {
  mGameEngine.stopGame();
  button.setText(R.string.start);
  playPauseButton.setEnabled(false);
}
else {
  mGameEngine.startGame();
  button.setText(R.string.stop);
  playPauseButton.setEnabled(true);
  playPauseButton.setText(R.string.pause);
}
}
```

Once again, we need a method in the GameEngine to know whether it is running or not. As we did for the previous one, we just mirror the status of UpdateThread:

```
public boolean isRunning() {
  return mUpdateThread != null && mUpdateThread.isGameRunning();
}
```

Once the basic connections are done, we can move to the really interesting bit: the game object we are creating. This object illustrates the use of each method from the GameObject class that we have been talking about:

```
public class ScoreGameObject extends GameObject {

  private final TextView mText;
  private long mTotalMilis;

  public ScoreGameObject(View view, int viewResId) {
    mText = (TextView) view.findViewById(viewResId);
  }

  @Override
  public void onUpdate(long elapsedMillis, GameEngine gameEngine)
  {
    mTotalMilis += elapsedMillis;
  }

  @Override
  public void startGame() {
    mTotalMilis = 0;
  }

  @Override
  public void onDraw() {
    mText.setText(String.valueOf(mTotalMilis));
  }
}
```

The `onUpdate` method just keeps adding milliseconds to the total. The total is reset when a new game starts and `onDraw` sets the value of the total number of milliseconds in the text view.

As expected, `onUpdate` is called a lot more often than `onDraw`. On the other hand, `onDraw` is executed on the `UIThread`, which is something we cannot afford to do with `onUpdate`.

We can now compile and run the example and check that the timer starts and stops when we start and stop the game engine. We can also check that pause and resume work as expected.

Moving forward with the example

Now we are going to change the example a bit. We are going to make a pause dialog from which we can resume or stop the game. This dialog will be shown if the user taps on the pause button and if he or she hits the back key.

Finally, we are going to add one fragment from which the player can start the game and we will separate the game fragment from the menu.

So, we'll be creating `MainMenuFragment.java` and `fragment_main_menu.xml`. The content of the layout will be extremely simple:

```xml
<?xml version="1.0" encoding="utf-8"?>
<FrameLayout xmlns:android="http://schemas.android.com/apk/res/
android"
  android:layout_width="match_parent"
  android:layout_height="match_parent">

  <TextView
    android:layout_gravity="center_horizontal|top"
    style="@android:style/TextAppearance.DeviceDefault.Large"
    android:layout_marginTop="@dimen/activity_vertical_margin"
    android:text="@string/game_title"
    android:layout_width="wrap_content"
    android:layout_height="wrap_content" />

  <Button
    android:id="@+id/btn_start"
    android:layout_width="wrap_content"
    android:layout_height="wrap_content"
    android:layout_gravity="center"
    android:text="@string/start" />

</FrameLayout>
```

This includes the app title on the screen and a button to start playing:

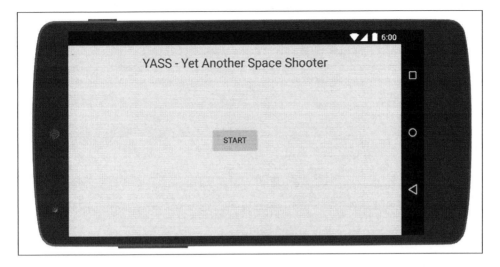

Inside this fragment, we add a listener to the start button and we make it call the startGame method. The code of the startGame method is very simple as well:

```
public void startGame() {
  getFragmentManager()
    .beginTransaction()
    .replace(R.id.container, new GameFragment(), TAG_FRAGMENT)
    .addToBackStack(null)
    .commit();
}
```

We are using the fragment manager to transition from the current fragment to GameFragment.

The beginTransition method creates the transition itself and we can configure it with chained methods.

We are replacing the fragment inside the view with the R.id.container id with a GameFragment. This will remove the old fragment. If we use add, both fragments will be shown instead.

Then, we add the fragment to the back stack with no tag, since we don't need any. This is very important, because it allows the system to handle the back key properly. Everything that is on the back stack of the fragment manager will pop up when the back key is pressed.

If we do not add the fragment to the back stack, the default behavior when we tap on the back key will be to close the app. With the fragment on the back stack, we can just rely on the system to handle fragment navigation properly.

Finally, we commit the transition so the fragment is replaced.

Inside the game fragment we have already, we will remove the start/stop dialog and modify the pause button to show a dialog from where we can resume or exit the current game.

We want the game to start immediately, so the onViewCreated method of the GameFragment will now look like this:

```
@Override
public void onViewCreated(View view, Bundle savedInstanceState) {
  super.onViewCreated(view, savedInstanceState);
  mGameEngine = new GameEngine(getActivity());
  mGameEngine.addGameObject(
    new ScoreGameObject(view, R.id.txt_score));
  view.findViewById(R.id.btn_play_pause)
    .setOnClickListener(this);
  mGameEngine.startGame();
}
```

We will also modify the onClick method, removing the old code to start or stop, so it looks like this:

```
@Override
public void onClick(View v) {
  if (v.getId() == R.id.btn_play_pause) {
    pauseGameAndShowPauseDialog();
  }
}
```

This simpler version only cares about pausing the game and showing a dialog when the pause button is clicked.

For now, we are going to create a default dialog using the AlertDialog framework:

```
private void pauseGameAndShowPauseDialog() {
  mGameEngine.pauseGame();
  new AlertDialog.Builder(getActivity())
  .setTitle(R.string.pause_dialog_title)
  .setMessage(R.string.pause_dialog_message)
  .setPositiveButton(R.string.resume,
  new DialogInterface.OnClickListener() {
    @Override
```

```
    public void onClick(DialogInterface dialog, int which) {
      dialog.dismiss();
      mGameEngine.resumeGame();
    }
  })
  .setNegativeButton(R.string.stop,
    new DialogInterface.OnClickListener() {
    @Override
    public void onClick(DialogInterface dialog, int which) {
      dialog.dismiss();
      mGameEngine.stopGame();
      ((MainActivity)getActivity()).navigateBack();
    }
  })
  .create()
  .show();
}
```

The positive button will resume the game, so it calls resumeGame in the game engine.

The negative button will exit the game, so it calls stopGame in the GameEngine and then navigateBack in the parent Activity.

The navigateBack method is nothing more than handling a back key pressed in the activity:

```
public void navigateBack() {
  super.onBackPressed();
}
```

Since we put the fragment in the navigation stack, the MainMenuFragment will be loaded again and the GameFragment will be destroyed. The following is how the Pause dialog looks:

Handling the back key

One of the things we want to do is to handle the back key properly. This is something that upsets Android users when it does not work as expected inside games, so we'll be paying some special attention to it. There are two places where it does not work as expected right now.

 Handling the back key properly is very important on Android.

- If we dismiss the **Pause** dialog using the back key, the game will not resume.
- While in the game fragment, the back key should pause the game. At the moment, the back key goes back to the GameFragment.

For the first problem, we need to add an OnCancelListener to the dialog. This is different from OnDismissListener, which is called every time the dialog is dismissed. The cancel method is only called when the dialog is canceled.

Also, OnDismissListener was introduced in API level 17. Since we don't need it, we will not worry about raising the minSDK of the game.

We update the creation of the **Pause** dialog with the following code:

```
new AlertDialog.Builder(getActivity())
  [...]
  .setOnCancelListener(new DialogInterface.OnCancelListener() {
    @Override
    public void onCancel(DialogInterface dialog) {
      mGameEngine.resumeGame();
    }
  })
  .create()
  show();
```

The remaining item is to pause the game when the back key is pressed during the game. This is something that needs to be handled in the fragment. As it happens, onBakPressed is a method available only for activities. We need to code a way to expand this to the current fragment.

We are going to make use of our `YassBaseFragment`, the base class for all the fragments in our game, to add the support to `onBackPressed`. We will create one `onBackPressed` method here:

```
public class YassBaseFragment extends Fragment {
  public boolean onBackPressed() {
    return false;
  }
}
```

In the `Activity`, we update `onBackClicked` to allow the fragments to override it if needed:

```
@Override
public void onBackPressed() {
  final YassFragment fragment = (YassFragment)
    getFragmentManager().findFragmentByTag(TAG_FRAGMENT);
  if (!fragment.onBackPressed()) {
    super.onBackPressed();
  }
}
```

If the fragment does not handle the back key press, it will return false. Then, we just call the super method to allow the default behavior.

`TAG_FRAGMENT` is very important; it allows us to get the fragment we are adding and it is set when we add the fragment to `FragmentTransition`. Let's review the `onCreate` method of `MainActivity`, which was created by the wizard, and add the `TAG_FRAGMENT` to the initial `FragmentTransition`:

```
@Override
protected void onCreate(Bundle savedInstanceState) {
  super.onCreate(savedInstanceState);
  setContentView(R.layout.activity_yass);
  if (savedInstanceState == null) {
    getFragmentManager().beginTransaction()
      .add(R.id.container, new MainMenuFragment(), TAG_FRAGMENT)
      .commit();
  }
}
```

It is also very important that all the fragments of the application must extend from `YassBaseFragment`, otherwise this method will throw a `ClassCastException`.

With all the pieces in place, we now override the onBackPressed method inside GameFragment to show the **Pause** dialog:

```
@Override
public boolean onBackPressed() {
  if (mGameEngine.isRunning()) {
    pauseGameAndShowPauseDialog();
    return true;
  }
  return false;
}
```

With this, the **Pause** dialog is shown when we click back while in the GameFragment. Note that we will only show the pause dialog if the GameEngine is running. When it is not running, we return false. The default behavior of Android will trigger and the **Pause** dialog, which must be showing, will be canceled.

Honoring the lifecycle

Our game should also be consistent with the Activity lifecycle; especially, it should pause whenever the Activity pauses. This is very important for mainly two reasons:

- If the game is put in the background, the user wants it to be paused when it returns
- As long as the game is running, the update thread will be updating as fast as it can, so it will make the phone feel slower

With the current implementation, none of this will happen. You can try pressing the home button, you will see that the device does not feel responsive. Also, if you put the game again in the foreground using the recent activities button, you will see that the timer is still counting.

 Not respecting the fragment lifecycle will result in performance problems and unhappy players.

Solving this is very simple, we just need to be consistent with the fragment lifecycle, by adding this code to the GameFragment:

```
@Override
public void onPause() {
  super.onPause();
  if (mGameEngine.isRunning()){
```

```
      pauseGameAndShowPauseDialog();
    }
  }

  @Override
  public void onDestroy() {
    super.onDestroy();
    mGameEngine.stopGame();
  }
```

With this, whenever the fragment is paused, we pause the game and show the dialog, so the player can resume again. Also, whenever the fragment is destroyed, we stop the game engine.

It is important to check whether the game engine is running or not before we pause it, since onPause is also called when we exit the game. So, if we forget to do this, exiting via the pause dialog will make the app crash.

Using as much screen as we can

We are building a game. We want to have all the screen space of the device and no distractions. There are two items that take this from us:

- **The Status bar**: The bar on the top of the screen where the time, battery, WiFi, mobile signal, and notifications are displayed.

- **The Navigation bar**: This is the bar where the back, home, and recent buttons are placed. It may be located in different places according to the orientation of the device.

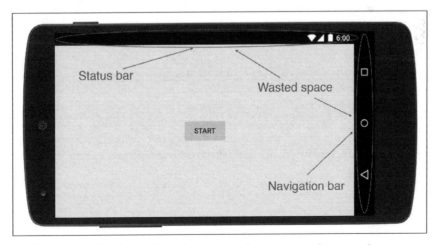

The Status and Navigation bars take up a significant amount of space on the screen

The **Navigation bar** was introduced on Ice Cream Sandwich as a replacement for physical buttons. But, even today, some manufacturers decide to use physical buttons instead, so it may or may not be there.

The first thing we can do is to tell the system that we want to be fullscreen. There is a flag with the SYSTEM_UI_FLAG_FULLSCREEN name, which seems to be what we are looking for.

The problem is that this flag was introduced in the early versions of Android when there was no **Navigation bar**. Back then, it really meant fullscreen but, from Ice Cream Sandwich onwards, it just means "remove the **Status bar**".

The SYSTEM_UI_FLAG_FULLSCREEN mode is not really fullscreen.

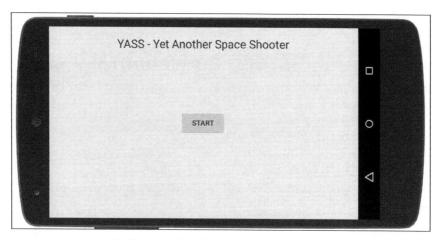

Fullscreen only makes the Status bar go away.

Along with the **Navigation bar**, some ways to handle fullscreen were added. The approach was revisited in KitKat. So, let's look at our options.

Before Android 4.4 – almost fullscreen

On Android 4.0, together with the **Navigation bar**, two new flags were added to handle the **Navigation bar** in addition to the existing fullscreen flag:

- SYSTEM_UI_FLAG_HIDE_NAVIGATION: This tells the system to hide the **Navigation bar**

- SYSTEM_UI_FLAG_LOW_PROFILE: This puts the device in "low profile" mode, dimming the icons on the **Navigation bar** and replacing them with just dots

While it is true that the "hide navigation" flag hides the Navigation bar completely, the bar will reappear as soon as you touch anywhere on the screen, since this mode is designed to be used for noninteractive activities such as video playback. So, SYSTEM_UI_FLAG_HIDE_NAVIGATION is not much use to us.

Using low profile to dim the navigation bar is a much more logical solution. Although we are not getting any extra screen space, the fact that the icons on the bar are reduced to small dots allows players to focus a lot more on the content. These icons will show when necessary (essentially, when the user taps on the bar) and dim again as soon as they are not needed.

Hiding the navigation bar will only work fine for noninteractive apps. The Navigation bar will appear again as soon as you touch the screen.

All in all, we have to be happy with just dimming the Navigation bar and getting rid of the Status bar.

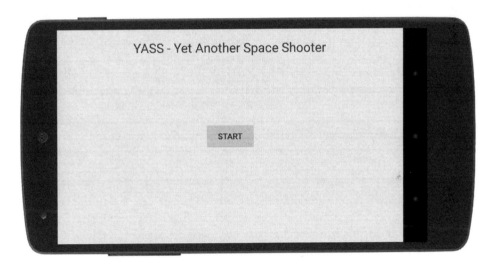

The low profile mode dims the Navigation bar so it is less obtrusive

This is the code we need to add to the MainActivity to remove the Status bar and put the device in a low profile mode:

```
@Override
public void onWindowFocusChanged(boolean hasFocus) {
  super.onWindowFocusChanged(hasFocus);
  if (hasFocus) {
    View decorView = getWindow().getDecorView();
```

```
decorView.setSystemUiVisibility(
View.SYSTEM_UI_FLAG_LAYOUT_STABLE
    | View.SYSTEM_UI_FLAG_LAYOUT_FULLSCREEN
    | View.SYSTEM_UI_FLAG_FULLSCREEN
    | View.SYSTEM_UI_FLAG_LOW_PROFILE);
    }
}
```

We are overriding the `onWindowFocusChanged` method in the main `Activity`. This is the recommended place to handle the flags, since it is called whenever the window focus changes. When the app regains focus, we don't know in which status the bars are. So, it is a good practice to ensure that things are the way we want them.

There are two more flags we haven't mentioned yet. They were introduced in API level 16 and are designed to take care of how the layout reacts to the appearance and disappearance of elements.

The `SYSTEM_UI_FLAG_LAYOUT_STABLE` flag means that the layout will be consistent, independent of the elements being shown or hidden.

The `SYSTEM_UI_FLAG_LAYOUT_FULLSCREEN` flag tells the system that our stable layout will be the one in the fullscreen mode—without the navigation bar.

This means that if/when the status bar is shown, the layout will not change, which is good, otherwise it will look like it is a glitch. It also means that we need to be careful with margins, so nothing important gets covered by the Status bar.

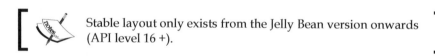

Stable layout only exists from the Jelly Bean version onwards (API level 16 +).

For Ice Cream Sandwich, `SYSTEM_UI_FLAG_LAYOUT_STABLE` does not work. But there are very few devices with this version and the Status bar is shown on very few occasions, so it is acceptable.

The real fullscreen mode was introduced in KitKat.

Android 4.4 and beyond – immersive mode

On KiKat, a new mode was introduced: the **immersive mode**.

Immersive mode hides the Status and Navigation bars completely. It is designed, as the name indicates, for fully-immersive experiences, which means games mostly. Even when the Navigation bar appears again, it is semitransparent instead of black and overlaid on top of the game.

 The sticky immersive mode has been designed almost specifically for games.

Immersive mode can be used in two ways: **normal** and **sticky**. Both of them are fullscreen and the user is shown a tip the first time the app is put in this mode with an explanation of how to get out of it:

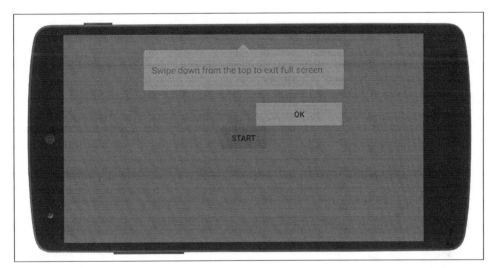

The immersive nonsticky mode will keep the Status and Navigation bars visible once they are shown, while the immersive sticky mode will hide them after a couple of seconds have passed, returning to the real fullscreen. The recommended mode for games is to use sticky immersion.

The code to put the app in the fullscreen sticky immersion mode is as follows:

```
@Override
public void onWindowFocusChanged(boolean hasFocus) {
  super.onWindowFocusChanged(hasFocus);
  if (hasFocus) {
    View decorView = getWindow().getDecorView();
    decorView.setSystemUiVisibility(
      View.SYSTEM_UI_FLAG_LAYOUT_STABLE
      | View.SYSTEM_UI_FLAG_LAYOUT_FULLSCREEN
      | View.SYSTEM_UI_FLAG_FULLSCREEN
      | View.SYSTEM_UI_FLAG_LAYOUT_HIDE_NAVIGATION
      | View.SYSTEM_UI_FLAG_HIDE_NAVIGATION
      | View.SYSTEM_UI_FLAG_IMMERSIVE_STICKY);
  }
}
```

In this case, as in the previous one, we are requesting the use of a stable layout, and we are making it as if it is fullscreen. This time, we include a flag to make the stable layout the one with no Navigation bar (SYSTEM_UI_FLAG_LAYOUT_HIDE_NAVIGATION).

We also add the flags to hide the Status bar (fullscreen) and the Navigation bar (hide navigation). Finally, we ask for the immersive sticky mode. The result is a real fullscreen game:

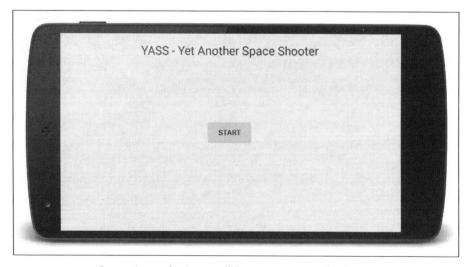

Immersive mode gives us all the screen space on the device

With this configuration, even when the user does a gesture to show the Status and Navigation bars, they are shown in a semitransparent way overlaid on top of our UI:

When the bars are shown while in sticky immersion mode, they are overlaid and semi transparent

Unfortunately, the sticky mode requires us to add the SYSTEM_UI_FLAG_HIDE_ NAVIGATION flag to put the Navigation bar in the sticky mode. This has a very bad side-effect in the previous versions of Android, making the Navigation bar appear and disappear continuously as soon as you touch the screen, since this flag without the immersive mode means something different.

In addition to this, the SYSTEM_UI_FLAG_LOW_PROFILE flag does not have any effect on the versions in which the immersive mode is available. This makes sense, since it is considered a replacement and an improvement on it.

Putting fullscreen together

Since we have two different modes for requesting fullscreen, one prior to KitKat (low profile) and one from KitKat (immersive mode), and the flags for hiding the Navigation bar do not play together nicely, we need to make a different configuration based on which version of Android the device is running on:

```
@Override
public void onWindowFocusChanged(boolean hasFocus) {
  super.onWindowFocusChanged(hasFocus);
  if (hasFocus) {
    View decorView = getWindow().getDecorView();
    if (Build.VERSION.SDK_INT < Build.VERSION_CODES.KITKAT) {
```

```
        decorView.setSystemUiVisibility(
          View.SYSTEM_UI_FLAG_LAYOUT_STABLE
           | View.SYSTEM_UI_FLAG_LAYOUT_FULLSCREEN
           | View.SYSTEM_UI_FLAG_FULLSCREEN
           | View.SYSTEM_UI_FLAG_LOW_PROFILE);
      }
      else {
        decorView.setSystemUiVisibility(
          View.SYSTEM_UI_FLAG_LAYOUT_STABLE
           | View.SYSTEM_UI_FLAG_LAYOUT_FULLSCREEN
           | View.SYSTEM_UI_FLAG_FULLSCREEN
           | View.SYSTEM_UI_FLAG_LAYOUT_HIDE_NAVIGATION
           | View.SYSTEM_UI_FLAG_HIDE_NAVIGATION
           | View.SYSTEM_UI_FLAG_IMMERSIVE_STICKY);
      }
    }
  }
}
```

With this code, we give the expected game experience to each one of the Android versions; a low profile with a dimmed Navigation bar on the versions older than KitKat and the full-immersive mode on the newer devices.

Good practices for game developers

In general, you should avoid premature optimization. This means, do not optimize your code unless you have a performance problem.

Nevertheless, in games, we have two methods (`onUpdate` and `onDraw`) for which the execution time is critical. So, we will be providing a few tips that should be enough to get performance under a reasonable threshold.

For the rest of the cases, your code will be probably good. If you find a performance problem, you should measure it carefully to find where the bottleneck is and only then optimize it. Most of the time, the problem is not where we think it is. Premature optimization can lead to a less readable code without significant improvement.

Object pools

The creation and destruction of objects is an expensive operation that should be limited. This is one area where a real-time game is a lot more sensitive than an app.

Every time you create an object, the garbage collector has a chance to be run. In the old versions of Android, it meant that everything stopped for 200ms. While it is no longer this bad, it may still be noticeable.

 We should avoid object creation as much as we can.

We want to avoid any expensive operation to be performed inside the onUpdate method—which must run as fast as it can—so we are going to take the creation and destruction of objects out of it.

The solution for this is a well-known software pattern called **object pool**.

Before we start the game, we will precreate the objects we are going to need and put them in a pool. The pool can be something as simple as a stack or list.

Instead of creating an object, we will pick one from the pool and initialize it. If the pool is empty, it means that we underestimated the number of objects. So as a lesser evil, a new instance of the object must be created.

Instead of destroying an object, we will put it back into the pool.

The fact that we have to return objects to the pool forces us to figure out when an object is no longer needed instead of just relying on the garbage collector to do that for us. While it requires a bit of effort, this mental exercise will improve the game performance and structure. If you have ever worked with C++, this should be easy-peasy for you.

We will use object pools for all the game objects in the code; this means enemies and bullets basically.

Avoiding enhanced loop syntax in lists

Related to the object creation, we should avoid the use of an enhanced loop syntax in the lists. While the for-each syntax is easier to read, it creates an iterator on-the-fly, which makes the execution slower and gives the garbage collector a chance to be run.

In the case of the `onUpdate` method of `GameEngine`, we could have written it using the for-each syntax like this:

```
public void onUpdate(long elapsedMillis) {
  for (GameObject gameObject : mGameObjects) {
    gameObject.onUpdate(elapsedMillis, this);
  }
}
```

But this is significantly slower than using the standard for loop syntax. This is why it looks like this instead:

```
public void onUpdate(long elapsedMillis) {
  int numGameObjects = mGameObjects.size();
  for (int i=0; i<numGameObjects; i++) {
    mGameObjects.get(i).onUpdate(elapsedMillis, this);
  }
}
```

In the particular case of arrays, the enhanced syntax is as fast as the traditional one on the devices with the **JIT (just-in-time)** compiler—which should be the case for all devices nowadays—so there is no drawback in always using the default loop syntax instead of the enhanced one.

It is also important to use a variable for the size instead of requesting it for every iteration, which leads us to the next tip.

Precreating objects

Related to the inefficiency of creating objects inside the `onUpdate` loop, we should always precreate the objects we are going to use.

A good example of this practice is the `Runnable` objects that are created inside the `GameObject` to run `onRemovedFromGameUiThread` and `onAddedToGameUiThread`.

We could create them on-demand inside the game engine as a part of `addGameObject` and `removeGameObject`, but it will be much less efficient.

Accessing variables directly

As often as we can, we will use a direct variable access instead of using getters and setters. This is a good practice in general, since accessors are expensive and the compiler does not inline them.

In the case of games, it makes sense to extend this practice to variables of other classes. As we mentioned several times before, the execution time of onUpdate and onDraw is critical; a difference of just milliseconds counts. This is why, when variables from the game objects are accessed by other game objects, we make them public and work with them directly.

This is a bit counter-intuitive for Java developers, since we are used to encapsulating everything through getters and setters. In this case, efficiency is more important than encapsulation.

Being careful with floating points

In the case of doing calculations, integer operations are about twice as fast as float operations.

When integers are not enough, there is no real difference in speed between float and double. The only difference is in space, where doubles are twice as large.

Also, even for integers, some processors have hardware multiply, but lack hardware divide. In such cases, integer division and modulus operations are performed in the software. All in all, this is a case where premature optimization can harm you.

Performance myths – avoid interfaces

On the older versions of Android, before the JIT compiler was introduced, accessing methods via an interface instead of the exact type was slightly more efficient. In these versions, it made sense to declare a variable of ArrayList instead of the generic List interface to access the class directly.

In the modern versions of Android, however, there is no difference between accessing a variable via an interface and doing it directly. So, for the sake of generality, we will be using the generic interface instead of the class, as seen inside the GameEngine:

```
private List<GameObject> mGameObjects = new
  ArrayList<GameObject>();
```

Summary

After a quick introduction to the question of which tools are best to make which types of games, we have described the pros and cons of using the bare Android SDK for making games.

We have set up a project and defined the main activity and its orientation. We have created a basic game engine, included it in the project, and checked whether it works as expected.

Later, we have extended the project with a second fragment and a pause dialog, managed the lifecycle of the game properly, and defined a way to get a proper fullscreen for different Android versions.

Finally, we have covered a few tips on optimizing the code inside the critical sections of the game.

We are ready to start handling the user input.

Managing User Input

2

In this chapter, we will learn how to handle user input in a generic way and later expand it to be either a virtual joystick, sensors, or an external controller.

To get a visual feedback of the input, we will be placing a spaceship on the screen and moving it around. We will also make it fire some bullets. This will also help you understand the interaction between the game objects and the game engine.

We will extend the generic `InputController` class to make the simplest keypad controller possible to understand how the class fits in the existing architecture and how the input is processed and read inside the game objects.

Once we get the basic keypad working, we will implement a virtual joystick, which is a much better way of handling user input.

Managing physical controllers is also important for the game we are writing, so we will see how to detect them and handle different options.

Finally, we will talk a bit about using sensors as controls. They are not a good fit for this type of game, but we will cover the basics and provide some links if you want to explore further.

The InputController base class

It does not matter how we want to control the game; it can always be abstracted as a two-axis joystick and a button to fire. For other games this could be different, but you should always be able to extract basic actions from the user and create an `InputController` that handles them. The `InputController` we are building is useful for any game that uses directional control.

[Input controllers are quite specific to each type of game.]

We are going to consider a normalized horizontal and vertical axis as an input (going from -1 to 1). In the case of a controller that does not have a range, we will just set it to the maximum. This will allow us to handle user input with precision when the type of input allows us to, as is the case with virtual and real joysticks as well as with sensors.

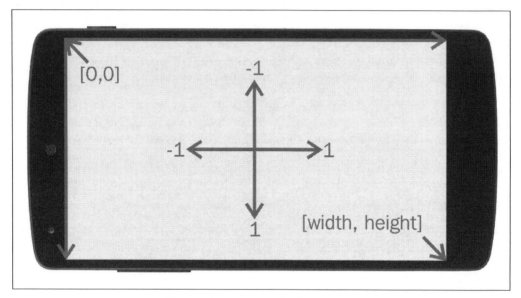

The coordinate system of a phone screen

Just as a reminder, the coordinates on a computer screen have [0,0] in the top-left corner and go positive towards to the right and down. The bottom-right corner has coordinates **[width, height]**. This is different from the standard coordinate system we are used to, but it is very important that you remember it.

This is why moving left is -1 and moving to the top is -1 as well.

The base class for all the input controllers in our game is going to be as follows:

```
public class InputController {

    public double mHorizontalFactor;
    public double mVerticalFactor;

    public boolean mIsFiring;

    public void onStart() {
    }

    public void onStop() {
    }

    public void onPause() {
    }

    public void onResume() {
    }
}
```

Note that this is a class with public variables. It is done this way to avoid reading the values via a method. We mentioned that in the previous chapter as a performance improvement.

Each implementation of this class will be responsible for having these variables populated with the updated values. The game objects can read them during `onUpdate`. By doing this, we separate the action of using the values from the game objects from the reading of the user input.

 `InputController` isolates the reading of the input from its usage via the game objects.

`InputController` is a part of the `GameEngine`. We just add a variable of this type to the engine and create a method to set it:

```
public InputController mInputController;

public void setInputController(InputController controller) {
    mInputController = controller;
}
```

The methods `onStart`, `onStop`, `onPause`, and `onResume` are called from the `GameEngine`, when the game is started, stopped, paused, or resumed. Some input controllers will need to do special actions in such situations.

Finally, we add the input controller to the `GameEngine` during the initialization of the engine inside the `GameFragment`:

```
mGameEngine = new GameEngine(getActivity());
mGameEngine.addGameObject(new ScoreGameObject(view,
  R.id.txt_score));
view.findViewById(R.id.btn_play_pause).setOnClickListener(this);
mGameEngine.setInputController(new InputController());
mGameEngine.addGameObject(new Player(getView()));
mGameEngine.startGame();
```

For now, we are adding an input controller that does nothing. We are also adding a `Player` game object, which we are going to work on before going into the different input controllers in more detail.

Note that we are no longer using the `ScoreGameObject` from the previous example and it should not be added to the game engine.

The Player object

The first version of the `Player` game object we are going to build will just initialize its coordinates in the middle of the screen. Then, it will update them based on the information in the input controller and, finally, it will display the value as [x, y] in the `TextView` we have on the layout.

After this, we will make it display a spaceship located at the coordinates. But for now, we will focus on how `onUpdate` is implemented.

The code for `onUpdate` and `onDraw` of the first version of the `Player` class is as follows:

```
@Override
public void onUpdate(long elapsedMillis, GameEngine gameEngine) {
  InputController inputController = gameEngine.inputController;
  mPositionX +=
    mSpeedFactor*inputController.mHorizontalFactor*elapsedMillis;
  if (mPositionX < 0) {
    mPositionX = 0;
  }
```

```
    if (mPositionX > mMaxX) {
      mPositionX = mMaxX;
    }
    mPositionY +=
      mSpeedFactor*inputController.mVerticalFactor*elapsedMillis ;
    if (mPositionY < 0) {
      mPositionY = 0;
    }
    if (mPositionY > mMaxY) {
      mPositionY = mMaxY;
    }
  }

  @Override
  public void onDraw() {
    mTextView.setText("["+(int) (mPositionX)+","+(int)
      (mPositionY)+"]");
  }
```

So, in each run of onUpdate, we will increase the x and y position using the corresponding factor (which we read from the input controller), a speed factor, and the elapsed milliseconds. This is nothing more than the classic formula *distance = speed * time*.

The rest of the code ensures that the *x* and *y* positions stay inside the boundaries of the screen.

The onDraw method is equivalent to the one of ScoreGameObject, but it just sets text in TextView.

Now there are a few values in this code that we have not initialized. They are as follows:

- mSpeedFactor: The speed converted into pixels per millisecond.
- mMaxX: The maximum value for x. It will be the width of the view minus the paddings.
- mMaxY: The maximum value for y. It is the height of the view minus the padding.
- mTextView: The view in which we set the current coordinates.

All these elements are initialized on the constructor of the `Player` object that receives the parent view as a parameter:

```java
public Player(final View view) {
  // We read the size of the view
  double pixelFactor = view.getHeight() / 400d;
  mSpeedFactor = pixelFactor * 100d / 1000d;
  mMaxX = view.getWidth() - view.getPaddingRight() -
    view.getPaddingRight();
  mMaxY = view.getHeight() - view.getPaddingTop() -
    view.getPaddingBottom();

  mTextView = (TextView) view.findViewById(R.id.txt_score);
}
```

We calculate the pixel factor of our screen, taking a height of 400 units as a reference. This is an arbitrary number and you can use whatever makes sense to you. It will help if you think of working with a 400 px tall screen and then let the code convert it to the real amount of pixels.

This is a concept that is similar to dips, but also different. While dips are meant to have the same physical size among all devices, the units make our game scale. So, all the items of the game will take the same amount of screen space regardless of the resolution or size of the device.

 We will define the game space in "units" so all the devices have the same screen height.

We want our ship to move at a speed of 100 units per second, so moving across the screen from its bottom to the top takes 4 seconds. Since we need the speed in pixels per millisecond, we need to multiply the desired speed with the pixel factor (pixels/unit) and divide it by 1,000 (milliseconds/second).

The next step is to read the width and height of the parent view and use them as the maximum width and height after subtracting the padding.

Finally, we get a hook into the `TextView` that we are going to use to display the coordinates.

Once we have finished the initialization, we still have the `startGame` method. In this one, we will position our player in the middle of the screen.

```
@Override
public void startGame() {
  mPositionX = mMaxX / 2;
  mPositionY = mMaxY / 2;
}
```

If you try and run the example now, you will see that the position stays at [0,0], indicating that something is going wrong.

The problem is that we are reading the width and height of a view straight after it is created (inside the `onViewCreated` method of the `GameFragment`). At this moment, the view has not yet been measured.

 You cannot obtain the width and/or height of a view during the constructor, as it has not been measured yet.

The solution for this is to delay the initialization of the `GameEngine` until the view has been measured. The best way to do this is to use `ViewTreeObserver`. Let's go to the `onViewCreated` of the `GameFragment` and update it:

```
@Override
public void onViewCreated(View view, Bundle savedInstanceState) {
  super.onViewCreated(view, savedInstanceState);
  view.findViewById(R.id.btn_play_pause).setOnClickListener(this);
  final ViewTreeObserver obs = view.getViewTreeObserver();
  obs.addOnGlobalLayoutListener(new
    ViewTreeObserver.OnGlobalLayoutListener() {
      @Override
      public void onGlobalLayout() {
        if(Build.VERSION.SDK_INT < Build.VERSION_CODES.JELLY_BEAN) {
          obs.removeGlobalOnLayoutListener(this);
        }
        else {
          obs.removeOnGlobalLayoutListener(this);
        }
        mGameEngine = new GameEngine(getActivity());
        mGameEngine.setInputController(new
          BasicInputController(getView()));
        mGameEngine.addGameObject(new Player(getView()));
        mGameEngine.startGame();
      }
    });
}
```

We get the `ViewTreeObserver` of the view that has just been created for the layout and add a new `OnGlobalLayoutListener` to it. We create the listener as an anonymous inner class.

This listener will be called every time a global layout is performed. To avoid being called multiple times and, therefore, initializing multiple engines, we need to remove the listener as soon as it is called.

Unfortunately, there was a typo in the name of the method used to remove the listener in Android versions prior to Jelly Bean, so we have to use one method name for versions before Jelly Bean and another one for later versions.

The rest of the code inside the method is the engine initialization, which was previously done directly inside `onViewCreated`. We just moved it inside `onGlobalLayout`.

Note that, while the views have not been measured yet, they have been created and they exist. So, there is no need to move the code that sets the `OnClickListener` for the pause button to the layout observer.

If we go on and run this version, we will see that the coordinates show the value of the center of the screen in pixels.

Displaying a spaceship

All this is not fun if we don't at least show a spaceship, so we can see that something is really happening.

We are going to take the graphics for the game from the OpenGameArt website (`http://opengameart.org`), which contains multiple free—as in freedom—graphics for games, most of them under a Creative Commons license, which means you have to credit the author.

 The OpenGameArt.org website is a great resource for game graphics.

The spaceships we are going to show were created by Eikesteer and we will use them throughout the game.

The spaceship set made by Eikesteer that we picked from Open Game Art

From the set, we will use the third from the right. We can extract it to a new image using a simple editor such as GIMP and place it under the `drawable-nodpi` directory.

Note that we are going to scale everything to be consistent with our 400 units of screen height, so it does not make sense to put the image in a drawable directory that has a density qualifier. This is why we are going to use `drawable-nodpi`.

The `drawable-nodpi` directory is meant to be independent from any density, while `drawable` is meant for images that do not have a qualifier. This means that the behavior is different when we try to read the intrinsic size of a drawable image. The intrinsic size will return the real size when placed under `nodpi` and will depend on the device when read from `drawable`.

 We will place our game object images in the `drawable-nodpi` folder.

The next step is to create an `ImageView` to display our spaceship. We are going to do this inside the constructor of the `Player` object:

```
public Player(final View view) {

  [...]

  // We create an image view and add it to the view
  mShip = new ImageView(view.getContext());
  Drawable shipDrawable = view.getContext().getResources()
    .getDrawable(R.drawable.ship);
  mShip.setLayoutParams(new ViewGroup.LayoutParams(
    (int) (shipDrawable.getIntrinsicWidth() * mPixelFactor),
    (int) (shipDrawable.getIntrinsicHeight() * mPixelFactor)));
  mShip.setImageDrawable(shipDrawable);

  mMaxX -= (shipDrawable.getIntrinsicWidth()*mPixelFactor);
  mMaxY -= (shipDrawable.getIntrinsicHeight()*mPixelFactor);

  ((FrameLayout) view).addView(mShip);
}
```

The first part of the constructor remains unchanged. We then add the code to create the `ImageView` and load the `Drawable` into it.

First, we create an `ImageView` using the `Context` of the parent view and we store it as a class variable.

Then, we load the `Drawable` of the ship from the resources and assign it to the `shipDrawable` local variable.

We proceed to create a `LayoutParams` object for the `ImageView` and set it. Since we already have the drawable, we can specify the exact dimensions for it. For this, we read the intrinsic width and height of the `shipDrawable` and multiply it by the pixel factor.

This means that the `ImageView` of the spaceship will be scaled to the equivalent of a 400-unit screen in pixels. Another way to say this is that the spaceship is the exact same size as it would be if displayed on a 400-pixel-tall screen. The drawable is then set to the `ImageView`.

We also have to update the maximum value of x and y by subtracting the size of the ship. With this, it gets placed in the center and it does not go outside the borders.

Finally, the `ImageView` is added to the parent view, which is expected to be a `FrameLayout`. This new requirement comes from the need to be able to position the image anywhere.

This is something we need to update or we will get a `ClassCastException`. We are updating the `fragment_game.xml` layout to have a top layout of the `FrameLayout` type.

Now that we are touching the layout, we will also align the pause button to the top right, which is where the pause button for most games is:

```
<FrameLayout
    xmlns:android="http://schemas.android.com/apk/res/android"
    xmlns:tools="http://schemas.android.com/tools"
    android:layout_width="match_parent"
    android:layout_height="match_parent"
    android:orientation="vertical"
    android:paddingTop="@dimen/activity_vertical_margin"
    android:paddingLeft="@dimen/activity_horizontal_margin"
    android:paddingRight="@dimen/activity_horizontal_margin"
    tools:context="com.plattysoft.yass.counter.GameFragment">

    <TextView
        android:layout_gravity="top|left"
        android:id="@+id/txt_score"
        android:layout_width="wrap_content"
        android:layout_height="wrap_content"
        android:text="@string/hello_world" />

    <Button
        android:layout_gravity="top|right"
        android:id="@+id/btn_play_pause"
        android:layout_width="wrap_content"
        android:layout_height="wrap_content"
        android:text="@string/pause" />
</FrameLayout>
```

Finally, we need to update the `onDraw` method to make it display the spaceship in the right position. For this, we just translate the `ImageView` to the expected position on the screen using `translateX` and `translateY`.

This is far from optimal, but we will work on the drawing in the next chapter. For now, it serves the purpose of displaying the image at the right position:

```
@Override
public void onDraw() {
  mTextView.setText("["+(int) (mPositionX)+","+(int)
    (mPositionY)+"]");
  mShip.setTranslationX((int) mPositionX);
  mShip.setTranslationY((int) mPositionY);
}
```

If we launch our game, we can see the spaceship in the middle of the screen:

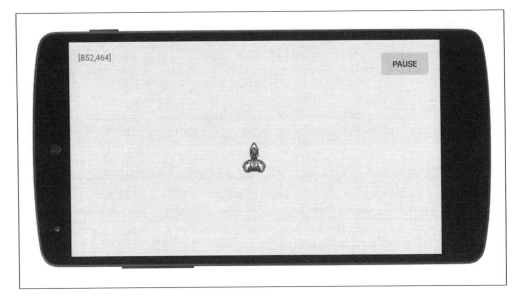

Now that we have a spaceship, it is time to add some bullets to the mix.

Firing bullets

The spaceship will fire bullets that will move upward until they are outside the screen.

As we mentioned in the Good practices for game developers section of the previous chapter, we will use an object pool for the bullets that we will create inside the Player class:

```
List<Bullet> mBullets = new ArrayList<Bullet>();
```

```
private void initBulletPool() {
  for (int i=0; i<INITIAL_BULLET_POOL_AMOUNT; i++) {
    mBullets.add(new Bullet(mPixelFactor));
  }
}

private Bullet getBullet() {
  if (mBullets.isEmpty()) {
    return null;
  }
  return mBullets.remove(0);
}

private void releaseBullet(Bullet b) {
  mBullets.add(b);
}
```

It initializes the number of bullets we want to have on the screen at a certain point. If you ask for a bullet when the pool has items it will just remove one and return it, but if the list is empty, it will return null. You can make this number a limitation to impact the gameplay or you can do the math and make the pool large enough.

In our case, we cannot fire more than 6 bullets, given the speed of the bullets and the time between shots.

Back to the pool, to release a bullet we will simply put it back into the list.

Now, during the onUpdate of the player, we check if we should fire a bullet:

```
@Override
public void onUpdate(long elapsedMillis, GameEngine gameEngine) {
  updatePosition(elapsedMillis, gameEngine.mInputController);
  checkFiring(elapsedMillis, gameEngine);
}

private void checkFiring(long elapsedMillis, GameEngine gameEngine) {
  if (gameEngine.mInputController.mIsFiring
      && mTimeSinceLastFire > TIME_BETWEEN_BULLETS) {
    Bullet b = getBullet();
    if (b == null) {
      return;
    }
```

```
        b.init(mPositionX + mShip.getWidth()/2, mPositionY);
        gameEngine.addGameObject(b);
        mTimeSinceLastFire = 0;
    }
    else {
        mTimeSinceLastFire += elapsedMillis;
    }
}
```

We check whether the input controller has the fire button pressed and whether the cool down time has passed. If we want and can fire a bullet we take one from the pool.

If there is no bullet available (the object b is null), we do nothing else and return.

Once we get a `Bullet` from the pool, we initialize it using the current position and place it in the middle of the spaceship. Then, we add it to the engine. To conclude, we reset the time since the last fire.

If we cannot or do not want to fire, we just add the elapsed milliseconds to the time since the last bullet was fired.

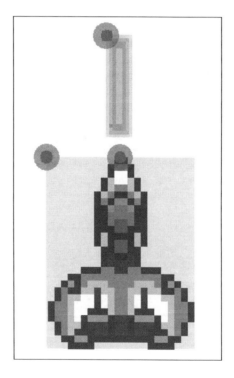

In the preceding image, we can see the relative position of the bullet with the spaceship and why passing the *x* coordinate as the center of the spaceship gives the right information to the bullet. But we still need to add some offsets to it.

From this moment on, all the logic regarding the movement of the bullet is done inside the `Bullet` object.

The Bullet game object

The `Bullet` extends `GameObject` as well. And, as the spaceship does, it also creates an `ImageView` and loads the drawable into it as part of the constructor:

```
public Bullet(View view, double pixelFactor) {
  Context c = view.getContext();

  mSpeedFactor = pixelFactor * -300d / 1000d;

  mImageView = new ImageView(c);
  Drawable bulletDrawable = c.getResources().getDrawable(R.drawable.
bullet);

  mImageHeight = bulletDrawable.getIntrinsicHeight() * pixelFactor;
  mImageWidth = bulletDrawable.getIntrinsicWidth() * pixelFactor;

  mImageView.setLayoutParams(new ViewGroup.LayoutParams(
    (int) (mImageWidth),
    (int) (mImageHeight)));
  mImageView.setImageDrawable(bulletDrawable);

  mImageView.setVisibility(View.GONE);
  ((FrameLayout) view).addView(mImageView);
}
```

The only difference between this constructor and the one for the `Player` object is that we set the visibility of `ImageView` to `GONE`, since the bullets are not supposed to be displayed unless they are being fired. The `Bullet` also has an `mPositionX` and `mPositionY` used for drawing.

These similarities come from the fact that both the game objects are what we call **sprites**. Sprite is a `GameObject` that has an image associated with it and gets rendered on the screen.

Sprite is a game object (generally a 2D image) that is displayed in a game and manipulated as a single entity.

In the next chapter, we will extract the common concepts of sprite and put them in a base class.

In the constructor, we also set the speed of the bullet to 300 units per second. This is 3 times faster than the spaceship. You can play with the values of speed and time between bullets, but remember to test that they do not overlap during continuous fire while the spaceship moves upward.

If you modify the bullet speed, you may also need to check the size of the pool. The worst case is to continuously fire with the spaceship placed at the bottom of the screen.

The next interesting point is initialization. This is done using the init method that receives the position of the spaceship:

```
public void init(Player parent, double positionX, double positionY) {
   mPositionX = positionX - mImageWidth/2;
   mPositionY = positionY - mImageHeight/2;
   mParent = parent;
}
```

It is worth mentioning that we want to position the bullet a bit ahead of the spaceship and properly centered. Since the member variables mPositionX and mPositionY are pointing to the top-left corner of the image, we have to apply an offset to the initial parameters based on the size of the bullet.

We are positioning the bullet only half way outside the spaceship on the vertical axis (*mImageHeight/2*) to improve the feeling of it being shot from the spaceship. We are also displaying it centered on the horizontal axis, which is why we also subtract *mImageWidth/2*.

The image in the previous section will also help you visualize this offset.

Because the Bullets are added and removed from the GameEngine, we need to change the visibility of the view when they are added and removed. This needs to be done on the UIThread. For this purpose, we use the callbacks we created in the previous chapter:

```
@Override
public void onRemovedFromGameUiThread() {
   mImageView.setVisibility(View.GONE);
}
```

```
@Override
public void onAddedToGameUiThread() {
    mImageView.setVisibility(View.VISIBLE);
}
```

 All changes to the view must be done on the UIThread, otherwise an exception will be thrown.

Since these bullets are also sprites, the onDraw method is almost identical to the one of the player. We do it again by animating the view and translating it:

```
@Override
public void onDraw() {
    mImageView.setTranslationX((int) mPositionX);
    mImageView.setTranslationY((int) mPositionY);
}
```

On the other hand, the onUpdate method is a bit different and it is interesting to look at it in detail:

```
@Override
public void onUpdate(long elapsedMillis, GameEngine gameEngine) {
    mPositionY += mSpeedFactor * elapsedMillis;
    if (mPositionY < -mImageHeight) {
        gameEngine.removeGameObject(this);
        // And return it to the pool
        mParent.releaseBullet(this);
    }
}
```

Similar to what we did with the player, we use the *distance = speed * time* formula. But, in this case, there is no influence from the InputController at all. The bullet has a fixed vertical speed.

We also check whether the bullet is out of the screen. Since we draw the items in the top-left corner, we need it to be completely gone. This is why we compare with mImageHeight.

If the bullet is out, we remove it from the GameEngine and we return it to the pool by calling releaseBullet.

This game object removal is done inside the onUpdate loop of the GameEngine. If we modify the list at this moment, we will get an ArrayIndexOutOfBoundsException while executing onUpdate in the GameEngine. This is why the removeGameObject method puts the objects in a separate list to be removed after onUpdate is called.

Now, all this is useless unless we can move the spaceship and fire the bullets. Let's build the most basic InputController.

The most basic virtual keypad

The simplest we can go is to build a simple keypad in the shape of a cross on the left-hand side of the screen and a fire button on its right-hand side. For this layout, we are going to create a new file under the layout folder and call it view_keypad. xml:

```xml
<?xml version="1.0" encoding="utf-8"?>
<RelativeLayout xmlns:android="http://schemas.android.com/apk/res/android"
    android:layout_gravity="bottom"
    android:padding="@dimen/keypad_size"
    android:layout_width="match_parent"
    android:layout_height="wrap_content">

    <Button
        android:id="@+id/keypad_up"
        android:layout_alignParentTop="true"
        android:layout_toRightOf="@+id/keypad_left"
        android:layout_width="@dimen/keypad_size"
        android:layout_height="@dimen/keypad_size" />

    <Button
        android:id="@+id/keypad_down"
        android:layout_below="@+id/keypad_left"
        android:layout_toRightOf="@+id/keypad_left"
        android:layout_width="@dimen/keypad_size"
        android:layout_height="@dimen/keypad_size" />

    <Button
        android:id="@+id/keypad_left"
        android:layout_alignParentLeft="true"
        android:layout_below="@+id/keypad_up"
        android:layout_width="@dimen/keypad_size"
        android:layout_height="@dimen/keypad_size" />
```

```
<Button
    android:id="@+id/keypad_right"
    android:layout_toRightOf="@+id/keypad_up"
    android:layout_below="@+id/keypad_up"
    android:layout_width="@dimen/keypad_size"
    android:layout_height="@dimen/keypad_size" />

<Button
    android:id="@+id/keypad_fire"
    android:layout_alignParentRight="true"
    android:layout_alignTop="@+id/keypad_left"
    android:layout_width="@dimen/keypad_size"
    android:layout_height="@dimen/keypad_size" />
</RelativeLayout>
```

We have a relative layout that covers the screen's full width. It has a `layout_gravity` set to `bottom`, so we are assured that it will be properly aligned.

We have our four-button pad arranged in a `RelativeLayout`. The left button is aligned to the left of the layout and the up button is aligned to the top of the layout. Then, the top and bottom buttons are set to the right of the left button. The right one is set below and to the right of the up button. Finally, the left one is set below the up button and the down button is just below the left. Sounds a bit too complicated, but the image is much clearer.

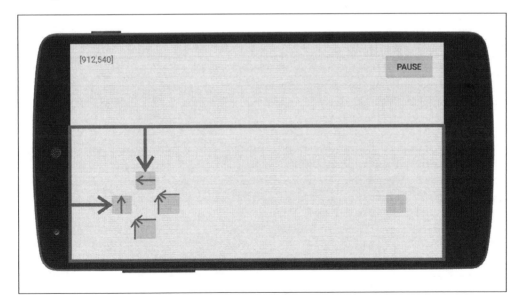

On the other side of the screen, aligned to the right of the parent and to the top of the left button, we have a fire button.

You may have noticed that all the buttons are using a special dimension named `keypad_size`. This is a very important point, not only to make them all look the same, but for usability in general. We are setting it to 42 dp, which is the recommended minimum size for a touch target.

 The smallest size a touchable item should have is 42 dp.

Feel free to play with the size of the buttons and observe by yourself that a smaller size button is very hard to touch. In fact, for a game, we should always use large-sized touch targets, sometimes larger than the area that provides visual feedback. The bigger you can make the touch area for a control, the better it is. In this example, the touch area of the fire button could be as large as the right half of the screen.

We are going to include this layout inside the game fragment, so we can see how it overlays. Since we already updated the top layout to be a `FrameLayout`, we just need to use an `include` tag.

```
<FrameLayout
    xmlns:android="http://schemas.android.com/apk/res/android"
    xmlns:tools="http://schemas.android.com/tools"
    android:layout_width="match_parent"
    android:layout_height="match_parent"
    android:paddingTop="@dimen/activity_vertical_margin"
    android:paddingLeft="@dimen/activity_horizontal_margin"
    android:paddingRight="@dimen/activity_horizontal_margin"
    tools:context="com.plattysoft.yass.counter.GameFragment">

    <TextView
        android:layout_gravity="top|left"
        android:id="@+id/txt_score"
        android:layout_width="wrap_content"
        android:layout_height="wrap_content"
        android:text="@string/hello_world" />

    <Button
        android:layout_gravity="top|right"
        android:id="@+id/btn_play_pause"
        android:layout_width="wrap_content"
        android:layout_height="wrap_content"
        android:text="@string/pause" />
```

```
    <include layout="@layout/view_keypad" />
</FrameLayout>
```

If we just go on and run it, we can see how it looks all together.

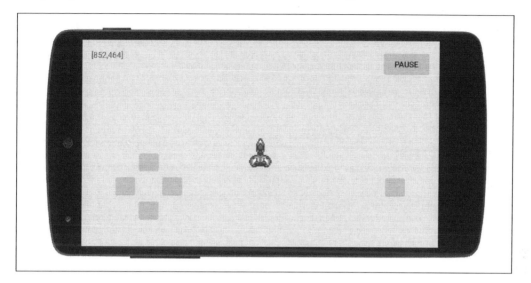

Now let's write the code for the `BasicInputController` to handle the buttons. Starting with the constructor, the code is as follows:

```
public BasicInputController(View view) {
    view.findViewById(R.id.keypad_up).setOnTouchListener(this);
    view.findViewById(R.id.keypad_down).setOnTouchListener(this);
    view.findViewById(R.id.keypad_left).setOnTouchListener(this);
    view.findViewById(R.id.keypad_right).setOnTouchListener(this);
    view.findViewById(R.id.keypad_fire).setOnTouchListener(this);
}
```

We are setting the game controller as the touch listener for all the buttons: up, down, left, right, and fire. It is important to note that we have to use `OnTouchListener` and not `OnClickListener`.

The `onClick` callback is only triggered when the button is pressed and then released. In our case, we need to know when the button is pressed and when it is released. We need to move the spaceship while the button is being pressed. This is why we need the more detailed callback that `OnTouchListener` provides.

The implementation of the method from `OnTouchListener` in the `BasicInputController` is as follows:

```java
@Override
public boolean onTouch(View v, MotionEvent event) {
  int action = event.getActionMasked();
  int id = v.getId();
  if (action == MotionEvent.ACTION_DOWN) {
    // User started pressing a key
    if (id == R.id.keypad_up) {
      mVerticalFactor -= 1;
    }
    else if (id == R.id.keypad_down) {
      mVerticalFactor += 1;
    }
    else if (id == R.id.keypad_left) {
      mHorizontalFactor -= 1;
    }
    else if (id == R.id.keypad_right) {
      mHorizontalFactor += 1;
    }
    else if (id == R.id.keypad_fire) {
      mIsFiring = false;
    }
  }
  else if (action == MotionEvent.ACTION_UP) {
    if (id == R.id.keypad_up) {
      mVerticalFactor += 1;
    }
    else if (id == R.id.keypad_down) {
      mVerticalFactor -= 1;
    }
    else if (id == R.id.keypad_left) {
      mHorizontalFactor += 1;
    }
    else if (id == R.id.keypad_right) {
      mHorizontalFactor -= 1;
    }
    else if (id == R.id.keypad_fire) {
      mIsFiring = false;
    }
  }
  return false;
}
```

It is important to note that we are calling `getActionMasked` instead of `getAction`. In the case of multiple touch pointers, `getAction` includes pointer information while that information is removed when requested as a masked action. This is why the recommended way to handle multitouch is to to use `getActionMasked` and `getActionPointer`. Otherwise, you need to use the OR operation to check for the action instead of the equal or it won't work when the pointers above the first one are being read.

 Using `getActionMasked` and `getPointerIndex` is the recommended way to deal with multitouch.

We have two cases. When the action is `MotionEvent.ACTION_DOWN`, it means that the user has pressed a button, so we check for the ID of the view that was touched and act accordingly.

If the view is up or down, we subtract or add 1 to the vertical factor. Similarly, we subtract or add 1 to the horizontal factor if the touched button was left or right.

The second part, where we handle the `MotionEvent.ACTION_UP` action, reverses the addition or subtraction to the corresponding factor.

We are adding and subtracting instead of setting the value to 1 or -1 for multitouch. For example, if you first tap on right and then on left, the spaceship should stop, since you are pressing on both buttons at the same time. Once you release one of them, the movement is restored.

For the fire button, we set `mIsFiring` to `true` when it is down and to `false` when it is up. Simple.

Finally, we return `false`. This is important, because it tells the system that the event was not consumed by our listener and, therefore, the chain of listeners can continue. This chain of listeners includes the button's own click listener, which is responsible for changing the background image to one consistent with the button's state. If we return true, updating the background will not happen.

 OnTouch implementation returns whether the event was consumed by this listener or not.

As simple as this—we can run the game now. We will see that the spaceship moves around the screen and also fires some bullets. At last, YASS starts to look like a game.

Limitations and problems

There are several limitations and problems with such a simple keypad. Apart from the fact that the buttons are quite small and hard to handle, the rest of the issues come from when users move the touch pointer.

If the user moves outside the button, Android versions before API level 17 will trigger an event of the `MotionEvent.ACTION_DOWN` type, but from this API level onwards they will not. If you want to handle this situation properly, you need to check on every move or action and validate whether it gets out of the rectangle for the original view to do a manual cancel. But this is not the only problem with move. If you tap on one button and move towards the opposite one, a new tap on the other button will not be detected, since it is an `ACTION_MOVE` and not an `ACTION_DOWN`.

The solution for this is to check the position of each pointer in each event, see whether it is inside the rectangle of a button, and act accordingly.

There is also the problem of not being able to handle diagonal movements.

We could try and solve these problems for this keypad. But since it is not a very elegant input controller anyway, we will just move forward and make an `InputController` that is a proper virtual joystick instead.

Creating a virtual joystick

We are going to improve the user input and we are going to do it by creating a virtual joystick.

A **virtual joystick** measures the distance from the touch position to its center and uses this information to set the values on the two axes. It behaves as a traditional analog joystick.

Since it is virtual, we are not constrained to have it at a specific position on the screen, so we can place it anywhere the player touches it.

We cannot, however, take the entire screen for the virtual joystick. There needs to be a fire button too.

We have experienced the frustration of small touch targets, so we are going to make the fire button as big as we can. This means that we are going to use half the screen for the virtual joystick and half the screen for the fire button.

The layout that we are going to use will have two views that fill the screen, each of them covering half of the width. We will name this layout `view_vjoystick.xml`:

```xml
<?xml version="1.0" encoding="utf-8"?>
<LinearLayout xmlns:android="http://schemas.android.com/apk/res/
android"
  android:orientation="horizontal"
  android:layout_width="match_parent"
  android:layout_height="match_parent">

  <View android:id="@+id/vjoystick_main"
    android:layout_height="match_parent"
    android:layout_width="match_parent"
    android:layout_weight="1"
  />
  <View android:id="@+id/vjoystick_touch"
    android:layout_height="match_parent"
    android:layout_width="match_parent"
    android:layout_weight="1"
  />
</LinearLayout>
```

The interesting bit of this layout is the usage of Android:`layout_weight` to equally divide the screen into two halves. You can modify the weight value to make one view larger than the other if you want a larger space for the virtual joystick or the fire button.

We will create a class to handle this user `InputController`. We will call it `VirtualJoystickInputController` and it will, obviously, extend `InputController`.

To handle the events of this `InputController`, we are going to use two internal classes. One for each view we want to listen to the events to:

```java
public VirtualJoystickInputController(View view) {
  view.findViewById(R.id.vjoystick_main)
    .setOnTouchListener(new VJoystickTouchListener());
  view.findViewById(R.id.vjoystick_touch)
    .setOnTouchListener(new VFireButtonTouchListener());

  double pixelFactor = view.getHeight() / 400d;
  mMaxDistance = 50*pixelFactor;
}
```

The mMaxDistance variable defines how far from the touch we consider the user to have reached the maximum. The value is, again, in screen units. You can imagine the maximum distance as the radius of the virtual gamepad. The smaller this distance is, the more sensitive the joystick is.

A small maximum distance will allow quick reactions, while a large one will allow better precision. Feel free to experiment with its size to make it work as you'd like.

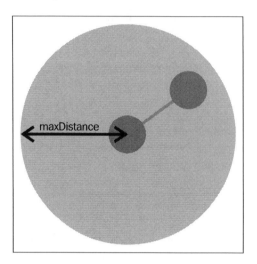

The fire button is easier to handle than the virtual joystick. We use the same logic as in the previous example. Set mIsFiring to true when the event is a down action and set it to false when the event is an up action:

```
private class VFireButtonTouchListener implements View.OnTouchListener
{
  @Override
  public boolean onTouch(View v, MotionEvent event) {
    int action = event.getActionMasked();
    if (action == MotionEvent.ACTION_DOWN) {
      mIsFiring = true;
    }
    else if (action == MotionEvent.ACTION_UP) {
      mIsFiring = false;
    }
    return true;
  }
}
```

The listener for the virtual joystick is more interesting. We record the position of the touch when a down action is performed, we also reset the values when the touch goes up. But, as long as it moves, we update the values of mHorizontalFactor and mVerticalFactor based on the distance to the original touch:

```
private class VJoystickTouchListener implements
  View.OnTouchListener {
  @Override
  public boolean onTouch(View v, MotionEvent event) {
    int action = event.getActionMasked();
    if (action == MotionEvent.ACTION_DOWN) {
      mStartingPositionX = event.getX(0);
      mStartingPositionY = event.getY(0);
    }
    else if (action == MotionEvent.ACTION_UP) {
      mHorizontalFactor = 0;
      mVerticalFactor = 0;
    }
    else if (action == MotionEvent.ACTION_MOVE) {
      // Get the proportion to the max
      mHorizontalFactor = (event.getX(0) - mStartingPositionX) /
        mMaxDistance;
      if (mHorizontalFactor > 1) {
        mHorizontalFactor = 1;
      }
      else if (mHorizontalFactor < -1) {
        mHorizontalFactor = -1;
      }
      mVerticalFactor = (event.getY(0) - mStartingPositionY) /
        mMaxDistance;
      if (mVerticalFactor > 1) {
        mVerticalFactor = 1;
      }
      else if (mVerticalFactor < -1) {
        mVerticalFactor = -1;
      }
    }
    return true;
  }
}
```

Please note that we want to keep mHorizontalFactor and mVerticalFactor between -1 and 1; thus, whenever the distance is larger than mMaxDistance, we do not consider it.

Finally, time to connect this new controller to the GameEngine. It is quite simple. We just have to update the layout for fragment_game.xml, including view_vjoystick.xml instead of view_keypad.xml, and then update the initialization of the GameEngine:

```xml
<FrameLayout
    xmlns:android="http://schemas.android.com/apk/res/android"
    xmlns:tools="http://schemas.android.com/tools"
    android:layout_width="match_parent"
    android:layout_height="match_parent"
    android:orientation="vertical"
    android:paddingTop="@dimen/activity_vertical_margin"
    android:paddingLeft="@dimen/activity_horizontal_margin"
    android:paddingRight="@dimen/activity_horizontal_margin"
    tools:context="com.plattysoft.yass.counter.GameFragment">

    <TextView
        android:layout_gravity="top|left"
        android:id="@+id/txt_score"
        android:layout_width="wrap_content"
        android:layout_height="wrap_content"
        android:text="@string/hello_world" />

    <Button
        android:layout_gravity="top|right"
        android:id="@+id/btn_play_pause"
        android:layout_width="wrap_content"
        android:layout_height="wrap_content"
        android:text="@string/pause" />

    <include layout="@layout/view_vjoystick" />

</FrameLayout>
```

As a reminder, the initialization of the GameEngine is done inside onViewCreated of the GameFragment. We only need to create an instance of the proper InputController:

```java
mGameEngine = new GameEngine(getActivity());
mGameEngine.setInputController(new
    VirtualJoystickInputController(get View()));
mGameEngine.addGameObject(new Player(getView()));
mGameEngine.startGame();
```

Time to run the game and try this controller.

General considerations and improvements

This input method is a huge improvement over the basic keypad we did before. The touch area is as big as the screen and the player does not need to look at this area of the screen to tap on small buttons. It will work anywhere.

This system handles diagonal as well as horizontal and vertical movements and also anything in between.

The player does not need to remove his/her finger from the screen to change the directions.

There is a lack of visual feedback, which can be solved by drawing the virtual gamepad as two circles when the player is using it. A big circle will show the range of the virtual joystick, while a smaller one will show the current touch pointer. On the other hand, you may not want to, since the lack of visual clutter makes the screen cleaner.

Physical controllers

Time to move into a type of controller that hardcore gamers love: physical ones.

There are a few devices that have a controller included as a part of their hardware. Some notable examples are XPeria Play — one of the pioneer phones that had a sliding gamepad — and Nvidia Shield, the latest in this category.

XPeria Play was one of the first devices with an integrated gamepad:

Nvidia Shield is one of the most powerful Android devices with a gamepad:

On the other hand, there are many brands that build game controllers for smartphones and they have been fairly popular among traditional gamers. All of them are Bluetooth controllers that can be connected to your phone or tablet. Some of them are designed to make your phone fit into it like Gametel (another pioneer) and most of the MOGA models.

MOGA controller with an adjustable strip to hold your phone

There are also a few Android-powered devices that use controllers as the main input source. Here, we are talking about microconsoles such as the OUYA or other TV-like devices such as the Amazon FireTV or Android TV.

The OUYA was the first of the Android microconsoles

These devices work in a very similar way to HID devices, either in the form of keyboards or as directional controls based on an axis (analog joysticks). All we have to do to handle them is to set the correct listeners.

Some controllers do have their own proprietary library. We won't cover this, since they are very specific and they provide detailed documentation on how to integrate them. This is the case with the MOGA Pocket (more advanced MOGA controllers support two modes: proprietary and HID).

 Most controllers work as HID, which is standard.

We can set listeners for the controller at the `Activity` level or `View` level. In any case, we will need to extend the class. There is no way to add a listener for these methods, they must be overridden. Since we are already extending the `Activity` class, we'll do it this way.

 We listen to `KeyEvent` and `MotionEvent` inside the Activity.

There are two types of events we need to listen for. They are as follows:

- KeyEvent: For all the button presses and, in some gamepads, also the directional cross
- MotionEvent: Events related to the movement along an axis: joysticks

We want to have the input controller separated from the Activity, so we will make a special listener that combines the two events we need and then make the Activity delegate on it.

The interface we need is very simple, we will call it GamepadControllerListener:

```
public interface GamepadControllerListener {

    boolean dispatchGenericMotionEvent(MotionEvent event);

    boolean dispatchKeyEvent(KeyEvent event);
}
```

Inside the Activity, we create a method to set a listener of GamepadControllerListener type. Since we only require one listener at a time, the method is set instead of add. To remove the listener, we just need to set it to null:

```
public void setGamepadControllerListener(GamepadControllerListener
    listener) {
  mGamepadControllerListener = listener;
}
```

Finally, we have to override dispatchGenericMotionEvent and dispatchKeyEvent inside our Activity:

```
@Override
public boolean dispatchGenericMotionEvent(MotionEvent event) {
  if (mGamepadControllerListener != null) {
    if (mGamepadControllerListener.dispatchGenericMotionEvent(event)
) {
      return true;
    }
  }
  return super.dispatchGenericMotionEvent(event);
}

@Override
public boolean dispatchKeyEvent (KeyEvent event) {
```

```
    if (mGamepadControllerListener != null) {
      if (mGamepadControllerListener.dispatchKeyEvent(event)) {
        return true;
      }
    }
    return super.dispatchKeyEvent(event);
}
```

Note that this method uses the convention of returning true if the event was consumed and false if it was not. In our case, we will return true only if the event was consumed by the listener. In other cases, we will return the result to delegate the event to the base class.

It is very important to call the corresponding method in the super class, as there is a lot of processing done inside the Activity class that we do not want to discard accidentally.

With these components in place, we can proceed to create our GamepadInputController, which will extend InputController and implement GamepadControllerListener:

```
public class GamepadInputController
  extends InputController
  implements GamepadControllerListener {

  public GamepadInputController(YassActivity activity) {
    mActivity = activity;
  }

  @Override
  public void onStart() {
    mActivity.setGamepadControllerListener(this);
  }

  @Override
  public void onStop() {
    mActivity.setGamepadControllerListener(null);
  }

  [...]
}
```

Hooking into the key and motion events of the Activity is something we want to limit as much as possible. This is why we override the onStop and onStart methods of the InputController to only set the listener while a game is running.

There are several possible controller layouts. In general, they usually have a cross control and/or an analog joystick. Some have several analog joysticks and, of course, buttons. All in all there are some important details about the events and how different gamepads may be configured:

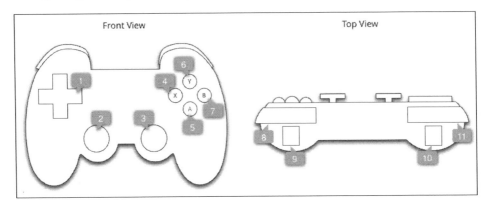

- The cross control can be made of buttons or it can be another analog joystick. If it has buttons, it will be handled as a KeyEvent with the same constants as a D-Pad. If it is an analog joystick, it will use AXIS_HAT_X and AXIS_HAT_Y.

- Analog joysticks are handled via MotionEvent and we can read them using the getAxisValue method of the MotionEvent. The default joystick will use AXIS_X and AXIS_Y.

- We are not going to map the second analog joystick for this game, but it is mapped on the AXIS_Z and AXIS_RZ.

- The buttons are mapped as a KeyEvent with the name of each button.

Handling MotionEvents

When we receive a MotionEvent, we need to first validate that the event is from a source we should read.

The source is part of the event and it is a composition of flags. The ones we are interested in are:

- SOURCE_GAMEPAD: It indicates that the device has gamepad buttons such as **A**, **B**, **X**, or **Y**.

- SOURCE_DPAD: It indicates that the device has a D-Pad.

- SOURCE_JOYSTICK: It indicates that the device has analog control sticks.

The only motion events we should process are the ones in which the source has the joystick flag set. Both gamepad and D-Pad sources will be sent as a KeyEvent.

The handling of receiving a `MotionEvent` is as follows:

```
@Override
public boolean dispatchGenericMotionEvent(MotionEvent event) {
  int source = event.getSource();

  if ((source & InputDevice.SOURCE_JOYSTICK) !=
    InputDevice.SOURCE_JOYSTICK) {
    return false
  }
  mHorizontalFactor = event.getAxisValue(MotionEvent.AXIS_X);
  mVerticalFactor = event.getAxisValue(MotionEvent.AXIS_Y);

  InputDevice device = event.getDevice();
  MotionRange rangeX = device.getMotionRange(MotionEvent.AXIS_X,
    source);
  if (Math.abs(mHorizontalFactor) <= rangeX.getFlat()) {
    mHorizontalFactor =
      event.getAxisValue(MotionEvent.AXIS_HAT_X);
    MotionRange rangeHatX =
      device.getMotionRange(MotionEvent.AXIS_HAT_X, source);
    if (Math.abs(mHorizontalFactor) <= rangeHatX.getFlat()) {
      mHorizontalFactor = 0;
    }
  }
  MotionRange rangeY = device.getMotionRange(MotionEvent.AXIS_Y,
    source);
  if (Math.abs(mVerticalFactor) <= rangeY.getFlat()) {
    mVerticalFactor = event.getAxisValue(MotionEvent.AXIS_HAT_Y);
    MotionRange rangeHatY =
      device.getMotionRange(MotionEvent.AXIS_HAT_Y, source);
    if (Math.abs(mVerticalFactor) <= rangeHatY.getFlat()) {
      mVerticalFactor = 0;
    }
  }
  return true;
}
```

First, we check the source. If it is not from a joystick, we just return `false`, since we won't be consuming this event.

Then we read the axis values for `MotionEvent.AXIS_X` and `MotionEvent.AXIS_Y` and assign them to our variables. This is meant to read the default joystick. But we are not done. It is possible that the controller has a cross that works as an analog joystick.

To decide whether we read the secondary joystick, we check if there was input on the default one. If not, we assign the value from the secondary one to our variables.

It is important to note that most analog joysticks are not perfectly aligned at 0, so comparing the value of mHorizontalFactor and mVerticalFactor with 0 is not a valid way to detect if the joystick was moved.

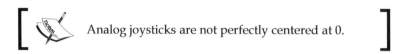 Analog joysticks are not perfectly centered at 0.

What we need to do is to read the flat value of the motion range of the device. It is much simpler than it sounds, since all this information is a part of the MotionEvent.

Then, if there was no input from the default axis, we assign the value of AXIS_HAT_X and AXIS_HAT_Y to our variables. We also check whether the input of the axis is above its flat value and set it to 0 if it is not. We need to do this or the spaceship will move very slowly without any input at all.

Finally, we return true to indicate that we have consumed the event.

Handling KeyEvents

The implementation of dispatchKeyEvent is very similar to the one we did for the basic controller with buttons on the screen:

```
@Override
public boolean dispatchKeyEvent(KeyEvent event) {
    int action = event.getAction();
    int keyCode = event.getKeyCode();
    if (action == MotionEvent.ACTION_DOWN) {
        if (keyCode == KeyEvent.KEYCODE_DPAD_UP) {
            mVerticalFactor -= 1;
            return true;
        }
        else if (keyCode == KeyEvent.KEYCODE_DPAD_DOWN) {
            mVerticalFactor += 1;
            return true;
        }
        else if (keyCode == KeyEvent.KEYCODE_DPAD_LEFT) {
            mHorizontalFactor -= 1;
            return true;
        }
```

```
      else if (keyCode == KeyEvent.KEYCODE_DPAD_RIGHT) {
        mHorizontalFactor += 1;
        return true;
      }
      else if (keyCode == KeyEvent.KEYCODE_BUTTON_A) {
        mIsFiring = true;
        return true;
      }
    }
    else if (action == MotionEvent.ACTION_UP) {
      if (keyCode == KeyEvent.KEYCODE_DPAD_UP) {
        mVerticalFactor += 1;
        return true;
      }
      else if (keyCode == KeyEvent.KEYCODE_DPAD_DOWN) {
        mVerticalFactor -= 1;
        return true;
      }
      else if (keyCode == KeyEvent.KEYCODE_DPAD_LEFT) {
        mHorizontalFactor += 1;
        return true;
      }
      else if (keyCode == KeyEvent.KEYCODE_DPAD_RIGHT) {
        mHorizontalFactor -= 1;
        return true;
      }
      else if (keyCode == KeyEvent.KEYCODE_BUTTON_A) {
        mIsFiring = false;
        return true;
      }
      else if (keyCode == KeyEvent.KEYCODE_BUTTON_B) {
        mActivity.onBackPressed();
        return true;
      }
    }
    return false;
}
```

The only significant difference is that we are comparing key codes to the constants for the D-Pad instead of view ID. But apart from this, the logic is exactly the same.

We also have to take care of mapping the button **B** to act as the back key. While this is already done on the latest versions of Android, it was not always the case, so we need to handle it. For this, we use the onBackPressed callback we already created in YassActivity.

Also, on Android 4.2 (API level 17) and before it, the system treated BUTTON_A as the Android back key by default. This is why we should always use BUTTON_A as the primary game action.

Detecting gamepads

It is a good practice to check whether a controller is connected when we launch the game. This allows us to display a help screen on how to play with a controller before the user starts playing. We should also check whether the controller is disconnected while the game is already running to pause it.

While checking for controllers can be done via the InputDevice class, checking for changes in the controllers was only introduced in API level 16 (we are using minSDK=15).

 Detecting changes in the controllers being connected or disconnected was only introduced in Jelly Bean.

We are not going to provide a backward-compatible solution to detect the connection and disconnection of controllers. If you need to do it, there are detailed steps in the official documentation at http://developer.android.com/training/game-controllers/compatibility.html; these basically use a polling mechanism over input devices and check for changes in the list.

We are going to check for gamepads during the onResume of the MainMenuFragment. The first time a controller is detected, we will show an AlertDialog that shows how to use the gamepad:

```
@Override
public void onResume() {
  super.onResume();
  if (isGameControllerConnected() && shouldDisplayGamepadHelp()) {
    displayGamepadHelp();
    // Do not show the dialog again
    PreferenceManager.getDefaultSharedPreferences(getActivity())
      .edit()
      .putBoolean(PREF_SHOULD_DISPLAY_GAMEPAD_HELP, false)
      .commit();
  }
}
```

```
private boolean shouldDisplayGamepadHelp() {
  return
    PreferenceManager.getDefaultSharedPreferences(getActivity())
    .getBoolean(PREF_SHOULD_DISPLAY_GAMEPAD_HELP, true);
}
```

We are using default shared preferences to store whether we have displayed the dialog already or not. Once it is displayed we set the value to false, so it is not shown again.

The method to check if there is a controller connected is as follows:

```
public boolean isGameControllerConnected() {
  int[] deviceIds = InputDevice.getDeviceIds();
  for (int deviceId : deviceIds) {
    InputDevice dev = InputDevice.getDevice(deviceId);
    int sources = dev.getSources();
    if (((sources & InputDevice.SOURCE_GAMEPAD) ==
        InputDevice.SOURCE_GAMEPAD) ||
        ((sources & InputDevice.SOURCE_JOYSTICK) ==
        InputDevice.SOURCE_JOYSTICK)) {
      return true;
    }
  }
  return false;
}
```

We iterate over the input devices and, if the source of any of them is a gamepad or a joystick, we return true.

If no device is found with these sources, we return false.

Note that each InputDevice also has a name. This can be useful to identify specific gamepads in case you want to show different help screens such as for Nvidia Shield.

To check whether a controller gets disconnected during gameplay, we need to register an InputDeviceListener on the InputManager and process the events. We will make GameFragment implement InputDeviceListener.

We do the registration right after creating the GameEngine and the unregistration after stopping the game in onDestroy. You need to either add some annotations to prevent int from giving an error for the method not being available on the minimum SDK or wrap it into an if block that checks the version, as we did before.

Then, it is as simple as pausing the game when a device is disconnected:

```
@Override
public void onInputDeviceRemoved(int deviceId) {
  if (!mGameEngine.isRunning()) {
    pauseGameAndShowPauseDialog();
  }
}
```

Note that this pauses the game when *any* device gets disconnected. It is unlikely that a device that is not a controller gets disconnected, but we could make sure it is a controller just by checking the source, as we did for `isGameControllerConnected`.

Sensors and InputControllers

Sensors are a common way to control games on smartphones. They work fine when the only controls in the game are left and right (like a car racing game). If you plan to also move up and down, you need to ask the player to do a calibration at the beginning of the game to make it usable. Note that, when you are using only one axis, such calibration is not necessary.

In addition to this, the up and down movement tends to interfere with the `sensorLandscape` orientation. So, the use of sensors is not a very good idea for YASS.

 Sensors are good controls only in certain cases.

You also have to consider that, while sensors are a replacement for directions, you still need to place the action buttons on the screen—in our case, the fire button.

We are not going to use sensors for YASS but, if you want to make a game that uses them, we will cover the basics.

You need to register a listener for the accelerometer and another one for the magnetic field. You should only listen to the sensors while the game is running, so we will override the life cycle methods to register and unregister sensors accordingly:

```
private void registerListeners() {
  SensorManager sm = (SensorManager)
    mActivity.getSystemService(Activity.SENSOR_SERVICE);
  sm.registerListener(mAccelerometerChangesListener,
    sm.getDefaultSensor(Sensor.TYPE_ACCELEROMETER),
    SensorManager.SENSOR_DELAY_FASTEST);
```

```
    sm.registerListener(mMagneticChangesListener,
      sm.getDefaultSensor(Sensor.TYPE_MAGNETIC_FIELD),
      SensorManager.SENSOR_DELAY_FASTEST);
  }

  private void unregisterListeners() {
    SensorManager sm = (SensorManager)
      mActivity.getSystemService(Activity.SENSOR_SERVICE);
    sm.unregisterListener(mAccelerometerChangesListener);
    sm.unregisterListener(mMagneticChangesListener);
  }

  @Override
  public void onStart() {
    registerListeners();
  }
  @Override
  public void onStop() {
    unregisterListeners();
  }
  @Override
  public void onResume() {
    registerListeners();
  }
  @Override
  public void onPause() {
    unregisterListeners();
  }
```

Note that we are using `SensorManager.SENSOR_DELAY_FASTEST`, which means that the sensors will give feedback as fast and as often as they can. This is very important for real-time games.

We are setting objects as listeners. Each listener will just copy the values of the sensor into a local array that we will process later on. For example, in the case of an accelerometer, we will do:

```
  @Override
  public void onSensorChanged(SensorEvent event) {
    System.arraycopy(event.values, 0, mLastAccels, 0, 3);
  }
```

To obtain the final value, we have to do some calculations. So, we will add a `onPreUpdate` method that will be called by the `GameEngine` just before calling `onUpdate`.

It is important to note that there are some special cases. They are as follows:

- There are devices that lack a magnetic field sensor. In such cases, we can use a simplified version using the value of the accelerometer. Nvidia Shield and specific versions of Nook are some of these devices.

- In all cases, the sensors are related to the default orientation of the device, which can be either landscape or portrait. We have to take this into consideration while processing the values.

All in all, the conversion for the horizontal axis can be done like this:

```
private double getHorizontalAxis() {
  if (SensorManager.getRotationMatrix(mRotationMatrix, null,
      mLastAccels, mLastMagFields)) {
    if (mRotation == Surface.ROTATION_0) {
      SensorManager.remapCoordinateSystem(mRotationMatrix,
        SensorManager.AXIS_Y, SensorManager.AXIS_MINUS_X,
        mRotationMatrix);
      SensorManager.getOrientation(mRotationMatrix, mOrientation);
      return mOrientation[1] * DEGREES_PER_RADIAN;
    }
    else {
      SensorManager.getOrientation(mRotationMatrix, mOrientation);
      return -mOrientation[1] * DEGREES_PER_RADIAN;
    }
  }
  else {
    // Case for devices which do NOT have magnetic sensors
    if (mRotation == Surface.ROTATION_0) {
      return -mLastAccels[0]* 5;
    }
    else {
      return -mLastAccels[1] * -5;
    }
  }
}
```

The `getHorizontalAxis` code does the following steps:

- Calculates the rotation matrix using the last data from the accelerometer and the magnetic sensor.

- If it returns true, all goes well. Based on the rotation of the device, we decide whether we need to remap the coordinate system or not and then return the orientation that is converted into degrees.

- If it could not be calculated (lack of a magnetic field sensor), the method returns false. We have to rely on an approximation using the accelerometer values. Based on the rotation of the device, we should use one or another axis.

The rotation of the device can be read in the constructor of the `InputController` with a single line of code.

```
mRotation = yassActivity.getWindowManager().getDefaultDisplay().
getRotation();
```

Finally, the `onPreUpdate` method:

```
@Override
public void onPreUpdate() {
  mHorizontalFactor = getHorizontalAxis()/ MAX_ANGLE;
  if (mHorizontalFactor > 1) {
    mHorizontalFactor = 1;
  }
  else if (mHorizontalFactor < -1) {
    mHorizontalFactor = -1;
  }
  mVerticalFactor = 0;
}
```

The is method just converts the reading (in degrees) into values in the range [-1,1] by using the maximum angle at which we consider it to be fully tilted. I recommend you to play with this constant and start with 30 degrees.

For more information on handling sensors, you can check the official documentation `http://developer.android.com/guide/topics/sensors/sensors_overview.html`.

Selecting control modes

It is common for games to ask the user to select the control mode they prefer, but it is also a good practice to avoid friction as much as possible by not asking what is not necessary.

YASS is only using a virtual joystick and the gamepad controls. There is no need to ask the user which one he or she wants. Both input modes are compatible, especially because the virtual joystick does not display anything on the screen when it is not used. The only thing we need to do is to modify the `GameEngine` to support more than one `InputController`.

We will support both input modes simultaneously.

The way to support both input modes at the same time is to create a `CompositeInputController` that uses the composition pattern to have both a `VirtualJoystickInputController` and a `GamepadInputController`, and combines the input from both.

To synchronize the readings from the two input controllers, we are going to use a method on the `InputController` called `onPreUpdate`, which will be called just before `onUpdate`. We will use it to populate the values of `mHorizontalFactor`, `mVerticalFactor`, and `mIsFiring` with the ones read from the other controllers.

```
public void onPreUpdate() {
  mIsFiring = mGamepadInputController.mIsFiring ||
    mVJoystickInputController.mIsFiring;
  mHorizontalFactor = mGamepadInputController.mHorizontalFactor +
    mVJoystickInputController.mHorizontalFactor;
  mVerticalFactor = mGamepadInputController.mVerticalFactor +
    mVJoystickInputController.mVerticalFactor;
}
```

We now have a game that can be controlled with a virtual joystick and a gamepad.

Summary

We have learned how to deal with input from users in several ways and how to make it transparent for the `GameEngine`.

To get a proper visual feedback from the controller, we created a `Player` game object that updates its position based on the values from the `InputController`. We also learned how to add and remove game objects to and from the `GameEngine` while playing.

We created a very basic keypad that later evolved into a virtual joystick. We also learned how to handle external controllers.

At this point, our game has a spaceship that moves along the screen and fires bullets. It can be controlled using a virtual joystick or a gamepad, independently.

The current implementation does lag occasionally and we have barely started drawing objects on the screen. It is time to fix this. Next stop: improve the rendering by drawing directly on the view instead of relying on positioning views on the screen.

3
Into the Draw Thread

In this chapter, we are going to improve the rendering of sprites for our game. For this, we are going to use a custom `GameView` that will perform low-level drawing. We will make two different implementations: one that extends from `View` and another one that extends from `SurfaceView`. We will let `DrawThread` be a real thread, to work better with this `GameView`.

We will refactor the project, creating a `Sprite` class that will be used for all the items that are drawn in the game. We will draw bitmaps on a `Canvas` and learn about the transformation matrix used to do this.

To continue improving the game, we will add enemies. They will be a wave of asteroids moving towards our spaceship. For this, we will learn the concept of `GameController` and the different ways of doing it, from static to procedural level generation.

As part of the rendering techniques, we will learn about occlusion culling and parallax backgrounds, which we will use to make the game look nicer.

Finally, we will add support for layers in the engine.

Using GameView

Until now, we have been using standard views and translating them to render the different elements of the game. While this is an easy way to draw elements on the screen, it is far from being efficient. We are relying on the system layout to do the drawing.

While this technique is fine for a turn-based game or any non-real-time game in general, it cannot render enough frames per second for a real-time game.

Working with standard Views is fine for non-real-time games.

We are going to create a custom `View` that we are going to call `GameView`. This view will be responsible for drawing the sprites.

We already noted the duplication of code and mentioned the concept of sprite in the previous chapter. We will now move forward and create a `Sprite` class that will take care of drawing an image at specific coordinates inside the `GameView`.

There are two ways of drawing at low level on Android. They are:

- Extending `View` and overriding `onDraw`
- Extending `SurfaceView` and using `SurfaceHolder`

In both cases, we will get a `Canvas` and draw our `GameObjects` on it. The main difference is that the `onDraw` method of the `View` is executed on the `UIThread`, while `SurfaceView` and `SurfaceHolder` are designed to perform the draw on a separate thread.

 Low-level drawing on Android is always done using a canvas.

According to the official documentation, it is more efficient to use `SurfaceView`. But, since Android 4.0, view rendering is hardware-accelerated (while `SurfaceView` is not). In the case of modern phones with high-resolution screens and faster processors, this may not always be the case.

 `SurfaceView` is not hardware-accelerated and may perform worse than normal `View`.

Anyway, you should know both and be able to swap them easily, even if it is just for testing purposes. We will create an interface named `GameView`, which will be implemented by the two classes, so they can be changed easily. The classes we will make are:

- `StandardGameView`: This will extend from `View`
- `SurfaceGameView`: This will extend from `SurfaceView`

The GameView interface

The GameView interface will have all the methods that are needed by the GameEngine to handle the View:

```
public interface GameView {
  void draw();
  void setGameObjects(List<GameObject> gameObjects);
  // Generic methods from View
  int getWidth();
  int getHeight();
  int getPaddingLeft();
  int getPaddingRight();
  int getPaddingTop();
  int getPaddingBottom();
  Context getContext();
}
```

There are basically two methods we need, one to trigger the drawing and one to pass the list of game objects to the GameView, so they can be drawn there:

- draw: This will trigger a draw on the GameView
- setGameObjects: This will set the list of GameObjects for the View

The rest of the methods are implemented in the View. We need to declare them, because we are using them on the GameEngine.

Let's explore each implementation in detail.

StandardGameView

The StandardGameView class extends View. We just provide the basic constructors for View, override the onDraw method, and then implement the methods from GameView:

```
public class StandardGameView extends View implements GameView {

  private List<GameObject> mGameObjects;

  public GameView(Context context) {
    super(context);
  }
```

```java
    public GameView(Context context, AttributeSet attrs) {
      super(context, attrs);
    }

    public GameView(Context context, AttributeSet attrs,
        int defStyleAttr) {
      super(context, attrs, defStyleAttr);
    }

    @Override
    protected void onDraw(Canvas canvas) {
      super.onDraw(canvas);
      synchronized (mGameObjects) {
        int numObjects = mGameObjects.size();
        for (int i = 0; i < numObjects; i++) {
          mGameObjects.get(i).onDraw(canvas);
        }
      }
    }

    @Override
    public void draw() {
      postInvalidate();
    }

    @Override
    public void setGameObjects(List<GameObject> gameObjects) {
      mGameObjects = gameObjects;
    }
  }
```

Basically, setGameObjects stores a reference to the game objects. The adding and removing of GameObjects are done in the GameEngine. When we draw the view, we iterate over the list of game objects, calling onDraw on all of them and passing the Canvas object on which we are drawing.

Note that the method is synchronized using the mGameObjects variable. This is important because, as we mentioned in *Chapter 1, Setting Up the Project*, the contents of the list can change during onUpdate and we do not want this to happen while we are iterating over the list.

The other important point is that the list of GameObjects is a reference to the one inside the GameEngine and not a copy, so whenever the list gets modified, the latest values are accessible from both places. This is also why synchronization is required.

The list of GameObjects is shared between the GameEngine and the GameView.

Performance-wise, it would not make sense to copy all the elements in the list to a new one in each execution of onDraw.

To trigger a draw, we just need to call postInvalidate. Remember that invalidating a view has to be done on the UIThread. This is why we need to call postInvalidate. This method will post a Runnable to be run on the UIThread that will then invalidate the View.

As we mentioned in the earlier chapters, once the view gets invalidated, Android makes sure that the onDraw method of the View is called and then the UI is updated. This is the connection between invalidating the view and the onDraw method, where we draw the game objects.

The onDraw method is obviously time-critical. We should avoid all unnecessary operations. In particular, lint shows a warning if you create an object inside onDraw. This is, to reiterate, a best practice for game developers: to always create the objects in advance.

 Never do object creation inside onDraw.

Also, it is worth remembering that Android has a fallback mechanism to avoid overload on the drawing. If a view has been invalidated but not yet redrawn, the call to invalidate will be ignored (the view is already going to be redrawn).

SurfaceGameView

To implement a GameView that extends SurfaceView, we need to define a Callback for SurfaceHolder—the class used to access the SurfaceView—and then, whenever we want to draw, we lock the canvas, draw on it, and unlock it again so it can be rendered by SurfaceView.

Let's see the code of SurfaceGameView:

```
public class SurfaceGameView extends SurfaceView implements
    SurfaceHolder.Callback, GameView {

    private List<GameObject> mGameObjects;
    private boolean mReady;
```

```java
    public SurfaceGameView(Context context) {
      super(context);
      getHolder().addCallback(this);
    }

    public SurfaceGameView(Context context, AttributeSet attrs) {
      super(context, attrs);
      getHolder().addCallback(this);
    }

    public SurfaceGameView(Context c, AttributeSet attrs,
        int defStyleAttr) {
      super(c, attrs, defStyleAttr);
      getHolder().addCallback(this);
    }

    @Override
    public void surfaceCreated(SurfaceHolder holder) {
      mReady = true;
    }

    @Override
    public void surfaceChanged(SurfaceHolder holder, int format,
        int width, int height) {

    }

    @Override
    public void surfaceDestroyed(SurfaceHolder holder) {
      mReady = false;
    }

    @Override
    public void setGameObjects(List<GameObject> gameObjects) {
      mGameObjects = gameObjects;
    }
```

```
@Override
public void draw() {
    if (!mReady) {
        return;
    }
    Canvas canvas = getHolder().lockCanvas();
    if (canvas == null) {
        return;
    }
    canvas.drawRGB(0,0,0);
    synchronized (mGameObjects) {
        int numObjects = mGameObjects.size();
        for (int i = 0; i < numObjects; i++) {
            mGameObjects.get(i).onDraw(canvas);
        }
    }
    getHolder().unlockCanvasAndPost(canvas);
    }
}
```

First, we have three constructors with different arguments that are intrinsic to SurfaceView. Note that they all include a call to set a Callback to the SurfaceHolder, which is also implemented by SurfaceGameView. This callback will inform us of when SurfaceView is ready or when things have changed.

The next methods are the implementation of the Callback interface. Those are the methods that are called when the SurfaceView is created, modified, or destroyed. We store the status of the view to know whether it is ready or not, so that it can be used to draw. A View is ready any time after it is created until it is destroyed.

Then, we move into implementing the methods from GameView.

To set the GameObjects, we do exactly as we did for StandardGameView, also with the same implications when it comes to handling a reference.

The draw method is where things are a bit different. We have to check whether the view is ready. If so, we lock the Canvas so we can draw on it.

Once we have the canvas, we need to clean it before we draw each frame. The canvas will have the previous image on it. (If we do not clean it, we will get rendering artifacts as shown in the following screenshot.) This cleaning is done by filling the canvas with a solid color using `drawRGB`.

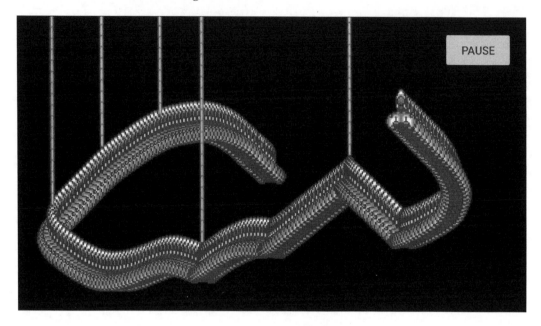

Once we have cleaned the canvas, we take the same drawing as for `StandardGameView` and just iterate over the game objects.

Finally, we unlock the canvas and post it. This is the point when we pass the `Canvas` back to the `SurfaceView` and post it to the `UIThread`. Note that all of the drawing has been done outside the `UIThread`. Only once the `Canvas` is fully rendered will it be passed back for drawing.

 `SurfaceView` performs the drawing on the `Canvas` outside the `UIThread`.

As mentioned before, `SurfaceView` is supposed to give better performance. But, since it is only software accelerated, in modern phones a standard `View`—with hardware acceleration—may be more efficient in some cases. A particular situation when `SurfaceView` performance is impacted is if we put other views on top of it (like the pause button), since a full alpha-blended composite will be performed each time the surface changes.

Updating GameEngine

The use of `GameView` has some implications from the `GameEngine` point of view. It means that it has to initialize the `GameView` and then trigger draws using the generic interface.

The `GameView` will be a parameter of the constructor of `GameEngine`. It will be initialized, passing a reference to the list of game objects. The updated constructor of `GameEngine` is like this:

```
public GameEngine (Activity a, GameView gameView) {
  mActivity = a;
  mGameView = gameView;
  mGameView.setGameObjects(mGameObjects);

  mWidth = gameView.getWidth()
    - gameView.getPaddingRight() - gameView.getPaddingRight();
  mHeight = gameView.getHeight()
    - gameView.getPaddingTop() - gameView.getPaddingBottom();

  mPixelFactor = mHeight / 400d;
}
```

From now on, we will also calculate the `pixelFactor` inside the `GameEngine`. We will store it in a public variable so it can be read by the game objects. This has several advantages, such as:

- If we decide to change the number of units of the screen, this is done in a single place
- Removing code duplications is always good for maintenance

On the other hand, the `onDraw` method of the `GameEngine` becomes extremely simple:

```
public void onDraw() {
  mGameView.draw();
}
```

Updating the game layout

Of course, we have to modify the `fragment_game.xml` layout to include the `GameView`. We will take this chance to do some other modifications to it, such as removing the `TextView` and changing the padding of the layout to be the margins on the pause button instead. This makes sure that the `GameView` is fullscreen while keeping the button margins as they were.

It is important to remember that in a `FrameLayout`, the order in the XML specifies the order in which the items are drawn (the z-index). We will put the `GameView` at the beginning of the layout to have the pause button drawn on top of it.

The new version of `fragment_game.xml` is as follows:

```xml
<FrameLayout
    xmlns:android="http://schemas.android.com/apk/res/android"
    xmlns:tools="http://schemas.android.com/tools"
    android:layout_width="match_parent"
    android:layout_height="match_parent"
    android:orientation="vertical"
    tools:context="com.example.yass.counter.GameFragment">

    <com.example.yass.engine.SurfaceGameView
        android:id="@+id/gameView"
        android:layout_width="match_parent"
        android:layout_height="wrap_content" />

    <Button
        android:layout_gravity="top|right"
        android:id="@+id/btn_play_pause"
        android:layout_marginTop="@dimen/activity_vertical_margin"
        android:layout_marginRight="@dimen/activity_vertical_margin"
        android:layout_width="wrap_content"
        android:layout_height="wrap_content"
        android:text="@string/pause" />

    <include layout="@layout/view_vjoystick" />

</FrameLayout>
```

Note that this is the place where we decide which variant of the `GameView` we are going to use. The rest of the code will access the methods via the `GameView` interface, so nothing else needs to be changed. We are going to use the `SurfaceGameView` from now on, but feel free to experiment with `StandardGameView` as well.

The layout is where we set which variant of GameView we are going to use.

Finally, inside GameFragment, we update the creation of the GameEngine by adding the GameView parameter:

```
GameView gameView = (GameView)
    getView().findViewById(R.id.gameView);
mGameEngine = new GameEngine(getActivity(), gameView);
```

Now we have a GameEngine that relies on a GameView to do the rendering. We still need to update the GameObject class to make use of it.

Before we get to the GameObject class, let's take a moment to improve DrawThread as well.

Improving DrawThread

To trigger the draw we have been using a Timer and TimerTask scheduled so we could get 30 frames per second. While this works, it gives better performance to do it like the UpdateThread: run as many calls to onDraw as we can.

This approach works great for SurfaceView since the drawing is done on the same thread. But it may give some message overflow problems while using StandardGameView, which just calls postInvalidate. To prevent the overflow, we will ensure that the time between the calls to onDraw is never shorter than 20 milliseconds, which is enough for 50 frames per second.

The code for the new DrawThread is exactly the same as for UpdateThread, except for the part in the run method that takes care of the overflow. It looks like this:

```
@Override
public void run() {
  long elapsedMillis;
  long currentTimeMillis;
  long previousTimeMillis = System.currentTimeMillis();

  while (mGameIsRunning) {
    currentTimeMillis = System.currentTimeMillis();
    elapsedMillis = currentTimeMillis - previousTimeMillis;
    if (mPauseGame) {
      while (mPauseGame) {
        try {
```

```
          synchronized (mLock) {
            mLock.wait();
          }
        } catch (InterruptedException e) {
          // We stay on the loop
        }
      }
      currentTimeMillis = System.currentTimeMillis();
    }
    if (elapsedMillis < 20) { // This is 50 fps
      try {
        Thread.sleep(20-elapsedMillis);
      } catch (InterruptedException e) {
        // We just continue.
      }
    }
    mGameEngine.onDraw();
    previousTimeMillis = currentTimeMillis;
  }
}
```

In the case of running two calls too close, we put the thread to sleep from the remaining time to a minimum of 20 milliseconds.

If an `InterruptedException` happens, we don't really have much to handle. So, we can just move on and call onDraw in the `GameEngine`.

Sprites

We have already mentioned the concept of a sprite being an entity that is drawn and handled at a specific position on a screen. Essentially, everything we see in a game are sprites. There are exceptions, such as game controllers (which do not draw anything) and backgrounds (which are drawn in a different way), but we will talk about them later in the chapter.

So, this is the code for the Sprite class that extends GameObject:

```
public abstract class Sprite extends GameObject {

  protected double mPositionX;
  protected double mPositionY;

  protected final double mPixelFactor;
```

```
    private final Bitmap mBitmap;
    protected final int mImageHeight;
    protected final int mImageWidth;

    private final Matrix mMatrix = new Matrix();

    protected Sprite (GameEngine gameEngine, int drawableRes) {
      Resources r = gameEngine.getContext().getResources();
      Drawable spriteDrawable = r.getDrawable(drawableRes);
      mPixelFactor = gameEngine.mPixelFactor;

      mImageHeight = (int)
        (spriteDrawable.getIntrinsicHeight()*mPixelFactor);
      mImageWidth = (int)
        (spriteDrawable.getIntrinsicWidth()*mPixelFactor);

      mBitmap = ((BitmapDrawable) spriteDrawable).getBitmap();
    }

    @Override
    public void onDraw(Canvas canvas) {
      mMatrix.reset();
      mMatrix.postScale((float) mPixelFactor, (float) mPixelFactor);
      mMatrix.postTranslate((float) mPositionX, (float) mPositionY);
      canvas.drawBitmap(mBitmap, mMatrix, null);
    }
  }
```

Sprite is an abstract class and there is no implementation of onUpdate at all. Sprites care about displaying an item on the screen, not about how this item moves.

The class has a series of member variables. Let's go through them:

- mPositionX, mPositionY: The position of the Sprite on the screen. The same concept we used for the Player and the Bullet objects. This position is in the top-left corner of the image.
- mPixelFactor: The same concept as before. The factor to convert screen units into pixels.
- mBitmap: The bitmap we are going to draw.
- mImageWidth, mImageHeight: The size of the bitmap as drawn on the screen. It is set here for convenience. We could always calculate it using the bitmap and the pixel factor, but it is faster to just store it for future use by the subclasses.

- mMatrix: This object is a transformation matrix. It is used for scaling, moving, and rotating the bitmap before rendering it on the canvas. For optimization purposes, it is reused among the onDraw executions instead of being created for each run.

The next piece of code is the constructor. We are passing a reference to the GameEngine and a drawable resource. In the previous chapter, we were passing the parent View, so we could add the newly created ImageView to it. This is no longer necessary. We just need the Context and the pixel factor, which we can get from the GameEngine.

The code in the constructor is very similar to the ones we have seen before. It does several things:

- Loads the Drawable from resources via the Context
- Gets the intrinsic size of the drawable and multiplies it by the pixel factor to store the width and height that the sprite will use in pixels for this particular device
- Gets the Bitmap from the Drawable and stores it in a class variable to use it during onDraw

Finally, we have the onDraw method that receives a Canvas. This method is now called from the GameView. The Canvas is obtained in a different way from a StandardGameView and SurfaceGameView, but the logic of drawing on it is the same in both cases.

A canvas works as a drawing interface for the actual surface upon which your graphics will be drawn. It provides us with a set of primitives to draw, including bitmaps, text, lines, rectangles, ovals, and so on. When using a canvas, the drawing is actually performed upon an underlying bitmap, which is then placed in the window.

[Canvas acts as a drawing interface that provides us with primitives.]

To draw the sprite, we use the drawBitmap method from the Canvas class. This method receives a transformation matrix as a parameter. Let's see what we can do with the Matrix:

- reset: We reset the transformation matrix from the values of the previous run. This is required to reuse the Matrix object from the previous run.
- postScale: We add a scale transformation at the end of the transformation list. The scale is the same as the mPixelFactor.

- `postTranslate`: This adds a translation transformation at the end of the transformation list. This means that this transformation will be performed after the scale. We translate the item to the location (`mPositionX`, `mPositionY`).

For now, this is all we will do with the transformation matrix. Later in the chapter, we will add rotation.

 The order of actions in a transformation matrix is very important. The results are impacted by the order of the transformations.

The transformation matrix is a very powerful tool to transform bitmaps. The key point while creating the matrix is to keep in mind that the order is very important. It does not matter when we only use translation and scale. But with rotation, the results are impacted by the order of the transformations.

Updating the spaceship and bullets

Now that we have a `Sprite` base class, we have to update the existing `Player` and `Bullet` classes to extend from it.

Most of the member variables from the `Player` object are now a part of the `Sprite`. We can also remove the old implementation of `onDraw` and rely on the one from the `Sprite`.

Finally, we have new simpler constructors that just receive the `GameEngine`. The one for the `Player` class is:

```
public Player(GameEngine gameEngine) {
   super(gameEngine, R.drawable.ship);
   mSpeedFactor = mPixelFactor * 100d / 1000d;

   mMaxX = gameEngine.mWidth - mImageWidth;
   mMaxY = gameEngine.mHeight - mImageHeight;

   initBulletPool(gameEngine);
}
```

The one for the `Bullet` object is:

```
public Bullet(GameEngine gameEngine) {
   super(gameEngine, R.drawable.bullet);
   mSpeedFactor = gameEngine.mPixelFactor * -300d / 1000d;
}
```

All in all, we have pushed a lot of code to the `Sprite` class, which will make the inclusion of new game elements easier.

Before this, let's also add a frame-per-second counter to the `GameView` and see how it is performing to be able to compare `StandardGameView` and `SurfaceGameView`.

Adding a frames-per-second (fps) counter

We have updated the `DrawThread` to run at an arbitrary number of frames per second, adapting to the time required to render instead of a fixed 30 fps, and we are using sprites. Now is the perfect time to add a frames-per-second counter. It is a very easy tool and is also handy to check performance.

We could have used a `TextView`, but there are some good reasons to draw it on the `Canvas` directly instead:

- The performance of `SurfaceView` suffers when we overlay other views on top of it
- It is an interesting example of other methods of drawing on the `Canvas`
- We can remove and add it without touching the layout

We will make a class named `FPSCounter` that extends from `GameObject` and looks like this:

```
public class FPSCounter extends GameObject {
  private final double mPixelFactor;
  private final float mTextWidth;
  private final float mTextHeight;

  private Paint mPaint;
  private long mTotalMillis;
  private int mDraws;
  private float mFps;

  private String mFpsText = "";

  public FPSCounter(GameEngine gameEngine) {
    mPaint = new Paint();
    mPaint.setTextAlign(Paint.Align.CENTER);
    mTextHeight = (float) (25*gameEngine.mPixelFactor);
    mTextWidth = (float) (50*gameEngine.mPixelFactor);
    mPaint.setTextSize(mTextHeight/2);
```

```
    }

    @Override
    public void startGame() {
      mTotalMillis = 0;
    }

    @Override
    public void onUpdate(long elapsedMillis, GameEngine gameEngine) {
      mTotalMillis += elapsedMillis;
      if (mTotalMillis > 1000) {
        mFps = mDraws*1000 / mTotalMillis;
        mFpsText = mFps+" fps";
        mTotalMillis = 0;
        mDraws = 0;
      }
    }

    @Override
    public void onDraw(Canvas canvas) {
      mPaint.setColor(Color.BLACK);
      canvas.drawRect(0, (int)(canvas.getHeight()-mTextHeight),
        mTextWidth, canvas.getHeight(), mPaint);
      mPaint.setColor(Color.WHITE);
      canvas.drawText(mFpsText, mTextWidth/2,
        (int)(canvas.getHeight()-mTextHeight/2), mPaint);
      mDraws++;
    }
  }
```

The logic is quite simple; we count the number of calls to onDraw and during onUpdate. Whenever we have been running for more than 1000 milliseconds, we do the calculation, store the result, and reset both variables.

The onDraw method draws a black square and then renders the text on it centered. We set the size of the square to 50 by 25 units and the text size to half the height of the square, so there is a margin. For this, we also need to use a Paint object.

The Paint class has methods to set colors, alignments, stroke width and type, and so on. Since we are mostly drawing bitmaps, we won't go into more detail on this.

Note that the Paint object is created once and reused, as we did with the Matrix on the Sprite, with (yet again) the premise that we should not do any object allocations inside onDraw.

Spawning enemies – the GameController

Now we are ready to spawn some enemies. For this, we are going to introduce a new concept: the GameController.

A GameController is a special type of GameObject that has no visual representation (it is not a sprite) and its mission is to control the evolution of the game using the calls to onUpdate.

One of the most typical tasks of a GameController is managing the environment. This includes spawning enemies with the right parameters when necessary.

Game controllers fall into two main groups:

- Procedural/random
- Deterministic/static

Procedural/random

This is a type of GameController that generates levels or enemies based on a set of parameters (or a function) that include some sort of random input.

The main advantage of procedural generation is that you do not have to create all the levels in detail, you just provide the parameters and an algorithm. It is complicated to tune it properly, but, once it is right, it potentially presents you with a different setup each time you play it. This improves replayability.

Some games that use procedural game controllers are Chalk Ball (survival mode), Fruit Ninja, and Eufloria. The most classic example of procedural-level generation are Rogue-like games, where each level of the dungeon is generated when you enter it.

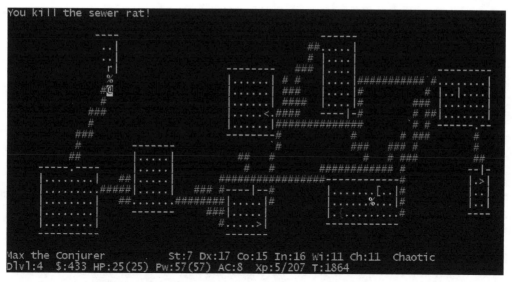

Nethack, one of the first games to use procedural-level generation.

Deterministic/static

Deterministic-level generation is used when the levels are fixed and they are always the same.

This implies a lot of attention to detail, which allows for fine-tuning difficulty in the levels. Obviously, it also takes a lot of time.

Most game puzzles and tower defense games are examples of this: Angry Birds, Cut the Rope, Anomaly, SpaceCat, among many others.

As a rule of thumb, while using a deterministic `GameController` you want to have the definition of the levels stored in some files that can be modified without touching the code. This allows you to tune a level or add new sets of levels independently of the code. You can even create an external editor to manage the levels.

The format of these files is completely up to you. I, personally, recommend the use of a structured language such as XML or JSON.

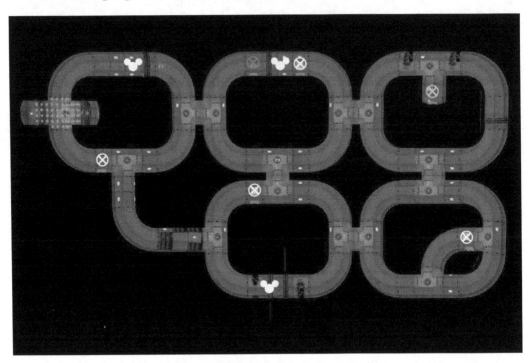

A level of SpaceCat as seen in the level editor

Hybrid approach

Game-level design is not black or white. There are many ways to define a `GameController` that is somewhere in between a procedural and a deterministic controller.

For example, Candy Crush Saga has a hybrid-level generation when the layout of the level is settled, but the candies that drop are different each time you play.

This gets the best of both worlds. It allows you to fine-tune the design of a level while it is still different each time you play it. It also takes a lot of time, because you have to tune both the static design and the algorithm.

Our approach

It does not make sense to have a deterministic GameController for YASS, so we will go for the procedural generation.

We are going to make asteroids fall from the top of the screen with an angle that varies in the range of [-30,30] degrees. We will restrict their position on the *x* axis to be in the 50 percent central area of the screen.

The speed is going to be constant and they will spawn at a given interval, also a constant.

The code of the GameController for handling the generation of Asteroids is as follows:

```
@Override
public void onUpdate(long elapsedMillis, GameEngine gameEngine) {
  mCurrentMillis += elapsedMillis;
  long waveTimestamp = mEnemiesSpawned*TIME_BETWEEN_ENEMIES;
  if (mCurrentMillis > waveTimestamp) {
    // Spawn a new enemy
    Asteroid a = mAsteroidPool.remove(0);
    a.init(gameEngine);
    gameEngine.addGameObject(a);
    mEnemiesSpawned++;
  }
}
```

We count the time the game has been running, then we calculate the time for the next enemy to spawn. This is the number of enemies we already created multiplied by the time between enemies.

If the current time of the game is greater than the time when the next enemy has to appear, then we spawn one and add it to the GameEngine.

To do so, we get an Asteroid from the pool of objects, just as we did with the bullets. We initialize it and add it to the GameEngine. Then, we add one to the number of enemies spawned.

The code spawns a new enemy, separating them by the number of milliseconds stated by TIME_BETWEEN_ENEMIES. We have set this at 500 milliseconds.

The object pool we are using for the asteroids is essentially the same as the one for the bullets. I won't bore you with the same details again.

The rest of the procedural generation is inside the `init` method of the `Asteroid`, which looks like this:

```
public void init(GameEngine gameEngine) {
    // They initialize in a [-30, 30] degrees angle
    double angle =
        gameEngine.mRandom.nextDouble()*Math.PI/3d-Math.PI/6d;
    mSpeedX = mSpeed * Math.sin(angle);
    mSpeedY = mSpeed * Math.cos(angle);
    // Asteroids initialize in the central 50% of the screen
    mPositionX = gameEngine.mRandom.nextInt(gameEngine.mWidth/2)+
        gameEngine.mWidth/4;
    // They initialize outside of the screen vertically
    mPositionY = -mImageHeight;
}
```

The `cos` and `sin` methods require the parameter to be radians, so we use `Random.getDouble` to get a double between [0,1], multiply it by PI/3, and then subtract PI/6. With this, we get a random value between [-PI/6,PI/6].

We use a random angle to get the components of speed on X and Y using `sin` and `cos`.

For the starting position we use the same technique. We get a random integer in the range [0,width/2] and then we add width/4, so the final value is in the range [width/4,width*3/4].

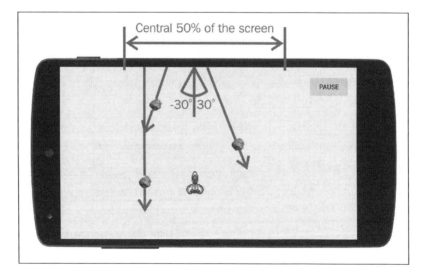

The asteroids

Finally, we need our Asteroid class, which is going to be a Sprite. As we did for the other graphics, we downloaded our art from the OpenGameArt website. This time we get a few asteroids with different shapes and colors.

The asteroid's implementation is reminiscent of the one for the bullets, except that this time the object is removed from the GameEngine when it gets out of the screen from the bottom and it has speed components on both axes.

The code for the Asteroid is as follows:

```
public class Asteroid extends Sprite {

    private final GameController mController;

    private final double mSpeed;
    private double mSpeedX;
    private double mSpeedY;

    public Asteroid(GameController gameController, GameEngine
        gameEngine) {
      super(gameEngine.getContext(), R.drawable.a10000,
        gameEngine.mPixelFactor);
      mSpeed = 200d*mPixelFactor/1000d;
      mController = gameController;
    }

    @Override
    public void onUpdate(long elapsedMillis, GameEngine gameEngine)
    {
      mPositionX += mSpeedX * elapsedMillis;
      mPositionY += mSpeedY * elapsedMillis;
      // Check of the sprite goes out of the screen
      if (mPositionY > gameEngine.mHeight) {
        // Return to the pool
        gameEngine.removeGameObject(this);
        mController.returnToPool(this);
      }
    }

    public void init(GameEngine gameEngine) {
      // We already saw that
    }
}
```

Thanks to the `Sprite` base class, this implementation is very easy. We just need to set the speed in the construction and then update the position on both axes using the speed and `elapsedMillis`.

Lastly, we check whether the object is out of bounds and, if so, we remove it from the engine and return it to the pool.

We can now compile and run and can see asteroids coming towards our spaceship.

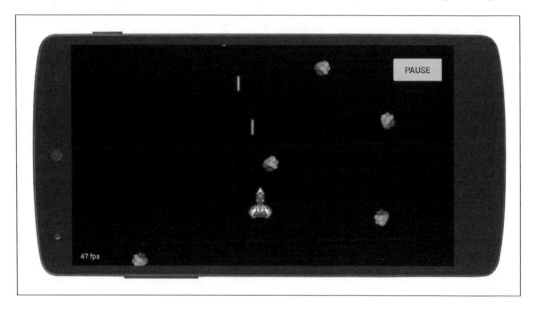

More on the transformation matrix

You may have noticed that the asteroids looked quite static. This is because the image is always the same. We can improve this with a nice simple trick: by adding rotation to them.

The first thing we need to do is to update the `Sprite` class to make it handle rotation as a part of the configuration of the transformation matrix:

```
@Override
public void onDraw(Canvas canvas) {
  mMatrix.reset();
  mMatrix.postScale((float) mPixelFactor, (float) mPixelFactor);
  mMatrix.postTranslate((float) mPositionX, (float) mPositionY);
  mMatrix.postRotate((float) mRotation,
    (float) (mPositionX + mImageWidth/2),
    (float) (mPositionY + mImageHeight/2));
  canvas.drawBitmap(mBitmap, mMatrix, null);
}
```

The order of the transformations is extremely important. The transformations are applied in order and a rotation does transform the reference axes. So, if we rotate 45 degrees and then translate 40 units to the right, since the initial rotation changes the reference for the coordinates, the end position will be down and left. On the other hand, if we first translate and then rotate, the coordinate system only gets affected at the end.

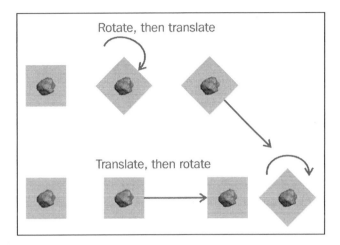

This can be counter-intuitive at first, but it is a very powerful tool to describe nonlinear movements. We will see more about transformations in *Chapter 8, The Animation Framework*.

For the sprites, we first do a translation and then a rotation, using the center of the sprite at the final position as the pivot for it.

 A rotation also affects the reference coordinate system of the object.

Once the `Sprite` knows how to handle rotation, we just need to initialize the rotation of the asteroid to a value that makes sense and is different for each asteroid.

First, we initialize the rotation to a random angle, so each asteroid has a different value. We add this line to the `init` method of the `Asteroid`:

```
mRotation = gameEngine.mRandom.nextInt(360);
```

Then we set the rotation speed proportional to the angle of the linear speed, so each asteroid has a rotation speed based on the inclination of the trajectory. This also goes inside the init method:

```
mRotationSpeed = angle*(180d / Math.PI)/250d;
```

We make the asteroid perform a rotation equivalent to the inclination angle for times each second.

Once the values have been initialized, we need to update them during the onUpdate call. We will add the following code to onUpdate:

```
mRotation += mRotationSpeed * elapsedMillis;
if (mRotation > 360) {
  mRotation = 0;
}
else if (mRotation < 0) {
  mRotation = 360;
}
```

We update the rotation and ensure that it is under the values that are valid [0-360].

 The rotation of a transformation matrix is provided in degrees.

Note that the transformation matrix uses the angles in degrees and not in radians, while the mathematical operators we used for the speed expect it in radians. Always double-check in which units the angles are expected.

If you run the game now, you will notice how such a simple tweak makes it look much nicer.

Occlusion culling

Occlusion culling is a technique that is broadly used in games, especially 3D ones. Since drawing is very expensive and has to be done many times, every optimization counts. The obvious optimization is to not draw the parts that are not going to be seen (for example hidden by something else). If we can draw each pixel on the screen only once, we are saving a lot of processing time.

The fact of drawing each pixel more than once is called overdraw. Having a high overdraw is one of the factors that impact performance the most.

In the case of 3D, drawing is especially expensive, and occlusion culling is something that most engines do automatically to a certain extent.

Occlusion culling optimizes the drawing time by not drawing what is not shown.

In our case, we may be drawing some pixels twice, but since we are only doing 2D, the cost of drawing is not that high and it is something we don't need to do.

There is one special case, however: drawing sprites that are outside the `GameView`.

Until now, we have been spawning the sprites as we needed them and removing them once they are out of the `GameView`. We could instead put them into place in the initialization of the level and just rely on the calls to `onUpdate` to make them appear on the screen. This is quite common for elements that are a part of the scenery or static enemies. In the case of a rogue-like game, we would be generating each dungeon level in the beginning and then spawning all the sprites and putting them into place.

Obviously, drawing things that are out of the player's view is a waste. So, we will make sure that the `Sprite` class performs this simple occlusion culling-like optimization:

```
@Override
public void onDraw(Canvas canvas) {
  if (mPositionX > canvas.getWidth()
      || mPositionY > canvas.getHeight()
      || mPositionX < -mImageWidth
      || mPositionY < -mImageHeight) {
    return;
  }
  mMatrix.reset();
  mMatrix.postScale((float) mPixelFactor, (float) mPixelFactor);
  mMatrix.postRotate((float) mRotation,
    (float) mImageWidth/2, (float) mImageHeight/2);
  mMatrix.postTranslate((float) mPositionX, (float) mPositionY);
  canvas.drawBitmap(mBitmap, mMatrix, null);
}
```

We just have to check if the positions on the x and y axes and see if the sprite is inside the drawing area. Remember that we use the points at the top-left corner of the image. This is why we have to check against the width and height in negative.

This will not make any difference in our game, but it may be crucial for other types of games, especially those with static content.

Parallax backgrounds

Another typical feature of 2D games that is deeply related to the `DrawThread` is parallax backgrounds.

The idea of a parallax background is to have an image that moves slower than the elements in the foreground, giving the impression of depth.

 Parallax backgrounds are used to create an illusion of depth in 2D games.

To make this effect better, we can use multiple background images at different speeds. This is commonly used in 2D scrollers. For example with trees in the near plane and mountains and clouds at the very back.

For YASS, we will use a star field that moves down slowly as a background.

We are going to use the same convention of units as we used for the sprites. The image we use for the background should be designed to be tiled, vertically in our case. This means that the end of the image fits with its beginning, so they are placed one after another and have continuity.

It should also be designed in a way that it is larger than the biggest screen. We can consider the tallest screens the ones with an 16:9 aspect ratio. So for a height of 400 pixels, this image should be at least 720 pixels wide (400 * 16 / 9 = 711.11).

A background is quite different from a sprite, mainly because of the size of the image and the fact that we may need to draw two of them to cover the screen is some cases.

We will create a new `ParallaxBackground` class for this:

```
public ParallaxBackground(GameEngine gameEngine, int speed,
    int drawableResId) {
  Drawable spriteDrawable = gameEngine.getContext().getResources()
    .getDrawable(drawableResId);
  mBitmap = ((BitmapDrawable) spriteDrawable).getBitmap();

  mPixelFactor = gameEngine.mPixelFactor;
  mSpeedY = speed*mPixelFactor/1000d;

  mImageHeight = spriteDrawable.getIntrinsicHeight()*mPixelFactor;
  mImageWidth = spriteDrawable.getIntrinsicWidth()*mPixelFactor;
```

```
    mScreenHeight = gameEngine.mHeight;
    mScreenWidth = gameEngine.mWidth;

    mTargetWidth = Math.min(mImageWidth, mScreenWidth);
}
```

The constructor is similar to the one `Sprite`. We load a bitmap, calculate the speed, and store the height and width of both the screen and image at its display size.

We have a new concept: the target width. This is used for optimization in case the image is larger than the screen, so we do not draw what is not going to be seen.

To begin with, we will do a simple implementation using the same transformation matrix concept that we used on the sprites:

```
@Override
public void onUpdate(long elapsedMillis, GameEngine gameEngine) {
    mPositionY += mSpeedY * elapsedMillis;
}

@Override
public void onDraw(Canvas canvas) {
    if (mPositionY > 0) {
        mMatrix.reset();
        mMatrix.postScale((float) (mPixelFactor),
            (float) (mPixelFactor));
        mMatrix.postTranslate(0, (float) (mPositionY - mImageHeight));
        canvas.drawBitmap(mBitmap, mMatrix, null);
    }
    mMatrix.reset();
    mMatrix.postScale((float) (mPixelFactor),
        (float) (mPixelFactor));
    mMatrix.postTranslate(0, (float) mPositionY);
    canvas.drawBitmap(mBitmap, mMatrix, null);

    if (mPositionY > mScreenHeight) {
        mPositionY -= mImageHeight;
    }
}
```

We are drawing the image at the y coordinate. When this coordinate is greater than 0, there will be space on the top of the view that needs to be filled with another image. This is what the first part of the code does; it draws the image one more time, but translates all the height of the image, so they tile.

In any case, we have to draw the background at `mPositionY`, which is what the second block does. Note that, when the position is smaller than 0, we only need to draw one image. The logic of the class ensures that the value of `Y` is never smaller than `mImageHeight – mScreenHeight`.

Once the `Y` position gets out of the screen, the second part of the drawing is no longer needed, so we subtract the image's height. With this, the image keeps the same position and scrolls smoothly, because the second part of the draw is now equivalent to the first one, which is not entered.

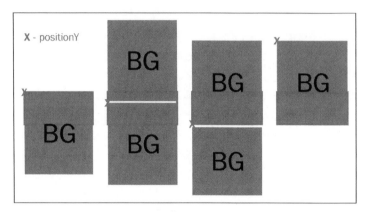

The different states of the background drawable.

While this code works, it is quite inefficient, because it does a lot of drawing that is not visible.

We can implement the drawing on `ParallaxBackground` using another variant of `drawBitmap` that receives the rectangle of the image we want to draw and the rectangle on the screen when it should be drawn.

The math for this case looks a bit complicated. Let's first look at the code:

```
private void efficientDraw(Canvas canvas) {
  if (mPositionY < 0) {
    mSrcRect.set(0,
      (int) (-mPositionY/mPixelFactor),
      (int) (mTargetWidth/mPixelFactor),
      (int) ((mScreenHeight - mPositionY)/mPixelFactor));
    mDstRect.set(0,
      0,
      (int) mTargetWidth,
      (int) mScreenHeight);
```

```
        canvas.drawBitmap(mBitmap, mSrcRect, mDstRect, null);
    }
    else {
      mSrcRect.set(0,
        0,
        (int) (mTargetWidth/mPixelFactor),
        (int) ((mScreenHeight - mPositionY) / mPixelFactor));
      mDstRect.set(0,
        (int) mPositionY,
        (int) mTargetWidth,
        (int) mScreenHeight);
      canvas.drawBitmap(mBitmap, mSrcRect, mDstRect, null);
      // We need to draw the previous block
      mSrcRect.set(0,
        (int) ((mImageHeight - mPositionY) / mPixelFactor),
        (int) (mTargetWidth/mPixelFactor),
        (int) (mImageHeight/mPixelFactor));
      mDstRect.set(0,
        0,
        (int) mTargetWidth,
        (int) mPositionY);
      canvas.drawBitmap(mBitmap, mSrcRect, mDstRect, null);
    }

    if (mPositionY > mScreenHeight) {
      mPositionY -= mImageHeight;
    }
  }
}
```

The handling is conceptually the same as for the previous algorithm, but now you have to keep in mind that the source rectangle has the original scale of the image, while the destination rectangle has the scale of the `GameView`. Other than this, the cases and how they work are the same.

While this drawing is more efficient under the draw-what-is-needed criteria, it is not so efficient in some cases.

When we use `drawBitmap` with two rectangles, a new bitmap is created and used. This bitmap is then discarded and another one is created for the next call to `onDraw`. With the other implementation, the bitmaps are not touched, so they can remain loaded in the memory, saving some processing time.

All in all, the performance depends on the size of the bitmaps, if you are using a `SurfaceView` or a normal `View`, and how good is the hardware of the device.

Though efficient, this way of drawing may not be faster. Bitmap manipulation and allocating memory are also time-consuming.

To add a background to the GameEngine, we have to remember that the drawing order in the GameView is the order in which the GameObjects were added to the GameEngine, so we must ensure that we add the background in the beginning, before the rest of the game objects.

The initialization of GameEngine inside GameFragment should look like this now:

```
mGameEngine = new GameEngine(getActivity(), (GameView)
  getView().findViewById(R.id.gameView));
mGameEngine.setInputController(
  new CompositeInputController(getView(), getYassActivity()));
mGameEngine.addGameObject(
  new ParallaxBackground(mGameEngine, 20,
  R.drawable.seamless_space_0));
mGameEngine.addGameObject(new GameController(mGameEngine));
mGameEngine.addGameObject(new Player(mGameEngine));
mGameEngine.startGame();
```

Our game is starting to look really good.

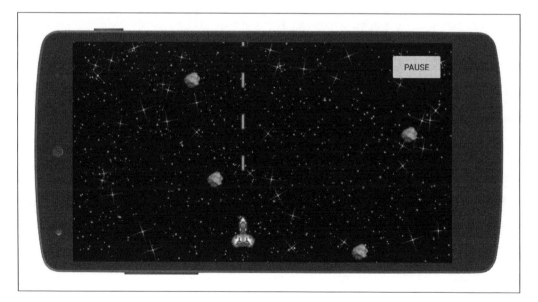

Multiple backgrounds

It is fairly easy to add another `ParallaxBackground` to the game with an additional set of stars at a different speed, so the two of them together give a better feeling of depth. This is as simple as adding another `ParallaxBackground` object with a different speed and a drawable that has transparency.

If we do it, we are going to see a dramatic decrease in performance.

This performance problem is caused by the number of pixel overdraws. With the second background, every point on the screen gets drawn at least twice (once for each background), and some of them thrice, when there is a sprite involved. Transparent pixels do count as overdraw.

Using two overlapping parallax backgrounds forces each pixel to be drawn at least twice per frame.

All in all, there are many parameters involved in the performance. In most cases, `SurfaceGameView`, together with efficient background drawing, will give the best results. But as soon as we overlay another `View` on top of `GameView`, the performance plummets. `StandardGameView` performance decays slower in this case.

There is not much of a difference in performance between the two implementations of `GameView` or background rendering methods when we use only one background. But again, it depends on the size of the bitmap used for the background. I recommend you to experiment and see the differences yourself.

While the effect of two parallax backgrounds is nice and our `GameView` can handle it with a decent refresh rate, we are going to use only one background in YASS. With this amount of overdraw, we are getting into the performance limit of what can be done with the standard Android SDK without using OpenGL.

If you want more complex backgrounds, you may want to move into using an OpenGL engine such as AndEngine, which uses the same concepts we have been using here.

Layers

Until now, the drawing sequence for the GameObjects is the order in which they are added to the GameEngine. This is inconvenient to say the least. We should improve it.

As most other drawing systems do, our engine should use layers.

Whenever we add a `GameObject` to the `GameEngine`, we will pass an integer to indicate the layer we want it to be added to. We will consider 0 to be the layer to add the background to. Think of layers as a z-index for the game objects.

We are going to use four layers. From the foreground to the background, we will display:

- The `Player` object: The spaceship
- Asteroids
- Bullets
- The background

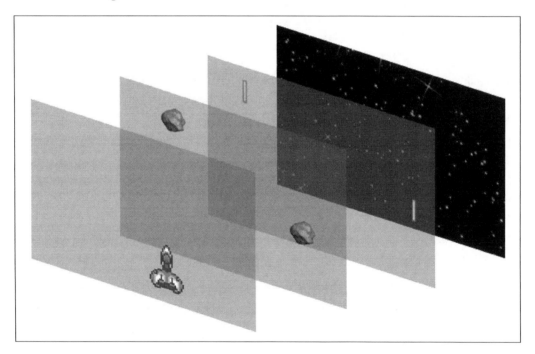

To add layer support, we need to modify the `GameEngine`, `StandardGameView`, and `SurfaceGameView` classes. For convenience, we will also update `GameObject` to know its layer.

On the top level, we will handle the layers as a list of lists of game objects. This is the data structure that we will store in the GameEngine and pass to the implementations of GameView. We will keep the old mGameObject list as a simple way to iterate over all the GameObjects.

We initialize the layers inside the constructor of GameEngine. We will add a parameter to the constructor showing the number of layers we expect to have, so they can be precreated:

```
private List<List<GameObject>> mLayers = new
  ArrayList<List<GameObject>>();

public GameEngine (Activity a, GameView gameView, int numLayers) {
  [...]
  for (int i=0; i<numLayers; i++) {
    mLayers.add(new ArrayList<GameObject>());
  }
}
```

The major changes are inside onUpdate:

```
public void onUpdate(long elapsedMillis) {
  mInputController.onPreUpdate();
  int numObjects = mGameObjects.size();
  for (int i=0; i<numObjects; i++) {
    mGameObjects.get(i).onUpdate(elapsedMillis, this);
  }
  synchronized (mLayers) {
    while (!mObjectsToRemove.isEmpty()) {
      GameObject objectToRemove = mObjectsToRemove.remove(0);
      mGameObjects.remove(objectToRemove);
      mLayers.get(objectToRemove.mLayer).remove(objectToRemove);
    }
    while (!mObjectsToAdd.isEmpty()) {
      GameObject gameObject = mObjectsToAdd.remove(0);
      addToLayerNow(gameObject);
    }
  }
}
```

The first part is the same as before. It iterates along all the GameObjects, calling onUpdate.

For the removal of objects, it is important that the GameObject knows its layer. Because of this, removing the object from the list of layers is just one more line of code.

Knowing the layer is also important when it comes to adding the `GameObjects`, especially when such addition is delayed to the end of `onUpdate`.

There is one new method called `addToLayerNow`. It is used also when the objects are added before the game starts. We can see how it is used in the `addGameObject` method of the `GameEngine`:

```
public void addGameObject(final GameObject gameObject, int layer) {
  gameObject.mLayer = layer;
  if (isRunning()){
    mObjectsToAdd.add(gameObject);
  }
  else {
    addToLayerNow(gameObject);
  }
  mActivity.runOnUiThread(gameObject.mOnAddedRunnable);
}
```

Note that the first thing we do when we add a new `GameObject` is to set the layer it is to be added to.

The `addToLayerNow` method takes care of the situation when we want to add a `GameObject` to a layer we have not defined. This should not happen if we defined the correct number of layers to be precreated. But it is a good safety measure to have in place, especially when you are not sure how many layers you will use:

```
private void addToLayerNow (GameObject object) {
  int layer = object.mLayer;
  while (mLayers.size() <= layer) {
    mLayers.add(new ArrayList<GameObject>());
  }
  mLayers.get(layer).add(object);
  mGameObjects.add(object);
}
```

The fact that `GameObject` knows the layer it has to be added to allows us to add it to the right layer in a single line of code. Note that we also add the `GameObject` to the list of all game objects.

Finally, the code that draws the game objects into the canvas has to be changed in both implementations of `GameView`. This is the place where the order of the layers is used to provide the drawing order:

```
int numLayers = mLayers.size();
for (int i = 0; i < numLayers; i++) {
  List<GameObject> currentLayer = mLayers.get(i);
  int numObjects = currentLayer.size();
  for (int j=0; j<numObjects; j++) {
    currentLayer.get(j).onDraw(canvas);
  }
}
```

Note that, inside each layer, the order of drawing is still the order of addition. Since we can now isolate the same type of items to the same layer, this should not be something to worry about any longer.

Also, note that the synchronization object is the same in the GameViews and in the GameEngine, now that synchronization is done using mLayers.

Summary

We have learned how to draw at low level using a standard View and also a SurfaceView. We have created a Sprite class to reuse the code of the items that are displayed on the screen.

The DrawThread has been updated to a more efficient one and we also added a frames-per-second counter to check the efficiency of each configuration.

Along the way, we learned about game controllers and the different ways to create levels. We also decided to spawn asteroids YASS using procedural generation, and put this into effect.

We also added support for parallax backgrounds and layers to the engine.

All in all, YASS is starting to look good, but we are clearly missing something: the bullets do nothing when they hit an asteroid and neither does our spaceship.

It is time to implement collision detection.

4

Collision Detection

In most games we need to detect when objects intersect with each other to trigger actions; this is called collision detection. We will use it to detect when a bullet hits an asteroid (to destroy it) and when the player is hit by an asteroid (to end the game). This detection can be done in a discrete or in a continuous way, and it can involve different types of shapes. We will use discrete detection with rectangular and circular shapes.

As mentioned in *Chapter 1, Setting Up the Project*, we are not going to do any Physics simulation. That is a completely separate topic and it is long enough to deserve its own book.

We will also discuss optimization techniques and implement one method called spatial partitioning that splits the area into smaller ones based on object density.

As a side note, all the concepts in this chapter can be easily extrapolated to collisions in 3D.

Detecting collisions

There are two main approaches to checking collisions:

- Discrete, or a posteriori
- Continuous, or a priori

For the discrete approach, we advance the state of the game items and then check if any of them are intersecting. It is a discrete simulation because we only do the evaluation at the end of each step. It is called a posteriori because it is done after the objects have moved. It is reactive. Most of the time we lack the exact point of contact; we only know that at the end of the simulation step the objects are colliding.

On the other hand, a continuous approach predicts the collision before applying the movement, based on the parameters of each object. It is calculated before the movement is performed. That's why it is called a priori. This method provides the exact point of contact and it is extremely useful when we require precision—such as for physics simulation.

The discrete method is generally one dimension simpler than the continuous one. This makes it much easier to understand and implement. It trades speed for precision.

 Discrete collision detection is faster but less precise.

Since we are not going to use physics and we don't really care about the exact point of contact, we will use the discrete approach.

Who can collide?

To be able to calculate GameObject collisions, we need to associate a shape (or body) to a GameObject. This association requires some information about the object on the screen, such as position on the *x* and *y* axes and also the width and height.

We are going to create a class named ScreenGameObject that extends from GameObject and will contain that information. In our game, Sprite is the only class that will extend from ScreenGameObject, but it may come in handy if you want to place non-visual items on the screen that trigger something when the player crosses them, which is a common technique in games.

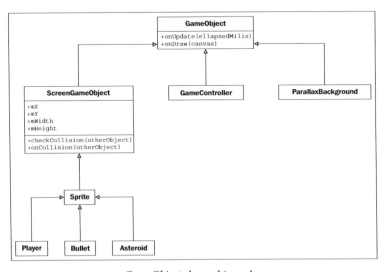

GameObject classes hierarchy

To collide with other objects you need a position on the screen and a size. `ScreenGameObject` will provide that.

All the logic for calculation collisions will be placed inside the `ScreenGameObject` class. The stub of the class is like this:

```
public abstract class ScreenGameObject extends GameObject {

    protected double mX;
    protected double mY;

    protected int mHeight;
    protected int mWidth;

    public Rect mBoundingRect = new Rect(-1, -1, -1, -1);

    public boolean checkCollision(ScreenGameObject otherObject) {
        return false;
    }

    public void onCollision(GameEngine gameEngine,
        ScreenGameObject sgo) {
    }
}
```

We take this opportunity to refactor the variables `width`, `height`, `X`, and `Y` to have shorter, more generic names. We will continue working with this class throughout the chapter.

The method `checkCollision` is where the action happens. That method will have a different implementation depending on the shapes we use to calculate the collisions.

Finally, `onCollision` is used to trigger an action when a collision occurs.

Updating GameEngine

To run discrete collision detection, we will use a method named `checkCollisions` during the execution of `onUpdate` on the `GameEngine`, so it will run every time the game objects are updated. We will place this method call after the update of the game objects and before the code that removes objects. Collisions are a typical reason why objects get removed.

Since only `ScreenGameObjects` can have collisions, we will create a special list containing them.

```
private List<ScreenGameObject> mCollisionableObjects;
```

And we will keep it updated whenever an object is added to or removed from the `GameEngine`, as we did for the separate layers in the previous chapter.

The code to check for collisions and to notify the game objects involved is as follows.

```
private void checkCollisions() {
  int numObjects = mCollisionableObjects.size();
  for (int i = 0; i < numObjects; i++) {
    ScreenGameObject objectA = mCollisionableObjects.get(i);
    for (int j = i + 1; j < numObjects; j++) {
      ScreenGameObject objectB = mCollisionableObjects.get(j);
      if (objectA.checkCollision(objectB)) {
        objectA.onCollision(gameEngine, objectB);
        objectB.onCollision(gameEngine, objectA);
      }
    }
  }
}
```

The code is as simple as a nested `for` loop that checks every `ScreenGameObject` against all the others. If a collision is detected, we will execute the method `onCollision` on both screen game objects involved in it, passing the object they have collided with as a parameter.

Keep in mind that this method has quadratic complexity, while all the other methods involved in `onUpdate` have linear complexity instead. Running collision detection is expensive.

 Checking for collisions has quadratic complexity $O(n^2)$.

Handling collisions

Regardless of the method we use to calculate the collisions, the actions we have to take for the player and the bullets are the same. Let's override the method `onCollision` for them.

In the case of the bullets, we have to check if the object it collides with is an asteroid and, if that's the case, we remove both objects from the GameEngine.

```
public void onCollision(GameEngine gameEngine,
    ScreenGameObject otherObject) {
  if (otherObject instanceof Asteroid) {
    // Remove both from the game (and return them to their pools)
    removeObject(gameEngine);
    Asteroid a = (Asteroid) otherObject;
    a.removeObject(gameEngine);
  }
}
```

Note that we are calling a method removeObject on the objects themselves. This method takes care of removing the GameObject from the GameEngine, and also returning it to the object pool.

The code for the player is almost identical to the one for the bullet: we just remove both colliding objects in the case of an asteroid.

It is worth mentioning that because of the way we are spawning the bullets, they do collide with the Player object when added to the scene because we want it to look like they appear from the spaceship. We have to discard that collision. It is good practice to always check what the object is colliding against.

 If we want to make a game with several lives, we should signal the GameEngine at that point to stop spawning waves, remove one life, spawn a new Player object, and then continue the game.

Let's see how the collisions are actually calculated.

Rectangular bodies

The first way we are going to implement detection is through the intersection of rectangles, which is also the simplest method.

We will use the bounding rectangle of the ScreenGameObject and check if it intersects with the bounding rectangle of the other ScreenGameObject.

The bounding rectangle changes each time we update the position of the sprite and, since we may be required to check with many other objects, it is best if we recalculate it after onUpdate. We are going to make a new method called onPostUpdate and do that inside it.

We have to add a new method to `ScreenGameObject`.

```
public void onPostUpdate(GameEngine gameEngine) {
  mBoundingRect.set(
    (int) mX,
    (int) mY,
    (int) mX + mWidth,
    (int) mY + mHeight);
}
```

If you need to override `onPostUpdate` on other objects, remember to always call the super method, otherwise collisions will misbehave.

Then, when checking for collisions, we do a check for rectangular ones:

```
@Override
public boolean checkCollision(ScreenGameObject otherObject) {
  return checkRectangularCollision(otherObject);
}
```

Finally, although calculating intersections of rectangles is a very easy operation, since the class `Rect` already provides us with a utility method to do it, we will use it.

```
private boolean checkRectangularCollision(ScreenGameObject other) {
  return Rect.intersects(mBoundingRect, other.mBoundingRect);
}
```

Adding visual feedback

Something that really helps when working with collisions is to get some visual feedback on what is happening. For that we are going to draw the bounding rectangle in yellow as a background for the sprites:

```
@Override
public void onDraw(Canvas canvas) {
  if (mX > canvas.getWidth() || mY > canvas.getHeight()
    || mX < -mWidth || mY < -mHeight) {
    return;
  }
  mPaint.setColor(Color.YELLOW);
  canvas.drawRect(mBoundingRect, mPaint);

  mMatrix.reset();
  [...]
  canvas.drawBitmap(mBitmap, mMatrix, null);
}
```

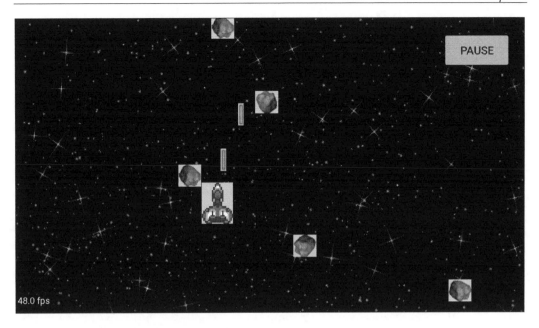

And it is time to try out our shiny collision detection method and see how it performs. Spoiler alert: not too good.

Pros and cons

This collision detection has some advantages:

- Easy to implement
- Fast to evaluate

But it also has some important flaws:

- If the sprite has padding, the collision area is too big and unrealistic.
- We are not rotating the rectangles when the Sprite rotates.
- Collisions are very strict. The system detects collisions where there are only transparent pixels. This is especially bad when the corners touch.

We can solve the first problem by clipping the sprites or by adding the possibility to set margins on the `ScreenGameObject`.

The second problem can be solved with some simple math, but it complicates the code and the result isn't a better solution than a circular collision body. This is outside the scope of this book and is left as an exercise for the reader.

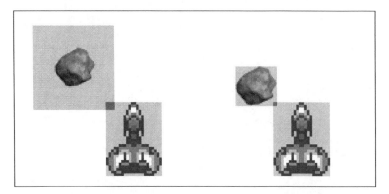

Rectangular bodies require no padding on the images and can still create false positives

Unfortunately, the last problem is something that is inherent to this approach and cannot be solved unless we use a bounding polygon or a combination of rectangles.

Circular bodies

The next type of body we can use to detect collisions is a circle. For that we are going to consider the diameter of the circle to be the largest of the dimensions of the sprite. We have to add a member variable to `ScreenGameObject` named `mRadius` and this code to the constructor of the sprite:

```
mRadius = Math.max(mHeight, mWidth)/2;
```

Note that other elements that inherit from `ScreenGameObject` may want to initialize the radius in a different way.

The calculation of a circular collision is fairly simple: we just have to measure the distance between the centers of the two circles and check if it is smaller than the sum of the radius.

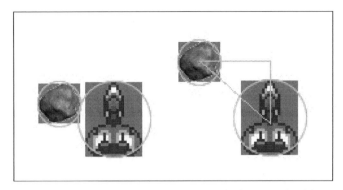

With circular bodies, the collision can occur outside the rectangle of the sprite

Because calculating square roots is a much more time consuming operation than a multiplication, we will use the square of the distance as defined by the Pythagorean theorem: $distance^2 = \Delta x^2 + \Delta y^2$.

The code to check circular collisions is like this:

```
private boolean checkCircularCollision(ScreenGameObject other) {
   double distanceX = (mX + mWidth /2) - (other.mX +
     other.mWidth /2);
   double distanceY = (mY + mHeight /2) - (other.mY +
     other.mHeight /2);
   double squareDistance = distanceX*distanceX +
     distanceY*distanceY;
   double collisionDistance = (mRadius + other.mRadius);
   return squareDistance <= collisionDistance*collisionDistance;
}
```

We calculate the distance on each axis, then get the `squareDistance` as the sum of the squares. The `collisionDistance` is the sum of the radius, and then we compare it with the square of the `collisionDistance`.

Adding visual feedback

As we did for rectangle collision detection, we will add some visual feedback to the sprite to show the collision area while playing. In this case we just need to draw a circle:

```
canvas.drawCircle(
    (int) (mX + mWidth / 2),
    (int) (mY + mHeight / 2),
    (int) mRadius,
    mPaint);
```

And, as simple as that, we can see the collision area of the sprites on the game.

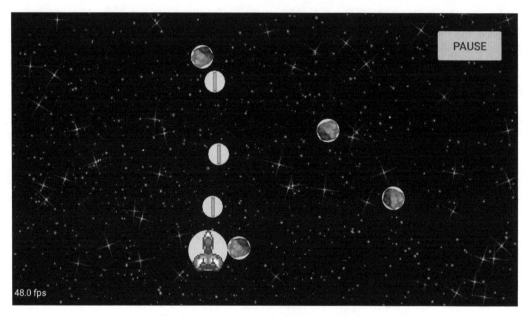

Circular bodies fit great the Asteroids, but are terrible for the Bullets

Pros and cons

This approach is not perfect either, but it has some advantages:

- It works better than rectangles for most sprites
- It is easy to implement
- It does not involve complex calculations

But it also has some problems— the most notable one is that when the image is mostly rectangular, the area of the collision is too big. We can see that clearly in the case of the bullets.

So, some sprites work better with rectangles, while others work better with circles. We could just have different body types for each `ScreenGameObject` and calculate collisions accordingly.

Mixed collision detection

We have seen that a single shape does not fit all cases, so we are going to update our game to allow us to define which body shape each `ScreenGameObject` uses for collisions. For this, we are going to create an enum of body types and have a variable to store that information in `ScreenGameObject`.

The enum `BodyType` is as follows:

```
public enum BodyType {
  None,
  Circular,
  Rectangular
}
```

In the case of sprites, we will add a parameter to the constructor that specifies body type. Note that we have a special type called `None`. This is used for sprites that do not collide with others. While there are none of those in our game yet, other types of games can have them—for example, floor tiles on a dungeon crawler.

 We may want to have some sprites that do not trigger collisions. This is done using `BodyType.None`.

We are going to use circular bodies for the asteroids and the player, and rectangular ones for the bullets.

Since we have a list of bodies that can collide, if a `ScreenGameObject` has a `BodyType` of `None` we will not add it to the list; therefore, we do not need to check its collisions. This piece of code goes inside the method `addToLayerNow` of `GameEngine`.

```
if (object instanceof ScreenGameObject) {
  ScreenGameObject sgo = (ScreenGameObject) object;
  if (sgo.mBodyType != BodyType.None) {
    mCollisionableObjects.add(sgo);
  }
}
```

Then we have to update the `checkCollision` method of the `ScreenGameObject` to check which types the bodies of the two objects are, and which method we have to apply:

```
@Override
public boolean checkCollision(ScreenGameObject otherObject) {
  if (mBodyType == BodyType.Circular
     && otherObject.mBodyType == BodyType.Circular) {
    return checkCircularCollision(otherObject);
  }
  else if (mBodyType == BodyType.Rectangular
     && otherObject.mBodyType == BodyType.Rectangular) {
    return checkRectangularCollision(otherObject);
  }
  else {
    return checkMixedCollision(otherObject);
  }
}
```

Note that at this point in the execution, we know that the object is a `ScreenGameObject` and that it has a `BodyType` that is not `None`.

If both objects involved have rectangular bodies, we use the rectangular collision detection method. If both have circular bodies, we use the circular collision detection method. In any other case one of them is circular and the other is rectangular, so we have a new method for this case: `checkMixedCollision`.

To calculate if a rectangle and a circle collide, we have to check if the point of the rectangle that is closest to the circle is inside it (the distance to the center of the circle is smaller than the radius).

The point of the rectangle that is closest to the circle can be easily calculated if we isolate the problem on each coordinate.

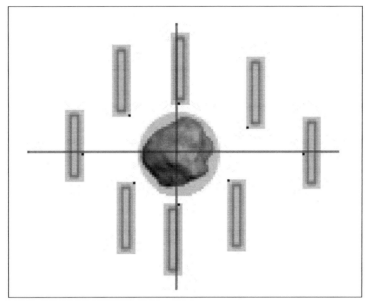

Possible relative positions of a circle and a rectangle and its closest point

We are going to discuss the vertical axis (this is easier to distinguish because the bullets are tall). The horizontal axis follows an equivalent logic:

- We draw a horizontal line that goes through the center of the circle.
- If that line intersects the rectangle, the point of intersection is the closest point. As we are considering only the vertical axis, that value is the y coordinate of the center of the circle.
- If the rectangle is below the line, the y coordinate of the closest point to the circle is the top position of the rectangle (the y coordinate).
- If the rectangle is above the line, the y coordinate of the closest point to the circle is the bottom position of the rectangle (y + `height`).

Remember that in computer graphics the [0,0] point is at the top left of the screen and the y axis is positive downwards.

Now that the algorithm is clear, let's look at the code:

```
private boolean checkMixedCollision(ScreenGameObject other) {
  ScreenGameObject circularSprite;
  ScreenGameObject rectangularSprite;
  if (mBodyType == BodyType.Rectangular) {
    circularSprite = this;
    rectangularSprite = other;
  }
  else {
    circularSprite = other;
    rectangularSprite = this;
  }

  double circleCenterX = circularSprite.mX +
    circularSprite.mWidth /2;
  double positionXToCheck = circleCenterX;
  if (circleCenterX < rectangularSprite.mX) {
    positionXToCheck = rectangularSprite.mX;
  }
  else if (circleCenterX > rectangularSprite.mX +
    rectangularSprite.mWidth) {
    positionXToCheck = rectangularSprite.mX +
    rectangularSprite.mWidth;
  }
  double distanceX = circleCenterX - positionXToCheck;

  double circleCenterY = circularSprite.mY +
    circularSprite.mHeight /2;
  double positionYToCheck = circleCenterY;
  if (circleCenterY < rectangularSprite.mY) {
    positionYToCheck = rectangularSprite.mY;
  }
  else if (circleCenterY > rectangularSprite.mY +
    rectangularSprite.mHeight) {
    positionYToCheck = rectangularSprite.mY +
      rectangularSprite.mHeight;
  }
  double distanceY = circleCenterY - positionYToCheck;

  double squareDistance = distanceX*distanceX +
    distanceY*distanceY;
  if (squareDistance <=
    circularSprite.mRadius*circularSprite.mRadius) {
    // They are overlapping
    return true;
  }
  return false;
}
```

We first identify which object has a circular body and which a rectangular one, and we set them to local variables.

Then we calculate the *x* and *y* coordinates of the closest point, following the logic we already described. This combination gives us nine possible relative positions, which you can see in the image.

Finally, we calculate the square distance from that point to the center of the circle and check if it is smaller than the square of the radius.

Adding visual feedback

Adding visual feedback is again very simple. We just need to run the code to draw a rectangle or the one to draw a circle, according to the type of body the sprite has.

```
mPaint.setColor(Color.YELLOW);
if (mBodyType == BodyType.Circular) {
  canvas.drawCircle(
    (int) (mX + mWidth / 2),
    (int) (mY + mHeight / 2),
    (int) mRadius,
    mPaint);
}
else if (mBodyType == BodyType.Rectangular) {
  canvas.drawRect(mBoundingRect, mPaint);
}
```

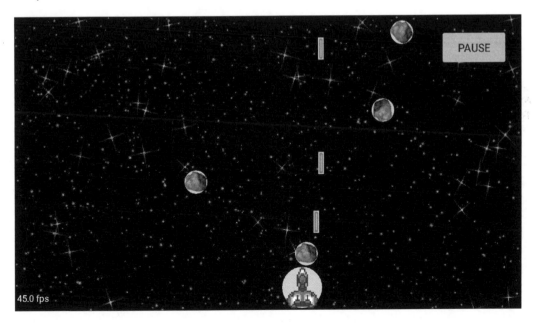

Other options for shapes

With this, we have covered the basic options for collision detection using simple shapes. To get a good feel for a game, you will need to pay special attention to the shape of each sprite and see which shape fits it best, maybe with modifications such as a smaller radius. For this I recommend you to keep the visual feedback on to check the approximation.

There is also the possibility of using polygons as shapes or multiple rectangles. These are reasonably easy ways to improve collision detection, and not too hard to implement. We leave it to the reader to explore the subject in more depth, as it requires fine-tuning.

In the case of the spaceship, the best shape would be a combination of 2 rectangles but, as we are happy with the circular body, we will leave it like that.

Different shape options for the spaceship

Optimization

Checking for collisions is an algorithm of quadratic complexity. If the number of objects to be checked grows, it may quickly become a bottleneck.

One option is to keep a record of the previous state of the comparison between the objects, and then either return the old value if both objects have not changed since the last check or use the old state as a parameter to the calculation of the new one. This is particularly handy for 3D games, where collision detection requires much more complex algorithms.

There is another optimization called spatial partitioning that exploits the proximity of the objects. This technique is based on the idea that objects can only collide with other elements that are close to them on the screen. Pretty obvious, right?

To implement spatial partitioning, we are going to use a data structure known as QuadTree.

Spatial partitioning and QuadTree

A QuadTree is similar to a binary tree, except that each node that is not a leaf has four children instead of two.

This is meant to represent the spatial partitioning of a space into four sectors, each sector represented by one of the children. Each child can have another four nodes, or just be a leaf. This design makes it possible to apply the partition recursively when it is needed.

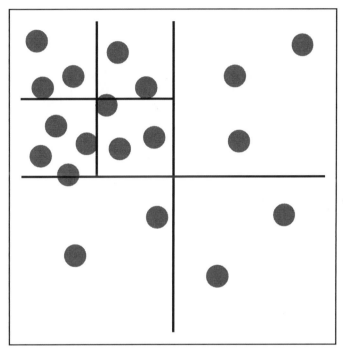

Example of recursive partitioning where the density is high.

We only need to partition the space if the number of objects in it is too large. This means that some sections with a high density of objects may be partitioned several times while others aren't.

When applying this concept to 3D games the data structure is called OctTree, because when we have three dimensions the space is divided into eight sections.

The algorithm to populate a `QuadTree` is quite straight forward:

- We check how many objects are in the space, and if the number is not too large (we use the constant `MAX_OBJECTS_TO_CHECK` for that), we will run the collision detection as before, checking each object with every other one
- Otherwise, divide the space into four quadrants or areas
- For each quadrant, check which objects are inside (an object may be in more than one quadrant)
- For each quadrant, apply this same algorithm recursively

Each `QuadTree` has a `Rect` member that designates its area and a list of objects to check.

Inside `GameEngine`, we will replace the list of objects to check for collision with the root node of a `QuadTree`. We will add objects to or remove them from this node as they are added to or removed from the `GameEngine` and delegate the `QuadTree` to check the collisions.

On the constructor of the `GameEngine`, we will set the area of the root node:

```
mQuadTreeRoot.setArea(new Rect(0,0,mWidth, mHeight));
```

The code to check the collisions on the `GameEngine` gets simplified to a single line:

```java
private void checkCollisions() {
  mQuadTreeRoot.checkCollisions(this);
}
```

Then, inside `QuadTree`, the code for checking the collisions is as follows:

```java
public void checkCollisions(GameEngine gameEngine) {
  int numObjects = mGameObjects.size();
  if (numObjects > MAX_OBJECTS_TO_CHECK && sQuadTreePool.size() >=
    4) {
    splitAndCheck(gameEngine);
  }
  else {
    for (int i = 0; i < numObjects; i++) {
      ScreenGameObject objectA = mGameObjects.get(i);
      for (int j = i + 1; j < numObjects; j++) {
        ScreenGameObject objectB = mGameObjects.get(j);
        if (objectA.checkCollision(objectB)) {
          objectA.onCollision(gameEngine, objectB);
          objectB.onCollision(gameEngine, objectA);
        }
      }
    }
  }
}
```

There are two possibilities. If we have too many objects and more than four `QuadTree` objects in the pool, we split the space and check the collisions on the children. If this isn't so, we just run the collision detection method as we did before, iterating among all the objects on the list.

The method `splitAndCheck` looks like this:

```
private void splitAndCheck(GameEngine gameEngine) {
  for (int i=0 ; i<4; i++) {
    mChildren[i] = sQuadTreePool.remove(0);
  }
  for (int i=0 ; i<4; i++) {
    mChildren[i].setArea(getArea(i));
    mChildren[i].checkObjects(mGameObjects);
    mChildren[i].checkCollisions(gameEngine);
    // Clear and return to the pool
    mChildren[i].mGameObjects.clear();
    sQuadTreePool.add(mChildren[i]);
  }
}
```

We take four `QuadTree` objects from the pool and assign them to the elements on the array of children. It is important to do this at the beginning, given the recursive nature of the algorithm.

For each child we define the area, which means dividing the current area into four equal rectangles, checking which objects are inside the area, and then checking for collisions, which is the recursive function again. Once that is done, we clear the child and return it to the pool.

On a final note—`getArea` just reuses a `Rect` object to set it to the values of the four quadrants.

```
private Rect getArea(int area) {
  int startX = mArea.left;
  int startY = mArea.top;
  int width = mArea.width();
  int height = mArea.height();
  switch (area) {
    case 0:
      mTmpRect.set(startX, startY,
        startX + width / 2, startY + height / 2);
      break;
    case 1:
      mTmpRect.set(startX + width / 2, startY,
        startX + width, startY + height / 2);
```

```
        break;
    case 2:
      mTmpRect.set(startX, startY + height / 2,
        startX + width / 2, startY + height);
      break;
    case 3:
      mTmpRect.set(startX + width / 2, startY + height / 2,
        startX + width, startY + height);
      break;
    }
  return mTmpRect;
}
```

To get an idea of the level of optimization of QuadTrees, let's imagine that we have 100 objects on the screen and that they are distributed in only two quadrants. This is one of those cases when this algorithm provides the best optimization.

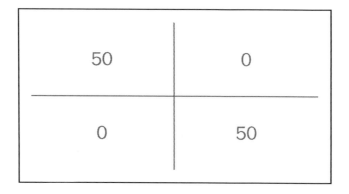

If we don't use the QuadTree technique, the number of collisions that need to be evaluated is 50.000. Iterating over the list twice gives $n^2/2$ collision checks.

When we split the space into four, the amount of collisions checked is 1.250 on the first and fourth quadrants ($50^2/2$) and none on the others. We have to add 400 operations, which are needed to see in which section each object is located (100 objects in four quadrants).

For us, checking which quadrant an object is in is of similar complexity to checking a collision, but for collisions in 3D the collision check is much more expensive.

Duplicated collisions

There is a special case we should be aware of when using spatial partitioning: some collisions can be detected twice.

When a collision occurs between two objects that are on the intersection of two quadrants, both objects are in both quadrants; when the algorithm checks for collisions, it is detected in each of them. In the worst case it would be detected four times, when the objects are placed on the intersection of the four quadrants.

To solve this, we will keep a list of collisions that have been detected and only process a collision if it has not been detected before.

The `Collision` class is very simple. It just contains two `ScreenGameObject` instances, an `equals` method, and a couple of static methods to handle its pool:

```
public class Collision {
  private static List<Collision> sCollisionPool = new
    ArrayList<Collision>();

  public static Collision init(ScreenGameObject objectA,
    ScreenGameObject objectB) {
    if (sCollisionPool.isEmpty()) {
      return new Collision(objectA, objectB);
    }
    Collision c = sCollisionPool.remove(0);
    c.mObjectA = objectA;
    c.mObjectB = objectB;
    return c;
  }

  public static void release(Collision c) {
    c.mObjectA = null;
    c.mObjectB = null;
    sCollisionPool.add(c);
  }

  public ScreenGameObject mObjectA;
  public ScreenGameObject mObjectB;

  public Collision(ScreenGameObject objectA,
    ScreenGameObject objectB) {
    mObjectA = objectA;
    mObjectB = objectB;
  }
```

```
    public boolean equals (Collision c) {
      return (mObjectA == c.mObjectA && mObjectB == c.mObjectB)
        || (mObjectA == c.mObjectB && mObjectB == c.mObjectA);
    }
  }
```

We add the list of detected collisions as a parameter to the checkCollisions method, and we make sure we clean it on GameEngine before checking it again. The updated checkCollisions on the GameEngine is like this:

```
private List<Collision> mDetectedCollisions = new
ArrayList<Collision>();

private void checkCollisions() {
  // Release the collisions from the previous step
  while (!mDetectedCollisions.isEmpty()) {
    Collision.release(mDetectedCollisions.remove(0));
  }
  mQuadTreeRoot.checkCollisions(this, mDetectedCollisions);
}
```

Note that, because we are using a pool, we cannot just clear the list; we need to release each element individually.

Finally, we verify that the collision has not been detected before, checking it on the QuadTree.

```
public void checkCollisions(GameEngine gameEngine, List<Collision>
detectedCollisions) {
  int numObjects = mGameObjects.size();
  if (numObjects > MAX_OBJECTS_TO_CHECK && sQuadTreePool.size() >=
    4) {
    // Split this area in 4
    splitAndCheck(gameEngine, detectedCollisions);
  }
  else {
    for (int i = 0; i < numObjects; i++) {
      ScreenGameObject objectA = mGameObjects.get(i);
      for (int j = i + 1; j < numObjects; j++) {
        ScreenGameObject objectB = mGameObjects.get(j);
        if (objectA.checkCollision(objectB)) {
          Collision c = Collision.init(objectA, objectB);
          if (!hasBeenDetected(detectedCollisions, c)) {
            detectedCollisions.add(c);
```

```
            objectA.onCollision(gameEngine, objectB);
            objectB.onCollision(gameEngine, objectA);
          }
        }
      }
    }
  }
}
```

Note that the list of collisions is required throughout the process, and it must be passed to the recursive method as part of the state of the calculation.

Summary

Now our game is really playable, we can detect when the bullets touch the asteroids and destroy them; additionally, we have to be careful because our ship can be destroyed by them as well.

We have learned how to do simple collision detection with rectangular and circular bodies, adjusting the body for each particular sprite.

We also learned some optimization techniques for collision detection and implemented one that makes use of spatial partitioning.

The next step in our roadmap is to add some juiciness to the game. Didn't you notice that the asteroids are missing some explosions? In the next chapter, we are going to talk about how to create particle systems for effects.

5
Particle Systems

Particle systems are a technique used widely in video games to simulate phenomena that are complicated to render with other methods. The typical usages for them include explosions, fireworks, smoke, fire, water, and so on. They are usually highly chaotic systems.

Their foundation is to use a large number of small sprites called particles. Their behavior is parametrized, so each particle has a different set of pseudo-random values. This makes each usage of the particle system different while it still looks similar.

Most game engines include a way to implement particle systems. Our engine will have them too.

We will base our code on the free software project Leonids, which is a library to display particle systems in the standard Android UI. We will adapt it to be used by our engine.

After explaining the basics of particle systems, we will implement a couple of examples of one-shot particle systems to simulate explosions, and also some continuous emitters to simulate a trail for the asteroids and the smoke of the spaceship's engine.

General concepts

We are going to make our particle system in a way that mimics the Leonids particle system library at `http://plattysoft.github.io/Leonids/`. This project is a free software library I made to use particle systems in the standard Android UI.

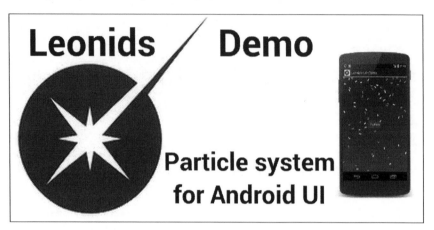

A demo of the Leonids library is available on Google Play

As a result of this, Leonids implements its own update and draw threads, as well as a simplified `GameView`. We already have all these, so we will adapt the code to suit our needs.

The concepts we are going to work with in this chapter are:

- **Particle**: Each of the sprites that are rendered
- **Particle system**: The entity that takes care of spawning, updating, and keeping track of the particles
- **Initializer**: A class that sets a value for a particle based on certain parameters (before being active)
- **Modifier**: A class that updates a value for a particle based on the elapsed time (while being active)

In our game, we will use only a few initializers and modifiers. If you need to extend the functionality of the particle system, you can visit Leonids' GitHub page to get ideas from it.

Let's get into the concepts.

Particles

Particles are a subclass of `Sprites`. Each particle is a small image with several particularities:

- Particles do not have a collision body
- Their movement is based on linear and angular speed
- They have a limited time to live

While, in theory, you could have a particle system in which the particles can collide — and this is handy to simulate effects such as a waterfall — the truth is that, unless you also have physics, this will not work properly. For simplicity, we are going to define our particles to have a `BodyType` of `None`.

A particle does have linear and angular speed and its `onUpdate` method is based on these variables. Each particle has these values initialized by the particle system.

There are a few properties of sprites that particles usually modify. They are alpha and scale. We are not using them on sprites yet, so we will modify the `onDraw` method of `Sprite` for it:

```
float scaleFactor = (float) (mPixelFactor*mScale);
mMatrix.reset();
mMatrix.postScale(scaleFactor, scaleFactor);
mMatrix.postTranslate((float) mX, (float) mY);
mMatrix.postRotate((float) mRotation,
   (float) (mX + mWidth*mScale / 2),
   (float) (mY + mHeight*mScale / 2));
mPaint.setAlpha(mAlpha);
canvas.drawBitmap(mBitmap, mMatrix, mPaint);
```

As it happens, we were using the scale as part of the transformation matrix to scale the sprite based on the pixel factor. Now, we also multiply this by the perceived scale and we are done.

Note that we also need to multiply the width and height by the scale to put the center of the rotation at the center of the scaled sprite.

Also, note that we do the scaling in the beginning. If we were to do the scaling after the translation, the movement would be scaled as well and this is not what we want. Again, the order of the transformations affects the result.

While the scale is a part of the transformation matrix, the alpha is a parameter of Paint. Its value goes from 0 (transparent) to 255 (opaque). It is important that you remember to initialize it to 255 or all our sprites will be transparent.

 Alpha values go from 0 (transparent) to 255 (opaque).

With regard to the time to live, we just need to check the total amount of time the particle has been active during onUpdate to remove it from the GameEngine and return it to the particle system when it has expired.

Particle is then a class that extends Sprite, which has a method to activate it. It runs its updates based on the values of linear and angular speed:

```
public class Particle extends Sprite {

    private long mTimeToLive;
    private long mTotalMillis;

    public double mSpeedX;
    public double mSpeedY;

    public double mRotationSpeed;

    protected Particle(
        ParticleSystem particleSystem,
        GameEngine gameEngine,
        int drawableRes) {
        super(gameEngine, drawableRes, BodyType.None);
        mParent = particleSystem;
    }

    @Override
    public void removeFromGameEngine(GameEngine gameEngine) {
        super.removeFromGameEngine(gameEngine);
        mParent.returnToPool(this);
    }

    public void activate(
        GameEngine gameEngine,
        long timeToLive,
        double x,
        double y,
```

```
    ArrayList<ParticleModifier> modifiers
    int layer) {
    mTimeToLive = timeToLive;
    mX = x-mWidth/2;
    mY = y-mHeight/2;
    addToGameEngine(gameEngine, layer);
    mModifiers = modifiers;
    mTotalMillis = 0;
  }

  @Override
  public void onUpdate(long elapsedMillis,
      GameEngine gameEngine) {
    mTotalMillis += elapsedMillis;
    if (mTotalMillis > mTimeToLive) {
      removeFromGameEngine(gameEngine);
    }
    else {
      mX += mSpeedX*elapsedMillis;
      mY += mSpeedY*elapsedMillis;
      mRotation += mRotationSpeed*elapsedMillis/1000d;
      for (int i=0; i<mModifiers.size(); i++) {
        mModifiers.get(i).apply(this, mTotalMillis);
      }
    }
  }
}
```

In the constructor, we pass a reference to the parent ParticleSystem, which we will use to return the particle to it when it is removed from the game engine. We also pass BodyType.None to the base class constructor so the particle is not involved in the collision detection.

When we activate the particle, we do several actions:

- Set a time to live
- Initialize the position on the *x* and *y* axes, adjusting it with the width and height of the image
- Add it to the specific layer of the GameEngine
- Store a reference to the list of modifiers to be used during onUpdate
- Set the total milliseconds to 0 to indicate that this particle has just been activated

It is worth noticing that we are keeping a reference to the list of modifiers. This list is shared among all the particles in the system and it is managed by the ParticleSystem class.

During onUpdate, we add the elapsed milliseconds to the total time and check whether the Particle has passed its time to live. If this is the case, we remove it from the GameEngine. Otherwise, we update the position and rotation based on the speed (linear and angular) and then apply all the modifiers.

You may have realized that we are using linear and angular speed values but, so far, we have not set them. This is done by the ParticleSystem through the initializers. This is why these variables are public.

Let's look at the system that handles the particles.

ParticleSystem

The ParticleSystem itself is the one that controls the emission of particles. It is similar to the GameController class in some ways. ParticleSystem takes care of the initializing, activating, and spawning of particles.

One of the responsibilities of the ParticleSystem is to manage the pool of Particle objects. Given that particle systems have a large number of particles that expire and get reused, this is one of the cases when using an object pool is most important.

 The ParticleSystem has a pool of Particles.

The pool is populated in the constructor of the ParticleSystem:

```
public ParticleSystem(
    GameEngine gameEngine,
    int maxParticles,
    int drawableRedId,
    long timeToLive) {
  mRandom = new Random();

    mModifiers = new ArrayList<ParticleModifier>();
    mInitializers = new ArrayList<ParticleInitializer>();
```

```
    mTimeToLive = timeToLive;
    mPixelFactor = gameEngine.mPixelFactor;
    for (int i=0; i<maxParticles; i++) {
      mParticlePool.add(new Particle(this, gameEngine, drawableRedId));
    }
  }
```

The constructor receives the maximum number of particles that will be used simultaneously. This is what we will use for the size of the pool.

Another important point about our particle system is that all the particles have the same image. This is passed to the `ParticleSystem` in construction. If you want to have different images, you should use a `ParticleSystem` for each one of them as we will do in one of the examples.

 All particles of a `ParticleSystem` have the same image.

In the constructor, we also create the lists of `ParticleInitializer` and `ParticleModifiers`. The initializers will be used while activating each particle. The modifiers list will be passed to each particle and it will be used inside the `onUpdate` method of `Particle` as we have already seen.

This is how the initializers are used during the activation of a particle:

```
  private void activateParticle(GameEngine gameEngine) {
    Particle p = mParticlePool.remove(0);
    for (int i=0; i<mInitializers.size(); i++) {
      mInitializers.get(i).initParticle(p, mRandom);
    }
    p.activate(gameEngine, mTimeToLive, mX, mY, mModifiers, mLayer);
    mActivatedParticles++;
  }
```

An important design concept in `ParticleSystem` is that it abstracts the initializers and modifiers via utility methods and each one of these utility methods return the `ParticleSystem` object, so the initialization can be chained, making the code shorter and easier to read.

Let's look at `ParticleInitializers` and `ParticleModifiers` in detail.

Initializers

Initializers are used by the `ParticleSystem` to set values for the particles based on parameters. To do this, we define `ParticleInitializer` as a very simple interface:

```
public interface ParticleInitializer {
  void initParticle(Particle p, Random r);
}
```

As an example, we will look at the utility method of `ParticleSytem` to set the initial rotation of the particles:

```
public ParticleSystem setInitialRotationRange (int minAngle,
    int maxAngle) {
  mInitializers.add(new RotationInitiazer(minAngle, maxAngle));
  return this;
}
```

When we set the initial rotation range for a `Particle`, we add an initializer of the `RotationInitializer` type to the `ParticleSystem`. Then we return this, so the methods can be chained.

Other methods that we can use to configure the initialization of particles are:

- `setRotationSpeedRange(double minRotationSpeed, double maxRotationSpeed)`

- `setSpeedRange(double speedMin, double speedMax)`

- `setSpeedModuleAndAngleRange(double speedMin, double speedMax, int minAngle, int maxAngle)`

- `setRotationSpeedRange(double minRotationSpeed, double maxRotationSpeed)`

We are not going to include the code of all the initializers we are going to use since all of them follow the same pattern:

- Receive a set of parameters and define the range(s)
- Generate a random value(s) from the range(s)
- Set the value(s) to the proper variable(s) of `Particle` (this may involve more than one field)

> Initializers get a random value(s) from a range and set it to a variable(s) of `Particle`.

As an example on how `ParticleInitializer` is implemented, let's look at the code of `RotationInitializer`:

```java
public class RotationInitiazer implements ParticleInitializer {

  private int mMinAngle;
  private int mMaxAngle;

  public RotationInitiazer(int minAngle, int maxAngle) {
    mMinAngle = minAngle;
    mMaxAngle = maxAngle;
  }

  @Override
  public void initParticle(Particle p, Random r) {
    int value = r.nextInt(mMaxAngle-mMinAngle)+mMinAngle;
    p.mRotation = value;
  }
}
```

Straightforward enough; the initializer stores the minimum and maximum values of the angle in member variables (`mMinAngle`, `mMaxAngle`). When it initializes a particle, it generates a random value in the range and sets it to the rotation variable of the particle.

All initializers work the same way; some are a bit more complex than others. For example, `SpeedModuleAndRangeInitializer` uses trigonometry to convert the speed from angle and module to coordinates:

```java
public class SpeedModuleAndRangeInitializer implements
  ParticleInitializer {

  private double mSpeedMin;
  private double mSpeedMax;
  private int mMinAngle;
  private int mMaxAngle;

  public SpeedModuleAndRangeInitializer(
      double speedMin, double speedMax,
      int minAngle, int maxAngle) {
    mSpeedMin = speedMin;
    mSpeedMax = speedMax;
    mMinAngle = minAngle;
    mMaxAngle = maxAngle;
  }
```

```
@Override
public void initParticle(Particle p, Random r) {
  double speed = r.nextDouble()*(mSpeedMax-mSpeedMin) +
    mSpeedMin;
  int angle;
  if (mMaxAngle == mMinAngle) {
    angle = mMinAngle;
  }
  else {
    angle = r.nextInt(mMaxAngle - mMinAngle) + mMinAngle;
  }
  double angleInRads = angle*Math.PI/180d;
  p.mSpeedX = speed * Math.cos(angleInRads)/1000d;
  p.mSpeedY = speed * Math.sin(angleInRads)/1000d;
  }
}
```

In this case, we have two ranges, one for the speed module and another for the angle. When we initialize a particle, we get a value for each one of them from their range, but then we need to use `sin` and `cos` to convert them into values that can be used for `Particle`, which are `mSpeedX` and `mSpeedY`.

In this case, we are initializing two variables of `Particle`. Note again that these fields of the `Particle` class are public, so we can modify them from this class easily.

Modifiers

Modifiers are a concept similar to initializers, but they are applied when the particle is active.

As for initializers, we define an interface that allows them to interact with the `Particle` class:

```
public interface ParticleModifier {
  void apply(Particle particle, long milliseconds);
}
```

For us, a modifier will have the same parameters for all the particles, while an initializer will generate a value for each particle. This is why the linear and angular speeds are *not* handled by modifiers and are variables of each particle that can—and most likely will—have different values for each one of them.

The `ParticleModifier` instances are also managed via utility methods of `ParticleSystem`, such as the one to set a fade out:

```
public ParticleSystem setFadeOut(long millisecondsBeforeEnd) {
  mModifiers.add(
    new AlphaModifier(255, 0, mTimeToLive-millisecondsBeforeEnd,
      mTimeToLive));
  return this;
}
```

This method creates an `AlphaModifier` to set a fade out (from an alpha of 255 to 0) based on the particle's time to live in the system.

In general, we can create our own `ParticleModifier` instances and add them to the `ParticleSystem` by calling `addModifier`:

```
public ParticleSystem addModifier(ParticleModifier modifier) {
  mModifiers.add(modifier);
  return this;
}
```

We are going to use only two modifiers: `AlphaModifier` for fade outs and `ScaleModifier`.

Let's examine the code for `AlphaModifier`:

```
public class AlphaModifier implements ParticleModifier {

    private int mInitialValue;
    private int mFinalValue;
    private long mStartTime;
    private long mEndTime;
    private float mDuration;
    private float mValueIncrement;

    public AlphaModifier(int initialValue, int finalValue,
        long startMilis, long endMilis) {
      mInitialValue = initialValue;
      mFinalValue = finalValue;
      mStartTime = startMilis;
      mEndTime = endMilis;
      mDuration = mEndTime - mStartTime;
      mValueIncrement = mFinalValue-mInitialValue;
    }
```

```
@Override
public void apply(Particle particle, long milliseconds) {
  if (milliseconds < mStartTime) {
    particle.mAlpha = mInitialValue;
  }
  else if (milliseconds > mEndTime) {
    particle.mAlpha = mFinalValue;
  }
  else {
    double percentageValue = (miliseconds-
      mStartTime)*1d/mDuration;
    int newAlphaValue = (int) (mInitialValue +
      mValueIncrement*percentageValue);
    particle.mAlpha = newAlphaValue;
  }
 }
}
```

Note that we have an initial value and a final value; we will set the alpha to the initial value if the time is less than the starting one and set it to the final value when the time is greater than the end one.

This allows us to do both, a fade in and a fade out, using the same class.

For modifiers, it is important to emphasize that the `apply` method receives the total amount of milliseconds spent. This is required because the modifier does not know anything about the `Particle`. It does not have any state, so all the information must be passed as parameters to the `apply` method.

 Modifiers are the same for all the particles and do not save any state.

The modifier has a start and an end time. When the time is outside the interval, we set it to the initial or final value. When the time is between these boundaries, it returns the value as a linear interpolation of the increment between the initial and final values.

It is quite easy to modify this code to use other types of interpolators. If you are curious about it, you can check the code of Leonids on GitHub, which supports interpolators.

`ScaleModifier` is almost identical to this one, except that the value is set to `mScale` instead of `mAlpha`.

Composite GameObjects and GameEngine

Until now, the GameObjects that we have been using are a single entity. From now on, we will also have GameObjects that include other GameObjects. In particular, the ParticleSystems used by each object will be owned by them.

This implies that the addition and removal of GameObjects to the GameEngine must be updated. The object will have two methods to add and remove itself from the GameEngine and we can override this method when we use a composite object to take care of them.

Our change will be to stop using the addGameObject and removeGameObject methods from GameEngine and start using new equivalent methods such as addToGameEngine and removeFromGameEngine on the GameObject instead.

This implies that we should go over the code of the project and replace all their occurrences. This is especially important in the case of the GameController, where the asteroids are spawned, and the initialization of the GameEngine inside GameFragment, when we add the Player object:

```
mGameEngine = new GameEngine(getActivity(), gameView, 4);
mGameEngine.setInputController(
  new CompositeInputController(getView(), getYassActivity()));
new ParallaxBackground(mGameEngine, 20,
  R.drawable.seamless_space_0)
  .addToGameEngine(mGameEngine, 0);
new GameController(mGameEngine).addToGameEngine(mGameEngine, 2);
new Player(mGameEngine).addToGameEngine(mGameEngine, 3);
new FPSCounter(mGameEngine).addToGameEngine(mGameEngine, 2);
```

Even though the use of the old methods would produce the same result on noncomposite objects, it is better to add all the GameObjects to the GameEngine in the same way to have consistent code.

The default implementations of addToGameEngine and removeFromGameEngine are actually extremely simple for a noncomposite GameObject:

```
public void addToGameEngine (GameEngine gameEngine, int layer) {
  gameEngine.addGameObject(this, layer);
}

public void removeFromGameEngine (GameEngine gameEngine) {
  gameEngine.removeGameObject(this);
}
```

When we override this methods on composite items, we must remember to call the super method to add and remove the object.

Making good particle systems

As a side note, particle systems are very powerful, but it is not trivial to tweak and design them.

The implementation details of a particle system are straightforward, as we have seen. But making a particle system that looks realistic and good is something else entirely.

The key to fine-tuning them is to play with the parameters and see how they look, again, and again, and again until we are happy with the result.

To try and throw some light on the obscure art of tweaking particle systems, we are going to do a few examples. You can play with the particles and parameters on your own to see how much of a difference small changes make.

There are two ways of using particle systems: one-shot and continuous emitter. Let's make some examples of both.

One shot

While using one shot, we make the ParticleSystem launch all the particles at once.

In this case, we do not need to add or remove the ParticleSystem to or from the GameEngine, because the onUpdate method of the ParticleSystem does not need to be called (it is only used to emit new particles).

While using one shot, it is only logical to initialize the particle pool with the same number of particles that we plan to use for the shot.

The oneShot method of the ParticleSystem class is as follows:

```
public void oneShot(GameEngine gameEngine, double x, double y,
    int numParticles) {
  mX = x;
  mY = y;
  mIsEmiting = false;
  for (int i=0; !mParticlePool.isEmpty() && i<numParticles; i++) {
    activateParticle(gameEngine);
  }
}
```

We set the *x* and *y* coordinates from which we will emit and then set isEmitting to false. While updating isEmitting is only necessary when the ParticleSystem is added to the GameEngine, we do it just to be safe. In this case, setting isEmitting to false will make onUpdate simply do nothing.

Once the parameters are set, we get the particles from the pool and `activate` them. Remember that we already saw the `activate` method while explaining the `ParticleSystem` class. As part of the activation, the particles are added to the `GameEngine`.

We are going to use this type of particle system for the explosion of `Asteroids` and the `Player`.

Asteroid explosions

For the explosion of asteroids, we are going to use a particle that has three small fragments of rock, so it will look like the asteroid has broken into multiple pieces. To enforce this effect, we will make the particles rotate and move in any direction, but not too far away.

We create and configure the `ParticleSystem` as part of the `Asteroid` creation. This will ensure that each asteroid has its own independent pool of particles:

```
public Asteroid(GameController gameController,
    GameEngine gameEngine) {
  super(gameEngine, R.drawable.a10000, BodyType.Circular);
  mSpeed = 200d*mPixelFactor/1000d;
  mController = gameController;
  mExplisionParticleSystem = new ParticleSystem(gameEngine,
    EXPLOSION_PARTICLES, R.drawable.particle_asteroid_1, 700)
    .setSpeedRange(15, 40)
    .setFadeOut(300)
    .setInitialRotationRange(0, 360)
    .setRotationSpeedRange(-180, 180);
}

public void explode(GameEngine gameEngine) {
  mExplisionParticleSystem.oneShot(gameEngine, mX + mWidth / 2,
    mY + mHeight / 2, EXPLOSION_PARTICLES);
}
```

The configuration of the particle system does the following:

* The particles will live for 700 milliseconds.
* They will be spawned in all directions with a speed that will vary between 15 and 40 units per second.
* In the last 300 milliseconds, they will have an alpha modifier to fade out smoothly.

- The particles will have any initial rotation. Note that the particle is not symmetrical; this is very important to prevent the particle from looking static.

- Finally, each particle will have an angular rotation speed between -180 and 180 degrees per second.

- EXPLOSION_PARTICLES is a constant for the Asteroid. We have set it at 15.

The explode method does trigger oneShot from the center of the asteroid, which will put all the particles in motion.

The last connection point is to trigger the explode method. This happens when a bullet collides with an asteroid or when the player collides with an asteroid. This is how it is done inside the Bullet class:

```
@Override
public void onCollision(GameEngine gameEngine, ScreenGameObject
    otherObject) {
  if (otherObject instanceof Asteroid) {
    removeFromGameEngine(gameEngine);
    Asteroid a = (Asteroid) otherObject;
    a.explode(gameEngine);
    a.removeFromGameEngine(gameEngine);
  }
}
```

This is it. Quite simple, right? Since the ParticleSystem is using a oneShot, it does not need to be added or removed to or from the GameEngine.

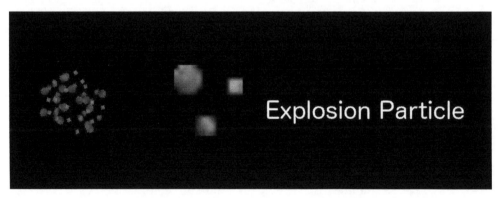

Detail of the explosion particle and particle system.

Spaceship explosions

For the `Player` explosion, we will use a different approach. We want it to look more dramatic. We will have a larger value for the speed than for the asteroid to give the impression of a much more aggressive explosion with an extended range. We will also use two different particles with different colors instead of one with several shards.

Since each `ParticleSystem` is designed to hold only one type of `Particle` (one image), we will have two `ParticleSystem` instances in the `Player` class that will be initialized in the constructor:

```
mExplisionParticleSystem1 = new ParticleSystem(gameEngine,
EXPLOSION_PARTICLES, R.drawable.particle_ship_explosion_1, 600)
  .setSpeedRange(30, 150)
  .setInitialRotationRange(0,360)
  .setFadeOut(200);
mExplisionParticleSystem2 = new ParticleSystem(gameEngine,
EXPLOSION_PARTICLES, R.drawable.particle_ship_explosion_2, 600)
  .setSpeedRange(30, 150)
  .setInitialRotationRange(0,360)
  .setFadeOut(200);
```

In this case, each particle is very small and symmetrical, so we don't need rotational speed. Since they are much faster than before, the time to live is also a bit shorter and the fade out is sharper.

In this case, `EXPLOSION_PARTICLES` is set to 20, so there are 40 particles in total.

When the `Player` object explodes (as a part of `onCollision`), we trigger `oneShot` on both `ParticleSystem` instances:

```
mExplisionParticleSystem1.oneShot(gameEngine, mX + mWidth / 2,
  mY+mWidth/2, EXPLOSION_PARTICLES);
mExplisionParticleSystem2.oneShot(gameEngine, mX+mWidth/2,
  mY+mWidth/2, EXPLOSION_PARTICLES);
```

As you can see, if you run it now, the explosion has a completely different feeling from the one for the asteroid:

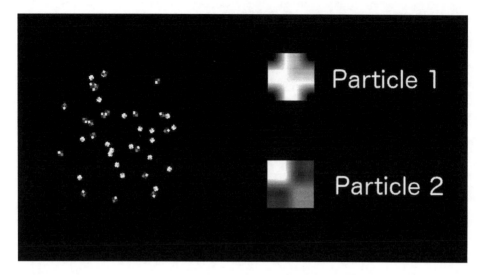

Emitters

The other way to use particle systems is to configure them as emitters. This means that there is a ratio of particles per second that your system emits while it is active.

Calculating the right pool size is quite easy. It is just a formula based on the particle's time to live and the number of particles per second you want. For example, using 20 particles per second with 500 milliseconds time to live, you only need a pool of 10 particles, since they are returned to the pool as they die.

It is important to remember that a `ParticleSystem` working as an emitter needs to be added and removed from the `GameEngine`, since the `onUpdate` method is required to check for the spawning of more particles. The `onUpdate` method of the `ParticleSystem` looks like this:

```
@Override
public void onUpdate(long elapsedMillis, GameEngine gameEngine) {
  if (!mIsEmiting){
    return;
  }
  mTotalMillis += elapsedMillis;
  // We have to make sure that we have to keep emiting
  while ( !mParticlePool.isEmpty() && // We have particles in the
    pool
```

```
    mActivatedParticles < mParticlesPerMillisecond*mTotalMillis) {
    // and we are under the number of particles that should be
      launched
    // Activate a new particle
    activateParticle(gameEngine);
  }
}
```

The code is quite simple. First we check weather the system is emitting or not. If the system is not emitting, we do not need to update anything, so we can simply return.

If it is emitting, we check whether we have to activate a particle. For this, we compare the number of particles that we have activated with the number of particles that should have been activated (*particlesPerMillisecond*totalMilliseconds*). We also need to be sure that we can have a particle from the pool (it is not empty).

Once we know that we need to spawn a particle and we have some particles available, we proceed to the activation. The last line on the `activateParticle` method increases the counter of activated particles.

Note that the number of activated particles is the total number of particles that have been activated by the emitter and not the current number of active particles.

The emit method from `ParticleSystem` is as follows:

```
public void emit (int particlesPerSecond) {
  mActivatedParticles = 0;
  mTotalMillis = 0;
  mParticlesPerMillisecond = particlesPerSecond/1000d;
  mIsEmiting = true;
}
```

Easy enough; it resets the number of activated particles and the time counter. It also calculates the rate of particles per millisecond (the parameter is passed as particles per second) and then sets `mIsEmitting` to `true`, so the `onUpdate` method should work.

Finally, to stop emitting we just need to set `mIsEmitting` to `false`:

```
public void stopEmiting() {
  mIsEmiting = false;
}
```

Let's look at some examples of emitters.

Asteroid trails

Asteroids will look a lot cooler if they leave a trail behind them. Inside the constructor of the `Asteroid` class, we will create a `ParticleSystem` for the trail in the same place as the one for the explosion:

```
mTrailParticleSystem = new ParticleSystem(gameEngine, 50,
    R.drawable.particle_dust, 600)
 .addModifier(new ScaleModifier(1, 2, 200, 600))
 .setFadeOut(200);
```

For this trail, we are using a particle, that is two small pieces. To give a better feel of a trail, we add a `ScaleModifier` together with the fade out.

We want an initialization that depends on the values of the asteroid. To do so, we will set all the initializers during the call to `init` of the asteroid:

```
public void init(GameEngine gameEngine) {
  [...] // Standard initialization
  mTrailParticleSystem.clearInitializers()
    .setInitialRotationRange(0,360)
    .setRotationSpeed(mRotationSpeed * 1000);
    .setSpeedByComponentsRange(
      -mSpeedY * 100, mSpeedY * 100,
      mSpeedX * 100, mSpeedX * 100);
}
```

First, we clean all the initializers and then set it to have any rotation. The rotation speed will be the same as the rotation speed of the asteroid. Then, the linear speed will be proportional and swapped from the asteroid components. This will make the trail move perpendicular to the asteroid.

The point of emission of the `ParticleSystem` needs to be updated on each run of `onUpdate` on the asteroid to keep emitting from the right position:

```
mTrailParticleSystem.setPosition(mX + mWidth / 2,
  mY + mHeight / 2);
```

Since it is an emitter, it needs to be added to and removed from the `GameEngine` together with the `Asteroid`. For this, we have already defined the `addToGameEngine` and `removeFromGameEngine` methods. We will override them now:

```
@Override
public void addToGameEngine (GameEngine gameEngine, int layer) {
  super.addToGameEngine(gameEngine, layer);
```

```
    mTrailParticleSystem.addToGameEngine(gameEngine, mLayer-1);
    mTrailParticleSystem.emit(15);
}

@Override
public void removeFromGameEngine(GameEngine gameEngine) {
    super.removeFromGameEngine(gameEngine);
    mTrailParticleSystem.stopEmiting();
    mTrailParticleSystem.removeFromGameEngine(gameEngine);
}
```

Note that we add it to the GameEngine one layer below the asteroids, so the particle system always goes behind them and not the other way around.

With this, we have all the pieces in place and we can see how much nicer our asteroids look now:

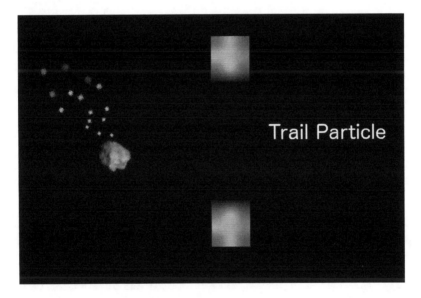

The spaceship's engine

For the last effect, we will add some smoke to the spaceship. Because it is an emitter, it needs to honor the GameObject lifecycle by adding and removing it from the GameEngine together with the player object, as we did for the asteroid trail:

```
@Override
public void removeFromGameEngine(GameEngine gameEngine) {
```

```
        super.removeFromGameEngine(gameEngine);
        mEngineFireParticle.removeFromGameEngine(gameEngine);
    }

    @Override
    public void addToGameEngine(GameEngine gameEngine, int layer) {
        super.addToGameEngine(gameEngine, layer);
        mEngineFireParticle.addToGameEngine(gameEngine, mLayer - 1);
        mEngineFireParticle.emit(12);
    }
```

Inside the onUpdate method, we have to synchronize the position of the player with the emitter of the ParticleSystem, as we did with the asteroid:

```
mEngineFireParticle.setPosition(mX+mWidth/2, mY+mHeight);
```

Note that we are setting the emitter at the bottom of the spaceship instead of the center. This makes the smoke appear in the right place.

Finally, we will create the ParticleSystem in the constructor of the Player object at the same place we are already creating the other two for the explosions:

```
mEngineFireParticle = new ParticleSystem(gameEngine, 50, R.drawable.
particle_smoke, 600)
    .setInitialRotationRange(0, 360)
    .setRotationSpeedRange(-30, 30)
    .setSpeedModuleAndAngleRange(50, 80, 60, 120)
    .setFadeOut(400);
```

These configuration methods are all well-known to us by now.

We have the whole range of the initial rotation [0-360] and a rotation speed that goes from -30 to 30 degrees per second. We also have a much longer fade out for other systems to make it dissolve in a smooth way.

We also use setSpeedModuleAndAngleRange, which sets the speed in terms of the angle and module. We want the smoke to get out of the spaceship in the range of [60-120] degrees (that is, an arc of 60 degrees going to the bottom of the spaceship) and with a speed that does not vary much.

You can run it now and see how it looks:

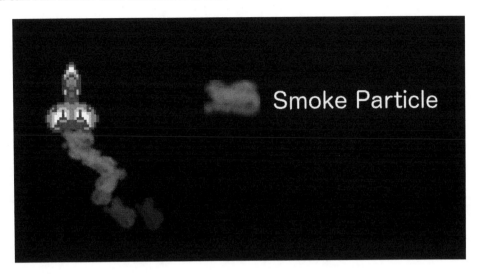

While looking at a static image, you can see each particle, but when they are in motion, it feels really good.

Optionally, you could start this particle system if there is some user input during onUpdate and stop it if not, which will give a more dynamic look and feel, since the smoke will appear only when the spaceship is moving.

Summary

We have learned how particle systems work and how to integrate them into our game. We included ParticleSystem and the particles themselves into our GameEngine. We also learned about initializers and modifiers and how to create new ones to extend the system if we want to.

Then we saw how to compose a GameObject that has other GameObject instances inside it. In particular, particle systems do normally belong to another GameObject. For this, the ParticleSystem hooks into the lifecycle of the GameObject. We updated the GameEngine to make it easier to add GameObjects that are compositions.

Finally, we examined two examples of one shots and two examples of emitters that covered a variety of different parameters.

All in all, these four ParticleSystem instances make the game feel much more alive. Let's move on to the last step of making the game feel alive: sound effects.

6

Sound FX and Music

A game feels incomplete without sound. In this chapter we will explore the different options for playing sound effects and music in Android, we will build a `SoundManager` class to handle them, and we will see how it interacts with the `GameEngine`.

For sound effects we will use `SoundPool`, which has been specifically designed for playing small sounds by preloading them in memory. To trigger the sound effects, we will introduce the concept of `GameEvent` and learn how they are propagated through the `GameEngine`.

In the case of background music, we will use `MediaPlayer` directly since long tracks do not work well with `SoundPool`, and `MediaPlayer` is the generic solution for playing all types of media files.

Finally, we will add controls to enable and disable sound effects and music on the home screen and make `SoundManager` take care of them.

SoundManager

To manage sounds and music, we are going to have a class called `SoundManager`. This class will be instantiated only once along the `Application` code and it will be done at `onCreate` of `YassActivity`. There are several reasons to do this:

- Sound effects do take a little time to be loaded, so it is better to load them in advance
- We may want to use sounds and music in the menus
- Loading sounds and music requires memory; it does not make sense to duplicate that

Let's look at the modifications we need to make to `YassActivity`:

```
private SoundManager mSoundManager;

@Override
protected void onCreate(Bundle savedInstanceState) {
  super.onCreate(savedInstanceState);
  [...]
  setVolumeControlStream(AudioManager.STREAM_MUSIC);
  mSoundManager = new SoundManager(getApplicationContext());
}

public SoundManager getSoundManager() {
  return mSoundManager;
}
```

We have a field that contains the `SoundManager`, and we initialize it during the `onCreate` method. We also provide a getter method for it.

There is another line that requires special mention:

```
setVolumeControlStream(AudioManager.STREAM_MUSIC);
```

This code sets the volume control stream of the application to be music. It tells the operating system that, when we press the physical volume keys while our application is running, we want it to modify the music volume instead of the default volume. There are seven stream types on Android, one for each sound type, from system and ring tone volumes to alarms and notifications.

 To make the volume keys act over the music volume if pressed while the game is running, we should call `setVolumeControlStream` `(AudioManager.STREAM_MUSIC)` in the Activity.

Since we will be playing sound, this small tweak is very important to allow the user to control the volume of sounds during the course of the game.

`SoundManager` will take care of the sounds and music using different classes from the Android SDK. It will also provide different methods to access them. Sound effects and music are independent features in the `SoundManager` class, so we will look at each of them separately.

Sound FX

Sound effects will be used for events in the game such as explosions, firing bullets, and so on, but also could be used in other cases such as menu clicks and dialogs appearing. In our game we will add sound effects to the explosions of the asteroids and the spaceship as well as for laser firing.

We will begin discussing some ways to get sound effects for games. We cannot work if we don't have sound files, right?

Once we have our sounds in place, we will update `GameEngine` to provide a way to signal events in the game, and we will let `SoundManager` know when one of those events happens.

Finally we will explain how `SoundPool` works and how to include it in our `SoundManager`, associating a game event to a sound effect.

Hands on—let's get some sound files.

How to create sound FXs

For indie developers, there are a few places where you can get sound effects. The already mentioned `OpenGameArt` not only has graphics but also sounds. One of the best places to find sound effects for games is the website `www.freesound.org` (formerly "The Free Sound Project").

In its own words: Freesound aims to create a huge collaborative database of audio snippets, samples, recordings, bleeps, and so on released under Creative Commons licenses that allow their reuse. Freesound provides new and interesting ways to access these samples, allowing users to browse the sounds in new ways using keywords, a "sounds-like" type of browsing, and more.

 Freesound.org is a great sound database under Creative Commons licenses.

It may take you a while to browse to the sounds you need, but this is a really useful resource. We used it when making Chalk Ball and SpaceCat at The Pill Tree.

For games that require simple sounds in a retro style, there is another project that is interesting: Bfxr (www.bfxr.net/)

 Bfxr is a simple and handy utility to create retro-style sound effects.

Bfxr allows you to do a lot with sound waves, but you do not need to be an expert because it also has some buttons that will generate a new random sound based on certain parameters. These buttons are used for shoots, pickup, powerups, hits, and so on. Bfxr is inspired by as3sfxr, which is also simpler.

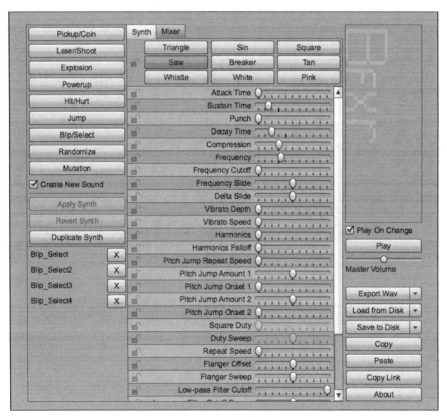

The UI of the web version of bfxr

You have full rights to all sounds made with bfxr, therefore you are free to use them for any purposes, commercial or otherwise.

For YASS we have used bfxr to generate a few explosions and laser sounds and then picked the ones we liked better. You can make your own and it will take you only a few minutes.

Now that we have the sounds, we need a place to put them inside our project. We could store the sounds as raw resources (under `res/raw`) but it is more handy to have them inside the `assets` folder, where we can have a hierarchical structure and there is no restriction on the file naming.

[We store the sound files under the `assets` folder.]

We have to create the `assets` folder under the `src/main` directory of the project. Inside the `assets` folder we will create another folder called `sfx` for all our sound files.

GameEvents

As we mentioned, we are going to link sound effects to `GameEvents`, so first we need our `GameEngine` to have support for such `GameEvents`. For that we create an enum that contains the `GameEvents` we are interested in:

```
public enum GameEvent {
    AsteroidHit,
    SpaceshipHit,
    LaserFired
}
```

`GameEvents` will be propagated across the `GameEngine` in a way similar to a `BroadcastReceiver` or an `EventBus`. We create a new method `onGameEvent` in `GameEngine`. This method will be called when a `GameEvent` happens.

```
public void onGameEvent (GameEvent gameEvent) {
    mSoundManager.playSoundForGameEvent(gameEvent);
}
```

When a `GameEvent` arrives, we communicate it to the `SoundManager`. It will be easy to have all `GameObjects` subscribed to `GameEvents` by just adding a loop over the `GameObjects` inside this method.

The only thing left is to trigger the events when they happen. Let's see the ones triggered from the `Player` object:

```
private void checkFiring(long elapsedMillis, GameEngine
  gameEngine) {
  if (gameEngine.mInputController.mIsFiring
    && mTimeSinceLastFire > TIME_BETWEEN_BULLETS) {
    [...]
    gameEngine.onGameEvent(GameEvent.LaserFired);
  }
  else {
    mTimeSinceLastFire += elapsedMillis;
  }
}


@Override
public void onCollision(GameEngine gameEngine,
  ScreenGameObject otherObject) {
  if (otherObject instanceof Asteroid) {
    [...]
    gameEngine.onGameEvent(GameEvent.SpaceshipHit);
  }
}
```

Because the `GameEvents` happen during `onUpdate`, we always have a reference to the `GameEngine` at hand, and sending the event is as simple as adding a method call in the right place. The `Player` object now communicates the events of `LaserFired` and `SpaceshipHit` to the `GameEngine`.

Bullet does trigger a `GameEvent` as well.

```
@Override
public void onCollision(GameEngine gameEngine, ScreenGameObject
otherObject) {
  if (otherObject instanceof Asteroid) {
    [...]
    gameEngine.onGameEvent(GameEvent.AsteroidHit);
  }
}
```

Now that the events are triggered and they reach the `SoundManager`, we have to actually play the specific sound when the event arrives. For that we need to build and configure the `SoundPool`.

Using SoundPool

`SoundPool` is a utility designed to play multiple short sound files with low latency playback. It does preloading of the files and it allows us to play several of them at the same time. The initial constructor for `SoundManager` will look like this:

```
public SoundManager(Context context) {
  mContext = context;
  loadSounds();
}
```

We are going to have a method that loads the sounds. At the moment this is used only once but later on, when we add a setting to enable or disable them, the sounds could be loaded and unloaded multiple times.

There is a specific method to handle the creation of the `SoundPool` because the default constructor has been deprecated on Lollipop and the new way of building it is quite verbose and not backwards-compatible; we need to branch the code based on the OS version.

```
private void createSoundPool() {
  if (Build.VERSION.SDK_INT < Build.VERSION_CODES.LOLLIPOP) {
    mSoundPool = new SoundPool(MAX_STREAMS,
      AudioManager.STREAM_MUSIC, 0);
  }
  else {
    AudioAttributes audioAttributes = new
      AudioAttributes.Builder()
      .setUsage(AudioAttributes.USAGE_GAME)
      .setContentType(AudioAttributes.CONTENT_TYPE_MUSIC)
      .build();
    mSoundPool = new SoundPool.Builder()
      .setAudioAttributes(audioAttributes)
      .setMaxStreams(MAX_STREAMS)
      .build();
  }
}
```

Both ways of building the `SoundPool` receive the same kind of parameters, but while the old one is just one constructor, the new one uses a builder and `AudioAttributes`.

The parameters of the now deprecated constructor are:

* **Max streams**: Maximum number of simultaneous streams to be played.

- **Stream type**: the audio stream type as described in AudioManager. Games should use STREAM_MUSIC.
- **Src quality**: The sample-rate converter quality. It has no effect, so we just use 0.

The new way of building the SoundPool replaces the stream type with the usage and content type of AudioAttributes, but you could use the legacy system type instead of these parameters and set it to AudioManager.STREAM_MUSIC if you prefer.

The parameter of max streams has the exact same meaning as before. SoundPool tracks the number of active streams. If the maximum number of streams is exceeded, SoundPool will automatically stop a previously playing one, based first on priority and then by age within that priority.

[SoundPool is designed to play small sound files with low latency playback.]

Using SoundPool is quite easy. When we load a file into the SoundPool, it will return a sound ID, which we need to use to play the sound later.

To store those sound IDs we will have a map inside SoundManager that has a GameEvent as key and Integer as the type of the values.

```
private HashMap<GameEvent, Integer> mSoundsMap;
```

We now create a method that loads a file into the SoundPool and associates it to a GameEvent:

```
private void loadEventSound(Context context, GameEvent event, String
filename) {
  try {
    AssetFileDescriptor descriptor =
      context.getAssets().openFd("sfx/" + filename);
    int soundId = mSoundPool.load(descriptor, 1);
    mSoundsMap.put(event, soundId);
  } catch (IOException e) {
    e.printStackTrace();
  }
}
```

SoundPool has several methods for loading files regarding of where they are located. Since our sound files are in assets, we need to use the one that receives an AssetFileDescriptor.

The load method also receives the priority as a parameter. The official documentation says that this currently has no effect and we should use 1 for future compatibility, so we do.

Finally we store the sound ID into the map.

We can get an IOException if the file we are trying to open does not exist. It is interesting to print the stack trace if we miss some sounds while playing, to check for possible typos.

It is time to look at loadSounds, which effectively combines all the code that we have seen until now:

```
private void loadSounds() {
  createSoundPool();
  mSoundsMap = new HashMap<GameEvent, Integer>();
  loadEventSound(mContext, GameEvent.AsteroidHit,
    "Asteroid_explosion_1.wav");
  loadEventSound(mContext, GameEvent.SpaceshipHit,
    "Spaceship_explosion.wav");
  loadEventSound(mContext, GameEvent.LaserFired,
    "Laser_shoot.wav");
}
```

Simple enough—we create the SoundPool and the sounds map. Then we load three sound files and associate them to the GameEvents.

We also have a method to unload the sounds:

```
private void unloadSounds() {
  mSoundPool.release();
  mSoundPool = null;
  mSoundsMap.clear();
}
```

To unload the sounds, we release the sound pool and clear the sound map.

The official documentation tells us to release the SoundPool and set it to null; then create a new one when loading a new set of sounds instead of unloading each of the sound effects. That is why a new SoundPool is created at the beginning of loadSounds instead of in the constructor of SoundManager.

At last we are ready to play a sound when a `GameEvent` arrives:

```
public void playSoundForGameEvent(GameEvent event) {
  Integer soundId = mSoundsMap.get(event);
  if (soundId != null) {
    mSoundPool.play(soundId, 1.0f, 1.0f, 0, 0, 1.0f);
  }
}
```

We get the sound ID from the map and, if it is not null, we play it. This check is important to make the game future-proof, when we evolve it to support more `GameEvents` and some of them do not have sound associated.

The parameters for the play method of `SoundPool` are:

- **Left volume**: Self-explanatory. A float value between 0.0 and 1.0.

- **Right volume**: Also self-explanatory. A float value between 0.0 and 1.0.

- **Priority**: 0 means lowest priority; all our sounds will have the same priority. It is used to select the sound to stop when the maximum number of streams is reached.

- **Loop**: A loop value of -1 means loop forever, a value of 0 means don't loop, and other values indicate the number of repeats. We don't want to loop our sounds, so we pass 0.

- **Rate**: A value of 1.0 means play back at the original frequency. A value of 2.0 means play back twice as fast, and a value of 0.5 means playback at half speed. The range is from 0.5 to 2.0.

You could improve the feeling of the sound by tweaking the left and right volume based on the position of the event on the screen but we are not going to get into that, so we just use 1.0 for both left and right volumes.

The play method will return a stream ID that we could use to pause or resume this sound. Since we are using very short sounds that do not loop and are not interrupted, we do not need to store the stream ID at all.

Note that calling play may cause another sound to stop playing if the maximum number of active streams is exceeded.

With this architecture of `SoundManager`, it is very easy to add new sound effects by just associating them to a `GameEvent` and triggering the event from whatever `GameObject` produces it.

Playing music

The other type of sound that a game contains is background music. These tracks are usually longer than the sound effects and are played in a loop. In some cases there may be more than one track, for example, if we want a music for the menu and another one for the level, or if we want several levels with different background music tracks. We will work with a single one, but it is very easy to extend it to multiple tracks.

We are going to use `MediaPlayer` to play the background music in our game and we are going to abstract it via `SoundManager` as well, providing methods to pause and resume the music when the activity is paused and resumed.

Obtaining music

As with sound effects, we need some tracks to work with. When it comes to making games on a budget, one of the best places to look for music that can be used for free is Jamendo.com. There are lots of albums under Creative Commons license, some of them very reasonably priced when it comes to using them to make commercial products, and most of them only require attribution (also known as giving credit to the artist).

Jamendo is a great resource for Creative Commons music

We are going to use a track from Riccardo Colombo, entitled "Something mental", which has a nice ambient sound. We will also place that sound under the `sfx` folder we created inside `assets`.

On Android, MP3 files normally work fine, but OGG usually produces more consistent and reliable behavior among the different devices and hardware capabilities. You can convert any MP3 to OGG using an audio editor such as Audacity (`http://audacity.sourceforge.net/`).

MediaPlayer

`MediaPlayer` is quite straight forward to use, but it also has a complicated life cycle and it is very strict in its usage. It can give problems if not used exactly as intended.

The life cycle consists of several states and methods. While in a state, only a few methods can be called. Because of this, the invocation of the method calls must be done in precise sequence to move from one state to the next. If you call a method that is not allowed in the current state of `MediaPlayer`, it will crash with a cryptic error. Also, there is no method to know the current state of the MediaPlayer.

 If you call a method that is not allowed in the current state of `MediaPlayer`, it will crash with a cryptic error.

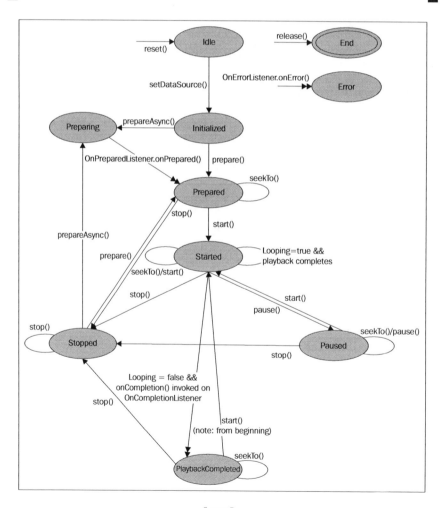

But do not worry, we are going to use it in the simplest way possible.

What we are going to do is take the following actions to load the track:

1. Create the `MediaPlayer` object, so it is in the **Idle** state.
2. Set the data source, so it becomes **Initialized**.
3. Call `prepare`. This moves `MediaPlayer` to the **Prepared** state.
4. From **Prepared**, we will call `start`, so it moves to **Started**.
5. While playing we may `pause` the stream, moving to **Paused**. And from **Paused** we can call `start` again to go back to **Started**.

We will also have a method to unload the track so the music can be enabled and disabled at any moment. To unload the track we just have to:

- **Call stop**. This will work from either **Started** or **Paused**. This call will make the music stop.
- **Call release**. This will move to the **End** status from any other state. Note that there is no way to get out of the **End** state, so when we want to load the music again, we need to create a new `MediaPlayer` and start again from the beginning.

The situation we need to take care of the most is to avoid calling `pause` while in the **Prepared** or **Paused** states. That method is not allowed there, and will `MediaPlayer` in to a non-working state. However, if you follow the steps provided here, you will not have to worry about it.

Let's look at the methods we have in `SoundManager` to handle background music:

```
private void loadMusic() {
  try {
    mBgPlayer = new MediaPlayer();
    AssetFileDescriptor afd = mContext.getAssets()
      .openFd("sfx/Riccardo_Colombo_-_11_-_Something_mental.mp3");
    mBgPlayer.setDataSource(
      afd.getFileDescriptor(),
      afd.getStartOffset(),
      afd.getLength());
    mBgPlayer.setLooping(true);
    mBgPlayer.setVolume(DEFAULT_MUSIC_VOLUME,
      DEFAULT_MUSIC_VOLUME);
    mBgPlayer.prepare();
  }
```

```
      catch (IOException e) {
        e.printStackTrace();
      }
    }

    private void unloadMusic() {
      mBgPlayer.stop();
      mBgPlayer.release();
    }

    public void pauseBgMusic() {
      mBgPlayer.pause();
    }

    public void resumeBgMusic() {
      mBgPlayer.start();
    }
```

The only points we haven't covered yet are the calls to `setLooping` and `setVolume`. They are quite clear on their own: `setLooping` sets the media player into looping or not-looping mode based on the parameter; `setVolume` sets the left and right volumes for this instance of `MediaPlayer`. For the volume we are using a constant `DEFAULT_MUSIC_VOLUME` that we have set to a value of 0.6, so the music is played more softly than the sound effects.

We can get an `IOException` when loading the music for the same reason we might have one with the sound effects: if the file does not exist. As we did earlier, if that happens we just log it and continue.

Of course we also need to load the music when we initialize the `SoundManager`, calling `loadMusic` just after we call `loadSounds`.

```
    public SoundManager(Context context) {
      mContext = context;
      loadSounds();
      loadMusic();
    }
```

Music and Activity life cycle

In this section we will handle pausing and resuming the music. For that, the only thing we need to do is link the `SoundManager` to the Activity life cycle. In the next section we will take care of unloading and loading the music on-demand when the user changes the preferences:

```
@Override
protected void onPause() {
   super.onPause();
   mSoundManager.pauseBgMusic();
}

@Override
protected void onResume() {
   super.onResume();
   mSoundManager.resumeBgMusic();
}
```

Remember that we create the `SoundManager` during `onCreate`. Now we add the method calls to pause the music when the activity calls `onPause` and resume it when the activity calls `onResume`.

This allows us to pause the music when another app comes to the foreground (or when the game is put to the background) and then resume it when it returns to the foreground.

Do not allow the user to manually pause or resume the background music; this can put `MediaPlayer` into an inconsistent state. Instead of pausing the music, we will allow the user to disable music, which is a different process and one that we will cover in the next section.

Enabling and disabling music and sound FX

Now we have music and sound effects working, but we are missing a very important point: allowing the user to disable them. If you add sounds to a game, you need to provide a way to disable them. Many people like to play in silence.

 Always provide a way for the user to disable music and sound effects individually.

To do this, we will add two buttons on the main screen (one for music and one for sounds) to enable and disable each one independently. These options should also be present on the **Pause** dialog, but we will get into that when we rework the dialogs in the next chapter.

On the one hand, we are going to update the layout and the code of MainMenuFragment; on the other hand, we will make SoundManager take care of this configuration.

To store the music and sound state we will use SharedPreferences, as it is the simplest and most convenient way to store key-value persistent data on Android.

Updating MainMenuFragment

Until now, a FrameLayout has been good enough for us. At this point we want to have the sound and music buttons on one side and together, so we need to replace it with a RelativeLayout.

The updated version of fragment_main.xml is as follows:

```xml
<?xml version="1.0" encoding="utf-8"?>
<RelativeLayout xmlns:android="http://schemas.android.com/apk/res/
android"
  android:layout_width="match_parent"
  android:layout_height="match_parent"
  >

  <TextView
    style="@android:style/TextAppearance.DeviceDefault.Large"
    android:layout_marginTop="@dimen/activity_vertical_margin"
    android:text="@string/game_title"
    android:layout_centerHorizontal="true"
    android:layout_width="wrap_content"
    android:layout_height="wrap_content" />

  <Button
    android:id="@+id/btn_start"
    android:layout_centerInParent="true"
    android:layout_width="wrap_content"
    android:layout_height="wrap_content"
    android:text="@string/start" />
```

```
<Button
    android:id="@+id/btn_sound"
    android:layout_margin="@dimen/activity_vertical_margin"
    android:layout_width="wrap_content"
    android:layout_height="wrap_content"
    android:layout_alignParentBottom="true"
    android:layout_alignParentRight="true"
    android:text="@string/sound_on" />

<Button
    android:id="@+id/btn_music"
    android:layout_width="wrap_content"
    android:layout_height="wrap_content"
    android:layout_alignBottom="@+id/btn_sound"
    android:layout_toLeftOf="@+id/btn_sound"
    android:text="@string/music_on" />
</RelativeLayout>
```

No specific comments are required. We just have `btn_sound` and `btn_music` added to the bottom right and with the correct margins, aligning the music button to the bottom of the sound one and placing it to the left of it.

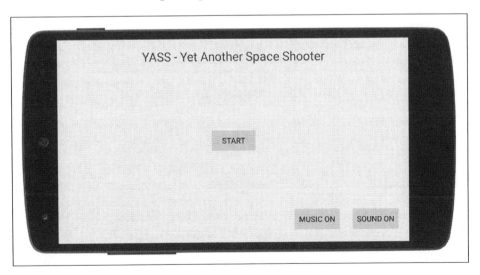

The code is a bit more interesting. We have to modify `MainMenuFragment` to handle the click on the new buttons as well as to place the correct text on them. For this we will modify `onViewCreated` and `onClick` and add a new method to place the correct text on each button.

First we have to add `MainMenuFragment` as a click listener to these buttons during `onViewCreated`:

```
@Override
public void onViewCreated(View view, Bundle savedInstanceState) {
  super.onViewCreated(view, savedInstanceState);
  view.findViewById(R.id.btn_start).setOnClickListener(this);
  view.findViewById(R.id.btn_sound).setOnClickListener(this);
  view.findViewById(R.id.btn_music).setOnClickListener(this);
  updateSoundAndMusicButtons();
}
```

Then we have to handle the click. For that we rely on methods we will create inside `SoundManager` to toggle the values. Once that is done, we update the text on the buttons.

```
@Override
public void onClick(View v) {
  if (v.getId() == R.id.btn_start){
    ((YassActivity) getActivity()).startGame();
  }
  else if (v.getId() == R.id.btn_music) {
    SoundManager soundManager =
      getYassActivity().getSoundManager();
    soundManager.toggleMusicStatus();
    updateSoundAndMusicButtons();
  }
  else if (v.getId() == R.id.btn_sound) {
    SoundManager soundManager =
      getYassActivity().getSoundManager();
    soundManager.toggleSoundStatus();
    updateSoundAndMusicButtons();
  }
}
```

Finally, the method `updateSoundAndMusicButtons` simply reads the state of sound and music from the `SoundManager` and sets the correct string resource on each button.

```
private void updateSoundAndMusicButtons() {
  SoundManager soundManager = getYassActivity().getSoundManager();
  TextView btnMusic = (TextView)
    getView().findViewById(R.id.btn_music);
  if (soundManager.getMusicStatus()) {
    btnMusic.setText(R.string.music_on);
  }
```

```
  else {
    btnMusic.setText(R.string.music_off);
  }
  TextView btnSounds= (TextView)
    getView().findViewById(R.id.btn_sound);
  if (soundManager.getSoundStatus()) {
    btnSounds.setText(R.string.sound_on);
  }
  else {
    btnSounds.setText(R.string.sound_off);
  }
}
```

As we mentioned, all the heavy work is done inside `SoundManager`, especially in the methods we have not implemented yet: `toggleMusicStatus` and `toggleSoundStatus`.

Let's get into `SoundManager` then.

Updating SoundManager

Our `SoundManager` is responsible for reading, changing, and restoring the values of the sound and music preferences. To do that we read them from `SharedPreferences` on construction and provide a method to change the setting that also takes care of the loading and unloading of the sound files as needed.

```
private boolean mSoundEnabled;
private boolean mMusicEnabled;

public SoundManager(Context context) {
  SharedPreferences prefs =
    PreferenceManager.getDefaultSharedPreferences(context);
  mSoundEnabled = prefs.getBoolean(SOUNDS_PREF_KEY, true);
  mMusicEnabled = prefs.getBoolean(MUSIC_PREF_KEY, true);
  mContext = context;
  loadIfNeeded();
}

private void loadIfNeeded () {
  if (mSoundEnabled) {
    loadSounds();
  }
  if (mMusicEnabled) {
    loadMusic();
  }
```

```
  }

  public boolean getSoundStatus() {
    return mSoundEnabled;
  }

  public boolean getMusicStatus() {
    return mMusicEnabled;
  }
```

With this initialization, we read the values from `SharedPreferences` and store them in the member variables `mSoundEnabled` and `mMusicEnabled`, which can be accessed at any time and don't need to be read from disk. Once the values are read, we load the sounds and music only if they are enabled.

We also provide the accessor methods `getSoundStatus` and `getMusicStatus`, which we were already using on `MainMenuFragment` to update the text on the buttons.

To change the value of each of the variables we have to use a method that will take care of saving the status and also to load or unload the required files. Let's see the method for the sounds:

```
  public void toggleSoundStatus() {
    mSoundEnabled = !mSoundEnabled;
    if (mSoundEnabled) {
      loadSounds();
    }
    else {
      unloadSounds();
    }
    // Save it to preferences
    PreferenceManager.getDefaultSharedPreferences(mContext).edit()
      .putBoolean(SOUNDS_PREF_KEY, mSoundEnabled)
      .commit();
  }
```

The method switches the value of the setting to the logical negation of what it was. Then it loads or unloads the sounds based on the new value. Finally it stores the updated value on `SharedPreferences` so the member variable and the stored one are in sync.

In the case of music, the method has the exact same logic but loads and unloads the music based on the value of `mMusicEnabled` and the preferences key is the constant `MUSIC_PREF_KEY` instead.

```
public void toggleMusicStatus() {
  mMusicEnabled = !mMusicEnabled;
  if (mMusicEnabled) {
    loadMusic();
    resumeBgMusic();
  }
  else {
    unloadMusic();
  }
  // Save it to preferences
  PreferenceManager.getDefaultSharedPreferences(mContext).edit()
    .putBoolean(MUSIC_PREF_KEY, mMusicEnabled)
    .commit();
}
```

To complete the functionality, we are yet to modify playSoundForGameEvent as well as pauseBgMusic and resumeBgMusic to only do something when the sounds or music are enabled. It is as simple as adding a check at the beginning of each one of the methods involved.

```
public void playSoundForGameEvent(GameEvent event) {
  if (!mSoundEnabled) {
    return;
  }
  Integer soundId = mSoundsMap.get(event);
  if (soundId != null) {
    mSoundPool.play(soundId, 1.0f, 1.0f, 0, 0, 1.0f);
  }
}

public void pauseBgMusic() {
  if (mMusicEnabled) {
    mBgPlayer.pause();
  }
}

public void resumeBgMusic() {
  if (mMusicEnabled) {
    mBgPlayer.start();
  }
}
```

Note that this check is very important because we can easily get NullPointerExceptions when trying to access uninitialized components.

Disabling system sounds

Android has default sounds for button clicks. If you want to use your own sounds for the click action, you also have to disable the system sounds. This is something that we will want almost every time. Luckily it is very easy to do. We just have to modify the application style we have already defined in `res/styles.xml` and tell it that we want to disable sound effects:

```
<style name="AppTheme" parent="Theme.AppCompat.Light.DarkActionBar">
  <item name="android:soundEffectsEnabled">false</item>
</style>
```

Summary

We have created a `SoundManager` that loads and unloads sound effects and music tracks from the assets folder, using the classes Android has for it—`SoundPool` and `MediaPlayer`—and we have learned the best use for each of them.

To play sounds we have added a `GameEvent` messaging system to the `GameEngine` that can be used for other purposes; this is a common mechanism for synchronizing `GameObject`s.

For music we have linked pausing and resuming the music with the Activity life cycle.

We have also added the possibility of enabling and disabling sounds and music independently at any time and stored the states in a persistent storage.

At this point the `GameEngine` is mostly complete. In the following chapters we are going to focus on the tools that Android provides to make the UI nicer and more compelling, improving the look and feel of the game overall.

7
Menus and Dialogs

Now that the game works, it is time to tweak the rest of the UI. When you make an app, the best practice is to use all the standard UI components. Games are different, they should have personality. For this we are going to see how to use custom fonts, buttons, and dialogs.

We will start by making all the fragments of the game use a custom font. Then we will tweak the main menu to make it look nicer by adding a background and customizing the buttons for sound and music; we will also customize the button that starts the game using special drawable types we can define in XML.

For `GameFragment`, we will make space to display the score and lives and will update the pause button as well. We will make the game take care of scoring and player deaths. For this we will also see how to use `GameEvents`, not just for playing sounds, but also for extending the functionality, and adding a few events.

We will also make `GameController` take more responsibility for the game situation by using a state machine. This technique can be applied to other cases such as new levels, etc.

Finally, since the Android framework for dialogs is quite limited, we'll see how we can create custom dialogs for quitting the game, pausing, and game over.

Custom fonts

For app developers, Google has always enforced the use of the system default font, especially since Robotto was introduced. That is the reason why there are no other fonts in the system. However, `TextView` can use custom fonts in True Type (`.ttf`) or Open Type (`.otf`) formats.

When choosing a font, you have lots of choices. There are websites that list lots of fonts that are free to use. Because YASS is meant to be a retro-style shooter, I picked a pixel-art style font called Adore64.

We will store the font files into a folder under `assets` that we will name `ttf`, in the same way as we did for sounds.

To load the font in a format that can be used by `TextView`, we have the `Typeface` class. The process of loading a font is expensive, so we will do it only once (inside `onCreate`) and we will keep the `Typeface` variable as a member of the `Activity`.

 Loading a Typeface is expensive; we should keep it in memory (at the Activity level).

The code we have to add to `YassActivity` for loading a font is very simple:

```
private Typeface mCustomTypeface;

@Override
protected void onCreate(Bundle savedInstanceState) {
  super.onCreate(savedInstanceState);
  [...]
  mCustomTypeface = Typeface.createFromAsset(getAssets(),
    "ttf/Adore64.ttf");
}
```

Once the font is loaded, we just need to apply it to all the text views of the hierarchy. This can be done easily using recursion:

```
public void applyTypeface (View view) {
  if (view instanceof ViewGroup) {
    // Apply recursively to all the children
    ViewGroup viewGroup = (ViewGroup) view;
    for (int i=0; i<viewGroup.getChildCount(); i++) {
      applyTypeface(viewGroup.getChildAt(i));
    }
  }
  else if (view instanceof TextView) {
    TextView tv = (TextView) view;
    tv.setTypeface(mCustomTypeface);
  }
}
```

The method receives a `View`. If it is an instance of `ViewGroup`, it means that it has (or can have) more views as children, so we iterate over all the children using this same method recursively.

If the view is an instance of `TextView`, we just call the method `setTypeface`, which only exists on `TextView`, and we can move on.

For any other type of views, we do nothing.

 Applying a typeface to all our views is easy to do using recursive algorithms.

Note that `instanceof` checks if the object complies with the class given. This means that objects from classes that extend from it will return true. This is key for this algorithm to work, since all the `Layout` classes are children of `ViewGroup` and all views that hold text (that is `Button`) extend from `TextView`.

The missing link is, where do we invoke this method and with which parameters? We will do it using the method `onViewCreated` of `YassBaseFragment`.

```
@Override
public void onViewCreated(View view, Bundle savedInstanceState) {
    super.onViewCreated(view, savedInstanceState);
    getYassActivity().applyTypeface(view);
}
```

Since all the fragments will extend from this one, they will all have the `Typeface` set automatically.

If we want to use more than one font in the game, the code starts to become complex and it is a better idea to use a library to take care of it. For this I recommend using Calligraphy (`https://github.com/chrisjenx/Calligraphy`), which hooks into the `ContextWrapper` to load the typeface when inflating the views instead of traversing the hierarchy later, and also supports XML attributes to set a specific font to a specific view.

 Calligraphy is a great library if you want to use multiple fonts in your Android project.

Working with backgrounds

Something that makes the game look bad is the plain white background we have at the moment. While we could set a background for the activity, this is not the best solution because background images are set to scale to fit, and that cannot be changed. When using a background image it will expand to cover all the view.

 The attribute `android:background` will stretch the image to make it fit in the view.

We do not want our background image to be stretched in one dimension. We want it to scale uniformly on both axes.

This can be improved with the use of a 9-patch as the background image, but in our case we will just use an `ImageView` that covers all the layout with `scaleType` set to `centerCrop`. This parameter does scale the image uniformly (maintaining the image's aspect ratio) so that both dimensions of the image (width and height) will be equal to or larger than the corresponding dimension of the `View`.

We will add an `ImageView` at the beginning of `fragment_main_menu.xml` with the desired `scaleType`:

```
<?xml version="1.0" encoding="utf-8"?>
<RelativeLayout
  xmlns:android="http://schemas.android.com/apk/res/android"
  android:layout_width="match_parent"
  android:layout_height="match_parent" >
  <ImageView
    android:layout_width="match_parent"
    android:layout_height="match_parent"
    android:scaleType="centerCrop"
    android:src="@drawable/seamless_space_0"/>
[...]
</RelativeLayout>
```

And just with the fonts and the background, the main menu looks much better already!

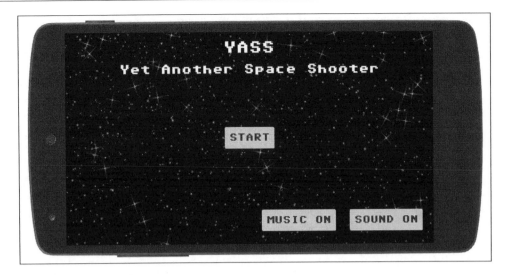

We could use a `GameView` instead of an `ImageView` to have a parallax background, I leave this as an exercise for readers interested in tweaking backgrounds even more.

The power of XML drawables

Until now we have used drawables that are images, but Android provides a very complete framework that allows us to use other types of resources. A drawable resource is a general concept for a graphic that can be drawn to the screen. There are several types of drawables that you can define in XML.

We are going to describe state lists and shape drawables, but there are a few more. In particular if you are not familiar with 9-patches, you should check them out as well.

 You can learn about all drawable resources in the official documentation: `http://developer.android.com/guide/topics/resources/drawable-resource.html`.

State list drawables

`StateListDrawable` is a drawable object defined in XML that uses several other drawables to represent the same graphic depending on the state of the object. The framework defines many states, but we will only use `pressed`, `focused`, and `default` (no state). There is also a state named `selected` that should not be confused with `focused`. In fact selected is hardly ever used.

The state list is described in an XML file that has `<selector>` as the root tag. Each graphic is represented by an `<item>` element which can use various attributes to describe the state in which it should be used as the graphic for the drawable.

When the state changes, the list is checked in sequential order and the first item that matches the current state is used. It is important to remember that this selection of state is not based on a best match but on a first match. The best practice for defining state lists is to put the most restrictive states at the beginning and to have a default state as the last item.

 The order of the states is very important. The first match on the list is the one that is used.

We are going to use state list drawables for the music and sound buttons. We will then have four state list drawables—music on, music off, sound on & sound off—and for each of them we will have three states: pressed, focused, and normal.

These views will not be buttons any longer but an `ImageView` instead. A bit of a code tweaking will be needed in order to make this change, basically inside `updateSoundAndMusicButtons`, which should use drawables now instead of texts.

Regarding the look and feel, we are going to make a circle of a color that represents the state, and then use the same icon for all of the states, just changing the color. We will also make the pressed state a bit smaller—to give the feeling of being pressed—by adding margins to the image.

We are using white for normal state, yellow for pressed, and blue for focused.

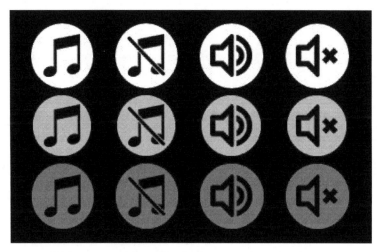

All the composed drawables for the states of sound and music

The state drawable files should be placed into the `res/drawable` directory because they are just a list of references and therefore they are independent of the density. On the other hand, we should provide density-specific versions of the drawables that are referenced as states.

Now, instead of providing 12 icons, since all of them use the same background we can configure this using 4 icons, 3 background states and 1 state drawable that will be the background for all of them. This will also allow us to reuse the background for other buttons.

This is the code of the state list drawable that we will use for the background:

```xml
<?xml version="1.0" encoding="utf-8"?>
<selector
  xmlns:android="http://schemas.android.com/apk/res/android">
  <item
    android:drawable="@drawable/icon_button_bg_pressed"
    android:state_pressed="true"/>
  <item
    android:drawable="@drawable/icon_button_bg_selected"
    android:state_focused="true"/>
  <item
    android:drawable="@drawable/icon_button_bg_normal"/>
</selector>
```

As we already said, the order is very important. We want to show the pressed state when it is pressed; we do not care if it is focused or not, so that is the first case. Then we want to show if it is focused. Finally we have a default case with no parameters that covers "everything else".

The backgrounds have been created using GIMP and the base icons are free ones that we found using an icon search website such as IconFinder (`https://www.iconfinder.com`). There are many icon search websites. Try several and see which one you like best.

Note that the naming convention is to use a name for the state list and then the same name followed by pressed, selected, or normal for each state.

State lists colors

We can use selectors to define colors as well as images. This can be used on the text that goes into a button or the background of a view. It works the same way as for drawables, but uses the `color` keyword instead of `drawable`. The files that define colors must be placed under the `res/colors` directory.

An example of a color state list that we will reference later is `btn_background.xml`.

```xml
<?xml version="1.0" encoding="utf-8"?>
<selector
  xmlns:android="http://schemas.android.com/apk/res/android">
  <item
    android:color="@color/btn_pressed"
    android:state_pressed="true"/>
  <item
    android:color="@color/btn_focused"
    android:state_selected="true"/>
  <item
    android:color="@color/btn_normal"/>
</selector>
```

And of course we need to define these colors as well. Note that these colors are not state lists, and therefore should be defined in a file under the `res/values` directory. We normally call this file `colors.xml` as a convention, but any name will work.

```xml
<?xml version="1.0" encoding="utf-8"?>
<resources>
  <color name="btn_selected">#39a29c</color>
  <color name="btn_normal">#ffffff</color>
  <color name="btn_pressed">#fdd33f</color>
</resources>
```

 State list color XML files are placed under `res/color`, but normal colors are defined as values in files under `res/values` instead.

As good practice, you should always externalize all the variables of the layouts . This is valid for colors, dimensions, and strings.

Shape drawables

Shape drawables are exactly what the name suggests: a way to define a generic shape in XML. We are going to use them to make all the button backgrounds.

The syntax for shape drawables is defined as this:

```xml
<?xml version="1.0" encoding="utf-8"?>
<shape
  xmlns:android="http://schemas.android.com/apk/res/android"
  android:shape=["rectangle" | "oval" | "line" | "ring"] >
  <corners
    android:radius="integer"
    android:topLeftRadius="integer"
    android:topRightRadius="integer"
    android:bottomLeftRadius="integer"
    android:bottomRightRadius="integer" />
  <gradient
    android:angle="integer"
    android:centerX="integer"
    android:centerY="integer"
    android:centerColor="integer"
    android:endColor="color"
    android:gradientRadius="integer"
    android:startColor="color"
    android:type=["linear" | "radial" | "sweep"]
    android:useLevel=["true" | "false"] />
  <padding
    android:left="integer"
    android:top="integer"
    android:right="integer"
    android:bottom="integer" />
  <size
    android:width="integer"
    android:height="integer" />
  <solid
    android:color="color" />
  <stroke
    android:width="integer"
    android:color="color"
    android:dashWidth="integer"
    android:dashGap="integer" />
</shape>
```

The top level tag of the shape drawable is `<shape>` and it has an attribute also named `shape` that defines its type. Possible values are:

- `rectangle`: a rectangle that fills the containing view. This is the default shape if none is specified.
- `oval`: an oval shape that fits the dimensions of the containing view.
- `line`: a horizontal line that spans the width of the containing view. This shape requires the `<stroke>` element to define the width of the line.
- `ring`: a ring shape. This shape allows some other attributes to be properly defined such as `innerRadius`/`innerRadiusRatio`, `thickness`/`thicknessRatio`, and `useLevel`.

The content of the shape can be a solid color or a gradient. For this, we use the tags `<solid>` or `<gradient>`.

The tag `<solid>` has the argument `color`, which can be provided as a hexadecimal value or a color resource. This color resource can also be a state list.

The tag `<gradient>` can be used instead of `<solid>` and its arguments are self-explanatory. We are not going to use them in our game.

We can define the padding of the containing view elements using the `<padding>` tag. It has four different attributes—`left`, `top`, `right`, and `bottom`—that can be provided as a dimension value or dimension resource.

The size of the shape is optional and can be defined using the tag `<size>`, which has `height` and `width` as attributes that can be a dimension value or resource.

The shape scales to the size of the container `View` proportionate to the dimensions defined here, by default. When you use the shape in an `ImageView`, you can restrict scaling by setting `android:scaleType` to `"center"`.

The border or outline of the shape is defined with the tag `<stroke>`. It accepts the following attributes:

- **Width**: the thickness of the line, as a dimension value or dimension resource.
- **Color**: the color of the line, as a hexadecimal value or color resource.
- **DashGap/DashWith**: the distance between line dashes and the size of each dash, both as dimension values and dimension resources. They need to be set together.

When using a rectangular shape, we can specify the corners to be rounded by using the `<corners>` tag; for that we can use just `radius` or we can specify a dimension for each of the corners: `topLeftRadius`, `topRightRadius`, `bottomLeftRadius`, and `bottomRightRadius`.

> The system requires every corner radius to be initialized with a value greater than 1 in the XML file. Otherwise no corners are rounded. To work around this you can override the corner radius value programmatically.

Now that we have seen the syntax in detail, let's create the shapes we are going to use in our game.

We are going to create an oval shape for the round buttons, and use a color that is also a color state list to replace the current drawable state list that has multiple shapes because it makes the code much more compact and easy to update.

```xml
<?xml version="1.0" encoding="utf-8"?>
<shape xmlns:android="http://schemas.android.com/apk/res/android"
  android:shape="oval">
  <solid
    android:color="@color/btn_backgound" />
  <padding android:bottom="@dimen/round_button_padding"
    android:left="@dimen/round_button_padding"
    android:right="@dimen/round_button_padding"
    android:top="@dimen/round_button_padding"/>
</shape>
```

We define the shape as oval, then set it to have a solid color that is the state list color resource we defined in the previous section. Finally we define some paddings that come from dimensions resources.

Next, we are going to define a shape for the square buttons (at the moment it is only used for the button to start the game):

```xml
<?xml version="1.0" encoding="utf-8"?>
<shape xmlns:android="http://schemas.android.com/apk/res/android"
  android:shape="rectangle">
  <solid
    android:color="@color/btn_backgound" />
  <padding android:bottom="@dimen/square_button_padding"
    android:left="@dimen/square_button_padding"
    android:right="@dimen/square_button_padding"
```

```
        android:top="@dimen/square_button_padding"/>
    <stroke android:color="@color/btn_border"
        android:width="@dimen/square_button_border" />
    </shape>
```

This shape is a rectangle with a border. The border is defined by the `stroke` tag.

All the dimensions we have used for this shape must be defined. We put them into a `dimens.xml` file under `res/values`.

```
    <dimen name="square_button_padding">18dp</dimen>
    <dimen name="square_button_border">6dp</dimen>
    <dimen name="round_button_padding">6dp</dimen>
    <dimen name="btn_sound_size">60dp</dimen>
```

We also added a couple more colors for the button border and the text color in `colors.xml`.

```
    <color name="text_color">#FFFFFF</color>
    <color name="btn_border">#AAAAAA</color>
```

Finally we are going to make use of styles to keep the code on the layouts cleaner. Styles on Android allow you to define several XML attributes and associate them with a name. Then you can reference the style by name on any layout and it will be applied.

The intention of styles is to define the look and feel in a single place so it can be changed and/or updated easily. The concept is similar to CSS for web pages.

 Styles are very handy for keeping layouts clean and having the definition of the look and feel in a single place.

We are going to define a style for the round buttons. This goes into the `styles.xml` file under `res/values` (and again, any name for the file will work, but it is better to follow the conventions).

```
    <resources>
      <style name="iconButton" >
        <item
          name="android:background">@drawable/icon_button_bg</item>
        <item name="android:layout_width">@dimen/btn_round_size</item>
        <item
          name="android:layout_height">@dimen/btn_round_size</item>
      </style>
    </resources>
```

To complete this section, let's look at the updated version of `fragment_main_menu.xml` with all these changes included:

```xml
<?xml version="1.0" encoding="utf-8"?>
<RelativeLayout
    xmlns:android="http://schemas.android.com/apk/res/android"
    android:layout_width="match_parent"
    android:layout_height="match_parent"
    >

    <ImageView
        android:layout_width="match_parent"
        android:layout_height="match_parent"
        android:scaleType="centerCrop"
        android:src="@drawable/seamless_space_0"/>

    <TextView
        android:textColor="@color/text_color"
        android:id="@+id/main_title"
        style="@android:style/TextAppearance.DeviceDefault.Large"
        android:layout_marginTop="@dimen/activity_vertical_margin"
        android:text="@string/game_title"
        android:layout_centerHorizontal="true"
        android:layout_width="wrap_content"
        android:layout_height="wrap_content" />

    <TextView
        android:textColor="@color/text_color"
        android:layout_below="@+id/main_title"
        style="@android:style/TextAppearance.DeviceDefault.Medium"
        android:layout_marginTop="@dimen/activity_vertical_margin"
        android:text="@string/game_subtitle"
        android:layout_centerHorizontal="true"
        android:layout_width="wrap_content"
        android:layout_height="wrap_content" />

    <Button
        android:id="@+id/btn_start"
        android:layout_centerInParent="true"
        android:layout_width="wrap_content"
        android:layout_height="wrap_content"
        android:background="@drawable/button_square_bg"
        android:text="@string/start" />
```

```
<ImageView
    android:background="@drawable/button_round_bg"
    android:id="@+id/btn_sound"
    android:layout_margin="@dimen/activity_vertical_margin"
    android:layout_width="@dimen/btn_sound_size"
    android:layout_height="@dimen/btn_sound_size"
    android:src="@drawable/sounds_on_no_bg"
    android:layout_alignParentBottom="true"
    android:layout_alignParentRight="true"/>

<ImageView
    android:background="@drawable/button_round_bg"
    android:id="@+id/btn_music"
    android:layout_width="@dimen/btn_sound_size"
    android:layout_height="@dimen/btn_sound_size"
    android:layout_alignBottom="@+id/btn_sound"
    android:src="@drawable/music_on_no_bg"
    android:layout_toLeftOf="@+id/btn_sound"/>
</RelativeLayout>
```

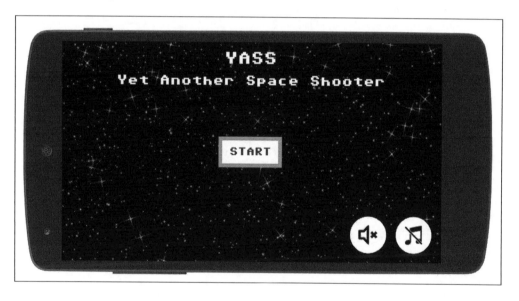

The GameFragment

Now that we have tweaked the main menu, it is time to work on the GameFragment.

There are two essential game features we have not even built yet: score and lives. We are going remedy that now. First we need to make space for them in the layout, then we have to write some code to actually take care of both features.

For the UI of the score and lives we are going to use standard Android components. We have built a lot of features into our GameEngine, but we do not want to reinvent the wheel. Since Android provides a good way to define layouts and make UIs we are familiar with, it would be a waste to not make use of it.

 Using the standard Android Views can save you a lot of time.

We are going to make the game area smaller by adding a column to each side. We will place the new UI elements there and we will link them to GameObjects to update them as the game progresses.

While we could overlay the controls on top of the GameView instead of having letterboxes, note that we are using a SurfaceView, and its performance plummets dramatically when other views are overlaid on top of it. We also think it looks nicer to have the gameplay area separated from the controls. If you want to use an overlay, you should change the GameView to be a StandardGameView.

Now that we are working with fragment_game.xml, it is a good moment to also update the Pause button with the same style we created for sound and music.

The new version of fragment_game.xml is like this:

```
<FrameLayout
    xmlns:android="http://schemas.android.com/apk/res/android"
    xmlns:tools="http://schemas.android.com/tools"
    android:layout_width="match_parent"
    android:layout_height="match_parent"
    android:background="@color/background"
    tools:context="com.plattysoft.yass.counter.GameFragment">
```

```
<RelativeLayout
  android:layout_width="@dimen/game_menu_width"
  android:layout_height="match_parent">
  <!-- Lives and score go here -->
</RelativeLayout>

<FrameLayout
  android:background="@color/game_view_frame"
  android:layout_weight="1"
  android:padding="4dp"
  android:layout_marginLeft="@dimen/game_menu_width"
  android:layout_marginRight="@dimen/game_menu_width"
  android:layout_width="match_parent"
  android:layout_height="match_parent">

  <com.plattysoft.yass.engine.SurfaceGameView
    android:id="@+id/gameView"
    android:layout_weight="1"
    android:layout_width="match_parent"
    android:layout_height="match_parent" />
</FrameLayout>

<include layout="@layout/view_vjoystick" />

<ImageView
  style="@style/iconButton"
  android:layout_gravity="top|right"
  android:id="@+id/btn_play_pause"
  android:layout_marginTop="@dimen/activity_vertical_margin"
  android:layout_marginRight="@dimen/activity_vertical_margin"
  android:src="@drawable/pause" />
</FrameLayout>
```

The GameView in now inside a FrameLayout that is centered and has margins to each side with values for the columns (R.dimen.game_menu_width). The FrameLayout is used to display a red frame around the GameView to clearly separate the play area from the rest of the UI.

The frame background is a rectangular shape drawable similar to the ones we have already defined:

```xml
<?xml version="1.0" encoding="utf-8"?>
<shape xmlns:android="http://schemas.android.com/apk/res/android"
  android:shape="rectangle">
  <solid
    android:color="@android:color/transparent" />
  <padding android:bottom="@dimen/game_frame_width"
    android:left="@dimen/game_frame_width"
    android:right="@dimen/game_frame_width"
    android:top="@dimen/game_frame_width"/>
  <stroke android:color="@color/game_view_frame"
    android:width="@dimen/game_frame_width" />
</shape>
```

On the left we have a `RelativeLayout`, which we will use to place the controls for the score and lives. In front of this we have the virtual joystick we were already using, and that covers the entire screen. Finally, we have the pause button, which has to remain in the foreground, otherwise the virtual joystick will capture the touch event. As we have already mentioned, the pause button is now using the same look and feel as the music and sound buttons on the main menu.

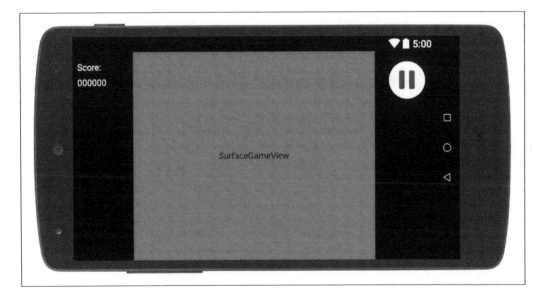

Now that we have the space, let's start adding items there! We are going to just display scores and lives, but you could use the space for anything relevant to the game, from top scores to In-App Purchases buttons.

Adding a score

Let's implement the score counter. For that we need to define a way to give points to the player as well.

We are going to use a TextView to display the score on the screen. To control this TextView, we will create a ScoreGameObject that is in many ways similar to the one we used in *Chapter 1, Setting Up the Project* to show the coordinates of the Player.

The score will be calculated inside the ScoreGameObject class and it will be updated based on game events. This also implies that the GameEngine must propagate the events to the game objects (until now it has only propagated them to the SoundEngine).

We will give 50 points each time the player hits an asteroid, and remove one point each time an asteroid escapes. An Asteroid escaping is a new GameEvent we will have to create and trigger. Both score modification values will be set as constants as good practice for readability and ease of change.

First things first: let's make GameEngine propagate GameEvents to all the GameObjects that are currently active. For this, we modify the method onGameEvent of GameEngine.

```
public void onGameEvent (GameEvent gameEvent) {
  // We notify all the GameObjects
  int numObjects = mGameObjects.size();
  for (int i=0; i<numObjects; i++) {
    mGameObjects.get(i).onGameEvent(gameEvent);
  }
  // Also the sound manager
  mSoundManager.playSoundForGameEvent(gameEvent);
}
```

Note that this implies creating a method named onGameEvent in GameObject, which will be empty by default.

We are going to use a new `GameEvent` that is triggered when the asteroid goes out of the screen (`AsteroidMissed`). We have to add that value to the `GameEvents` enum and also trigger the event from the `onUpdate` method of the `Asteroid`.

```
@Override
public void onUpdate(long elapsedMillis, GameEngine gameEngine) {
    [...]
    if (mY > gameEngine.mHeight) {
        gameEngine.onGameEvent(GameEvent.AsteroidMissed);
        removeFromGameEngine(gameEngine);
    }
}
```

Now let's add the `TextView` to the left column of our `fragment_game.xml`. We will have two new text views: one with the text "`Score:`" (`R.id.score_title`) and another one with the score itself (`R.id.score_value`).

```
<RelativeLayout
    android:layout_width="@dimen/game_menu_width"
    android:layout_height="match_parent">
    <TextView
        android:layout_marginTop="@dimen/activity_vertical_margin"
        android:layout_marginLeft="@dimen/menu_margin"
        android:id="@+id/score_title"
        android:layout_width="wrap_content"
        android:layout_height="wrap_content"
        android:layout_alignParentTop="true"
        android:textColor="@color/text_color"
        android:text="@string/score"/>
    <TextView
        android:id="@+id/score_value"
        android:layout_width="wrap_content"
        android:layout_height="wrap_content"
        android:layout_marginTop="@dimen/menu_margin"
        android:layout_below="@+id/score_title"
        android:layout_alignLeft="@+id/score_title"
        android:textColor="@color/text_color"
        android:text="000000"/>
</RelativeLayout>
```

We have everything in place, it is time to link them together with the
`ScoreGameObject` class. It is a fairly simple one:

```java
public class ScoreGameObject extends GameObject {

    private final TextView mText;
    private int mPoints;
    private boolean mPointsHaveChanged;

    private static final int POINTS_LOSS_PER_ASTEROID_MISSED = 1;
    private static final int POINTS_GAINED_PER_ASTEROID_HIT = 50;

    public ScoreGameObject(View view, int viewResId) {
        mText = (TextView) view.findViewById(viewResId);
    }

    @Override
    public void onUpdate(long elapsedMillis, GameEngine gameEngine) {}

    @Override
    public void startGame() {
        mPoints = 0;
        mText.post(mUpdateTextRunnable);
    }

    @Override
    public void onGameEvent(GameEvent gameEvent) {
        if (gameEvent == GameEvent.AsteroidHit) {
            mPoints += POINTS_GAINED_PER_ASTEROID_HIT;
            mPointsHaveChanged = true;
        }
        else if (gameEvent == GameEvent.AsteroidMissed) {
            if (mPoints > 0) {
                mPoints -= POINTS_LOSS_PER_ASTEROID_MISSED;
            }
            mPointsHaveChanged = true;
        }
    }

    private Runnable mUpdateTextRunnable = new Runnable() {
        @Override
```

```
    public void run() {
        String text = String.format("%06d", mPoints);
        mText.setText(text);
    }
};

@Override
public void onDraw(Canvas canvas) {
    if (mPointsHaveChanged) {
        mText.post(mUpdateTextRunnable);
        mPointsHaveChanged = false;
    }
}
}
```

This class sets the points to 0 when the game is started, and then reacts to
GameEvents by modifying the total points of the player. Once the value of the score
has been modified, we signal it with a boolean variable so we know it needs to be
updated during the next call to onDraw. This is done to prevent unnecessary redraws
on the TextView.

Remember that onDraw is invoked on the UIThread when we are using a
StandardGameView, but it is called from the UpdateThread in the case of a
SurfaceGameView. Since the views can only be updated on the UIThread, we use
a Runnable that gets posted to the UIThread, which then updates the value of the
TextView to make it work for both StandardGameView and SurfaceGameView.

 View modifications must always be done on the UIThread.

We use String.format to get a number consisting of 6 digits, filling in with 0s to
the left if the integer does not have enough digits. This just makes the score look
a lot nicer.

The only remaining link is to add this GameObject to the GameEngine initialization
in the GameFragment.

```
new ScoreGameObject(
    getView(),R.id.score_value).addToGameEngine(mGameEngine, 0);
```

We can now play the game and finally score some points.

Adding lives

We are also going to have a lives indicator in the left column. For this we have to update the game quite a lot since we only have one life currently and the game does not do anything when we die.

As we did for the score, we will have a `LivesCounter` object that takes care of the display, but in this case the lives count will rely on the `GameController`. The synchronization between the `GameController` and the `LivesCounter` will be done via `GameEvents`.

Another thing to consider is that once the player dies, the wave must stop. Only once the screen is empty can we spawn a new `Player` object and then restart the wave after a few seconds.

To manage this, we will have `GameController` be a state machine and transition from one state to the other based on `GameEvents`. This is a common technique for the controllers of games in general.

[Having the `GameController` be a state machine is a common technique for games.]

We are going to start with the modifications in `GameController` first and then `LivesCounter`.

For the state of the `GameController` we will create an enum that we will call `GameControllerState`.

```
public enum GameControllerState {
    StoppingWave,
    SpawningEnemies,
    PlacingSpaceship,
    Waiting,
    GameOver;
}
```

Let's describe each one of the states:

- `StoppingWave`: this state is time based. While the `GameController` is in it, no asteroids are spawned. Combined with the timeout it effectively stops the current wave. From this state the controller will transition either to `GameOver` if there are no lives left, or to `PlacingSpaceship` if there are.

- `SpawningEnemies`: the normal state. This is the equivalent of the behavior of the previous version without states. It transitions to `StoppingWave` when the spaceship is destroyed.

- `PlacingSpaceship`: the controller puts a `Player` object into play and sends a `GameEvent` about it. This transitions automatically to `Waiting`.

- `Waiting`: similar to `StoppingWave`, this state is also time based but it always transitions to `SpawningEnemies`. This state exists to allow the player some time to relax after the new spaceship is placed on the screen.

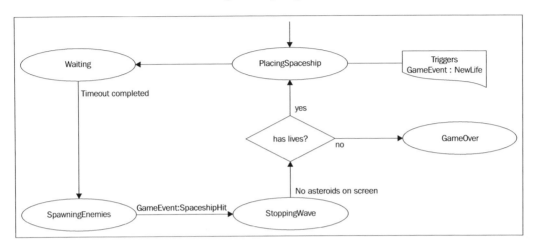

The `GameController` starts in the `PlacingSpaceship` state, which gets one life and places a spaceship on the screen. The `GameController` will move into `Waiting` and then into `SpawningEnemies`.

When a `SpaceshipHit` event arrives we move into `StoppingWave`. Once there are no more `Asteroids` on the screen, we check the number of lives remaining. If it is 0, that's `GameOver`, otherwise, we go to `PlacingSpaceship` (which triggers a `LifeLost` game event) and then moves to `Waiting` again until we can move to `SpawningEnemies`.

Let's see the code to start a game:

```
@Override
public void startGame(GameEngine gameEngine) {
  mCurrentMillis = 0;
  mEnemiesSpawned = 0;
  mWaitingTime = 0;
  for (int i=0; i<INITIAL_LIFES; i++) {
    gameEngine.onGameEvent(GameEvent.LifeAdded);
  }
  mState = GameControllerState.PlacingSpaceship;
}
```

First we reset all the counters and we run a loop over the amount of lives we have initially, sending the game event LifeAdded. This event is processed in this class as well as in the LivesCounter.

The main advantages to adding lives this way is that we can process lives that are given by other means than starting the game, that is, any extra lives. We also have the value of initial lives in a single place.

Finally we move to the state of PlacingSpaceship as we described before.

As an important note: since we are starting on PlacingSpaceship, we now don't need to add the player object to the GameEngine anymore because we do it from this class. We must remove that code from the initialization of the engine.

 The GameController now takes care of adding the Player to the game. We don't have to add it by hand on the GameEngine creation anymore.

We could start the GameController in the StoppingWave state as well. That would give us some time before the life is removed and then added. Play with this, and decide which one you like better.

Next let's look at the onGameEvent method of GameController:

```
@Override
public void onGameEvent(GameEvent gameEvent) {
  if (gameEvent == GameEvent.SpaceshipHit) {
    mState = GameControllerState.StoppingWave;
    mWaitingTime = 0;
  }
  else if (gameEvent == GameEvent.GameOver) {
    mState = GameControllerState.GameOver;
  }
  else if (gameEvent == GameEvent.LifeAdded) {
    mNumLives++;
  }
}
```

This does react to a SpaceshipHit event by moving into the StoppingWave state, and it also resets the waiting time. That state will check if there are remaining lives to be used or not and trigger the GameOver event if needed. We will see that when we look into onUpdate.

The method reacts to the `GameOver` event by putting itself in `GameOver` state. This event is only sent by the `GameController` at the moment, but it is nice to have it like this for future usage. Maybe we will want to have a very powerful enemy that can end the game in one go.

Finally, when `LifeAdded` arrives it increases the lives counter. Again, this event is only sent on construction of this class, but we could implement an extra life mechanic and then trigger it from somewhere else.

The real juice is inside the `onUpdate` method.

```
@Override
public void onUpdate(long elapsedMillis, GameEngine gameEngine) {
  if (mState == GameControllerState.SpawningEnemies) {
    mCurrentMillis += elapsedMillis;
    long waveTimestamp = mEnemiesSpawned * TIME_BETWEEN_ENEMIES;
    if (mCurrentMillis > waveTimestamp) {
      // Spawn a new enemy
      Asteroid a = mAsteroidPool.remove(0);
      a.init(gameEngine);
      a.addToGameEngine(gameEngine, mLayer);
      mEnemiesSpawned++;
      return;
    }
  }
  else if (mState == GameControllerState.StoppingWave) {
    mWaitingTime += elapsedMillis;
    if (mWaitingTime > STOPPING_WAVE_WAITING_TIME) {
      mState = GameControllerState.PlacingSpaceship;
    }
  }
  else if (mState == GameControllerState.PlacingSpaceship) {
    if (mNumLifes == 0) {
      gameEngine.onGameEvent(GameEvent.GameOver);
    }
    else {
      mNumLives--;
      gameEngine.onGameEvent(GameEvent.LifeLost);
      Player newLife = new Player(gameEngine);
      newLife.addToGameEngine(gameEngine, 2);
      newLife.startGame(gameEngine);
      // We wait to start spawning more enemies
      mState = GameControllerState.Waiting;
      mWaitingTime = 0;
    }
```

```
    }
    else if (mState == GameControllerState.Waiting) {
      mWaitingTime += elapsedMillis;
      if (mWaitingTime > WAITING_TIME) {
        mState = GameControllerState.SpawningEnemies;
      }
    }
  }
}
```

You can see that the code we had before is now the code for the SpawningEnemies state. There is nothing new about spawning asteroids.

To stop a wave we just have to wait some milliseconds. Since there are no new Asteroids being spawned, this timeout just needs to be longer than the time it takes an Asteroid to cross the screen. We could count the asteroids when they are returned to the pool instead, but this method always waits the same amount of time and feels better to the player.

The PlacingSpaceship state only lasts for one iteration. It will either send a GameOver event (which will move it to the GameOver state) or use a life, which includes:

- Sending the LifeLost event
- Creating a Player object, initializing it and adding it to the GameEngine
- Moving to the Waiting state and resetting the waiting time

At this time we are not doing anything when the GameOver event happens, but we will take care of this in the second part of the chapter, by showing a game over dialog.

Finally, while in the Waiting state we count the milliseconds, just as we do on the StoppingWave, and then we move to the SpawningEnemies state.

This is all we need to make the GameController handle the state machine properly. It is time to move on to the LivesCounter.

To show the lives on the screen we need to add some views to the layout and also implement the class that handles them. We want each life to be displayed as an icon of the spaceship on the left, under the score counter.

We need to add the following code to the left column of the `fragment_game.xml` layout:

```
<RelativeLayout>
  [...]
  <TextView
    android:layout_marginTop="@dimen/activity_vertical_margin"
    android:id="@+id/lives_title"
    android:layout_below="@+id/score_value"
    android:layout_alignLeft="@+id/score_value"
    android:layout_width="wrap_content"
    android:layout_height="wrap_content"
    android:textColor="@color/text_color"
    android:text="@string/lives" />
  <LinearLayout
    android:orientation="horizontal"
    android:id="@+id/lives_value"
    android:layout_marginTop="@dimen/menu_margin"
    android:layout_below="@+id/lives_title"
    android:layout_alignLeft="@+id/lives_title"
    android:layout_width="@dimen/game_menu_width"
    android:layout_height="wrap_content" />
</RelativeLayout>
```

We have a `TextView` that displays the text `"Lives"`: and a horizontal `LinearLayout` in which we will add and remove `ImageViews` when we receive the respective `GameEvents`.

The code for `LivesCounter` is as easy as this:

```
public class LivesCounter extends GameObject {

  private final LinearLayout mLayout;

  public LivesCounter(View view, int viewResId) {
    mLayout = (LinearLayout) view.findViewById(viewResId);
  }

  @Override
  public void startGame(GameEngine gameEngine) {}
```

```
    @Override
    public void onUpdate(long elapsedMillis, GameEngine gameEngine) {}

    @Override
    public void onDraw(Canvas canvas) {}

    @Override
    public void onGameEvent(GameEvent gameEvent) {
      if (gameEvent == GameEvent.LifeLost) {
        mLayout.post(mRemoveLifeRunnable);
      }
      else if (gameEvent == GameEvent.LifeAdded) {
        mLayout.post(mAddLifeRunnable);
      }
    }

    private Runnable mRemoveLifeRunnable = new Runnable() {
      @Override
      public void run() {
        // Remove one life from the layout
        mLayout.removeViewAt(mLayout.getChildCount()-1);
      }
    };

    private Runnable mAddLifeRunnable = new Runnable() {
      @Override
      public void run() {
        // Remove one life from the layout
        View spaceship = View.inflate(mLayout.getContext(),
          R.layout.view_spaceship, mLayout);
      }
    };
  }
```

As you can see, this class does not take into account the amount of lives that the player has. It only reacts to the events LifeAdded and LifeLost by adding or removing an item to the LinearLayout.

We add and remove views by posting a runnable object for the same reason as for the ScoreGameObject: modifying views must be done in the UIThread, and onDraw does run in the UpdateThread when we use SurfaceGameView.

The last piece is the layout `view_spaceship.xml` we are inflating, which is just an `ImageView`:

```xml
<?xml version="1.0" encoding="utf-8"?>
<ImageView
  xmlns:android="http://schemas.android.com/apk/res/android"
  android:src="@drawable/ship"
  android:scaleType="fitCenter"
  android:layout_width="@dimen/life_size"
  android:layout_height="@dimen/life_size" />
```

The dimension `life_size` is set to 30dp in the file `dimens.xml` file, so there is enough horizontal space for three spaceships.

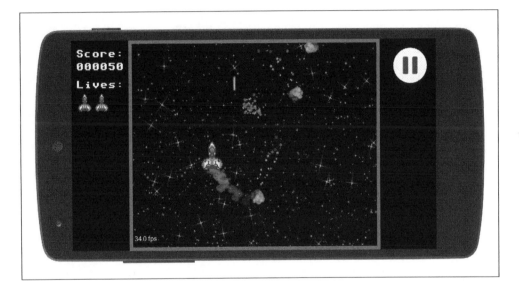

Custom dialogs

The next step in making our UI nicer is to stop using the standard Android dialogs and create our own custom ones instead. Once again this is something completely discouraged for apps but it makes a lot of sense for games.

There are many reasons why a custom dialog system is better for games:

- The default dialogs will look different in different Android versions. This is in fact great when you use `AlertDialog` in an app, since it mimics the dialogs of all the rest of the apps, but not the games. We want consistency.

- Default dialogs use the system font.

- If you try to set a custom background or a custom content view, `AlertDialogs` look terrible. Again, you should never do that in an app, but you definitely want it in a game.

- The standard dialogs ruin the immersive experience by showing the notifications and system bars when they are on screen.

- It is hard to replace the animations of `AlertDialog` with custom ones.

We are going to build a system that shows our dialogs on screen, with a gray semi-transparent overlay behind them. These dialogs will have a custom background made out of a shape drawable and will use the custom font we have selected for the game.

Finally, the dialog itself is just a layout we put in front of the content.

It is worth noting that we need to define a policy for what to do when we are showing a dialog and a new one is trying to display on top. In our game, the old dialog will stay and the new one will not be displayed, but nevertheless we will provide a method to dismiss the previous one and show the new one in case you want that behavior in your game.

We are going to describe the architecture first (including modifications to `YassBaseFragment`), and then we will start by making the dialog for quitting the game because it is the simplest one. After that we will replace the current pause dialog and finally we will make a new dialog for game over.

BaseCustomDialog

The custom dialog framework we are going to create is composed of three items:

- `BaseCustomDialog`: the base class of all the dialogs
- `my_overlay_dialog`: a layout that is the parent of all the dialogs
- Utility functions in the base fragment class

Most of the work is done in the `BaseCustomDialog` class, which provides methods to `setContentView`, `show`, and `dismiss`.

The complete code of `BaseCustomDialog` **class is as follows:**

```java
public class BaseCustomDialog implements OnTouchListener {

  private boolean mIsShowing;

  protected final YassActivity mParent;
  private ViewGroup mRootLayout;
  private View mRootView;

  public BaseCustomDialog(YassActivity activity) {
    mParent = activity;
  }

  protected void onViewClicked() {
    // Ignore clicks on this view
  }

  protected void setContentView(int dialogResId) {
    ViewGroup activityRoot = (ViewGroup)
      mParent.findViewById(android.R.id.content);
    mRootView = LayoutInflater.from(mParent).inflate(dialogResId,
      activityRoot, false);
    mParent.applyTypeface(mRootView);
  }

  public void show() {
    if (mIsShowing) {
      return;
    }
    mIsShowing = true;

    ViewGroup activityRoot = (ViewGroup)
      mParent.findViewById(android.R.id.content);
    mRootLayout = (ViewGroup)
      LayoutInflater.from(mParent).inflate(
      R.layout.my_overlay_dialog, activityRoot, false);
    activityRoot.addView(mRootLayout);
    mRootLayout.setOnTouchListener(this);
    mRootLayout.addView(mRootView);
  }
```

```
public void dismiss() {
  if (!mIsShowing) {
    return;
  }
  mIsShowing = false;
  hideViews();
}

private void hideViews() {
  mRootLayout.removeView(mRootView);
  ViewGroup activityRoot = (ViewGroup)
    mParent.findViewById(android.R.id.content);
  activityRoot.removeView(mRootLayout);
}

protected View findViewById(int id) {
  return mRootView.findViewById(id);
}

@Override
public boolean onTouch(View v, MotionEvent event) {
  // Ignoring touch events on the gray outside
  return true;
}

public boolean isShowing() {
  return mIsShowing;
}
}
```

During construction we store the reference to the main activity into the member variable mParent, to be used later.

There are a few other member variables in the class:

- mRootLayout: this is the layout we inflate that is common to all dialogs and which is used as a background.

- mRootView: the root of the content view. This is used to show and hide the dialog itself.

- mIsShowing: a variable to determine whether the dialog is showing or not.

During `setContentView`, we inflate the view for the dialog and store the reference in `mRootView`, but we do not add it to any `ViewGroup` yet. For inflation, we use the parameters of the content view of the app (`android.R.id.content`). The last parameter of the inflate method is used to determine if the system should add the view as a child of the parent or not. We pass `false`, so the view does not get added to the hierarchy. Finally we apply the custom typeface to it.

Note that `setContentView` is usually called during construction and not during show; that is the reason why the views are not added to the hierarchy at this point.

To show the dialog, we first check if it is already being shown and, if that is the case, we return and do nothing. Otherwise we set `mIsShowing` to `true` and proceed.

To properly show the dialog, we inflate the root layout and add it to the main content, then we add the root view to it. This makes the dialog the foremost item in the foreground of the view hierarchy.

We also add the class as a touch listener that does nothing to `mRootLayout`. This has the purpose of filtering out all the touch and click events in items that are behind the dialog. If we want a dialog to be dismissed when the user clicks outside its bounds, we just need to add a call to `dismiss` inside this listener.

Finally, `dismiss` first checks that the dialog is showing, and if so it removes the views from the hierarchy.

We also have utility methods such as `findViewById` and `isShowing`.

The layout for `mRootLayout` is just a gray semi-transparent overlay and its code is like this:

```xml
<?xml version="1.0" encoding="utf-8"?>
<FrameLayout
  xmlns:android="http://schemas.android.com/apk/res/android"
  android:background="#aa000000"
  android:layout_width="match_parent"
  android:layout_height="match_parent"/>
```

Note that this is already designed to make it easy to add animations to the process of showing and dismissing the dialog (discussed in the next chapter). This is particularly true when it comes to having a completely gray background independent of the content view.

The last stage in our dialog framework is to provide some utility methods in the base fragment to facilitate using our custom dialogs.

```
BaseCustomDialog mCurrentDialog;

public void showDialog (BaseCustomDialog newDialog) {
  showDialog(newDialog, false);
}

public void showDialog (BaseCustomDialog newDialog,
  boolean dismissOtherDialog) {
  if (mCurrentDialog != null && mCurrentDialog.isShowing()) {
    if (dismissOtherDialog) {
      mCurrentDialog.dismiss();
    }
    else {
      return;
    }
  }
  mCurrentDialog = newDialog;
  mCurrentDialog.show();
}

public boolean onBackPressed() {
  if (mCurrentDialog != null && mCurrentDialog.isShowing()) {
    mCurrentDialog.dismiss();
    return true;
  }
  return false;
}
```

We are going to show a dialog by calling the showDialog method on the fragment. This will store a reference to the dialog currently being displayed that can be used to determine if there is something else being shown and dismiss it if required.

By default we are going to not display a dialog if another one is already on the screen but, in the event you want to do it in your game, there is a version of showDialog that receives a boolean parameter to dismiss other dialogs, if present.

We also take care of handling the back key presses and use them to dismiss a dialog if it is being shown and return true, to indicate that the event has been consumed by the fragment.

Now that we have all the foundations, let's make a quit dialog for our game.

Quit dialog

The quit dialog has to appear when the back key is pressed while in the `MainMenuFragment`. It will display some text and two buttons to exit or continue playing.

This is a simple dialog that will help us understand how all the pieces fit into the architecture before we start creating more complex dialogs.

We will create the file `dialog_game_over.xml` under the `layouts` folder to define it. We are using a naming convention that gives all dialog layout definitions a name that starts with dialog (similar to the convention for fragments and activities).

The layout is as follows:

```xml
<?xml version="1.0" encoding="utf-8"?>
<RelativeLayout
  xmlns:android="http://schemas.android.com/apk/res/android"
  android:layout_gravity="center"
  android:background="@drawable/diablog_bg"
  android:layout_width="@dimen/dialog_width"
  android:layout_height="@dimen/dialog_height">

  <TextView
    android:layout_width="wrap_content"
    android:layout_height="wrap_content"
    android:textColor="@color/text_color"
    android:layout_marginTop="@dimen/activity_vertical_margin"
    android:layout_centerHorizontal="true"
    style="@android:style/TextAppearance.Large"
    android:text="@string/exit_confirm"/>

  <LinearLayout
    android:layout_alignParentBottom="true"
    android:layout_centerHorizontal="true"
    android:layout_marginBottom="@dimen/activity_vertical_margin"
    android:layout_width="wrap_content"
    android:layout_height="wrap_content">
    <ImageView
      style="@style/iconButton"
      android:layout_marginRight="@dimen/btn_sound_size"
      android:id="@+id/btn_resume"
      android:src="@drawable/resume"/>
```

```
      <ImageView
        style="@style/iconButton"
        android:id="@+id/btn_exit"
        android:src="@drawable/exit"/>
    </LinearLayout>
</RelativeLayout>
```

This is quite simple, but we still have a few remarks to make:

- The buttons will have the IDs `btn_exit` and `btn_resume`, and they use a transparent image we got from a free icon set.

- Both buttons use the style `iconButton` we created for the home screen, which sets the round state list background image.

- To make the buttons centered, we place them into a `LinearLayout` that is itself centered in the `RelativeLayout`. This is the easiest way to center several buttons.

- We use the drawable `dialog_bg` as background. It is a shape drawable similar to the one for the square buttons, but with different colors.

- The width and height of the dialog are extracted as dimensions. They will be the same for all dialogs. We have set them at 400x250dp.

The class that extends from `BaseCustomDialog` is quite simple as well:

```java
public class QuitDialog extends BaseCustomDialog implements View.
OnClickListener {
  private QuitDialogListener mListener;

  public QuitDialog(YassActivity activity) {
    super(activity);
    setContentView(R.layout.dialog_quit);
    findViewById(R.id.btn_exit).setOnClickListener(this);
    findViewById(R.id.btn_resume).setOnClickListener(this);
  }

  public void setListener(QuitDialogListener listener) {
    mListener = listener;
  }

  @Override
  public void onClick(View v) {
    if (v.getId() == R.id.btn_exit) {
      dismiss();
      mListener.exit();
    }
```

```
      else if (v.getId() == R.id.btn_resume) {
        dismiss();
      }
    }
  }

  public interface QuitDialogListener {
    void exit();
  }
}
```

In the constructor we set listeners to the buttons and then inside onClick we either just dismiss the dialog if resume is clicked, or dismiss the dialog and exit if exit is clicked.

This highlights the typical architecture we are going to use. The dialog has a custom listener associated, and there is a method in the listener for each particular action that can be triggered from the dialog.

 Each dialog will have a listener with methods for each particular option the dialog presents.

Using an interface instead of the fragment class from which the dialog is called allows us to decouple the functionality and invoke the dialog from other places. It is also good practice in itself.

Now, MainFragment is responsible for showing this dialog and is also the class that implements QuitDialogListener. Let's look at the code we have to change in the fragment to handle the dialog:

```
@Override
public boolean onBackPressed() {
  boolean consumed = super.onBackPressed();
  if (!consumed) {
    QuitDialog quitDialog = new QuitDialog(getYassActivity());
    quitDialog.setListener(this);
    showDialog(quitDialog);
  }
  return true;
}

@Override
public void exit() {
  getYassActivity().finish();
}
```

This is fairly simple. In the case of back pressed, we first check if the parent fragment handles the event (that is, if a dialog is being shown). If `false` is returned we create a `QuitDialog`, set this fragment to be the listener, and use the method `showDialog` of the base class to show it.

Either way the event is consumed by this fragment, so `onBackPressed` always returns `true`.

The method we have to implement because of the `QuitDialogListener` interface is `exit`, which is as simple as getting the parent `Activity` and calling `finish` in it.

Pause dialog

Let's do something a bit more complex. We are going to replace the existing Pause dialog with a custom one, and we will also add buttons to control sounds and music.

Again, we have some pieces that have to come together:

- A layout for the dialog
- A class that extends `BaseCustomDialog` to handle it
- A listener interface for the actions performed in the dialog
- Code in the `GameFragment` to handle it

Let's start with the layout. This one will have two groups of buttons, one at the bottom left for exit and resume, and one at the bottom right for the sound and music settings.

The layout is a simple RelativeLayout:

```xml
<?xml version="1.0" encoding="utf-8"?>
<RelativeLayout
  xmlns:android="http://schemas.android.com/apk/res/android"
  android:layout_gravity="center"
  android:background="@drawable/diablog_bg"
  android:layout_width="@dimen/dialog_width"
  android:layout_height="@dimen/dialog_height">

  <TextView
    android:layout_width="wrap_content"
    android:layout_height="wrap_content"
    android:textColor="@color/text_color"
    android:layout_marginTop="@dimen/activity_vertical_margin"
    android:layout_centerHorizontal="true"
    style="@android:style/TextAppearance.Large"
    android:text="@string/pause"/>

  <ImageView
    style="@style/iconButton"
    android:id="@+id/btn_resume"
    android:layout_margin="@dimen/activity_vertical_margin"
    android:src="@drawable/resume"
    android:layout_alignParentBottom="true"
    android:layout_alignParentLeft="true"/>

  <ImageView
    style="@style/iconButton"
    android:id="@+id/btn_exit"
    android:layout_alignBottom="@+id/btn_resume"
    android:src="@drawable/exit"
    android:layout_toRightOf="@+id/btn_resume"/>

  <ImageView
    style="@style/iconButton"
    android:id="@+id/btn_sound"
    android:layout_margin="@dimen/activity_vertical_margin"
    android:src="@drawable/sounds_on_no_bg"
    android:layout_alignParentBottom="true"
    android:layout_alignParentRight="true"/>
```

```
<ImageView
  style="@style/iconButton"
  android:id="@+id/btn_music"
  android:layout_alignBottom="@+id/btn_sound"
  android:src="@drawable/music_on_no_bg"
  android:layout_toLeftOf="@+id/btn_sound"/>

</RelativeLayout>
```

Each button is aligned to the left or right of another button or the dialog itself. Given how we have picked the dimensions of the dialog frame and the buttons, we can ensure that the four buttons will fit in the screen nicely. We are also sure that this dialog will look the same on all devices.

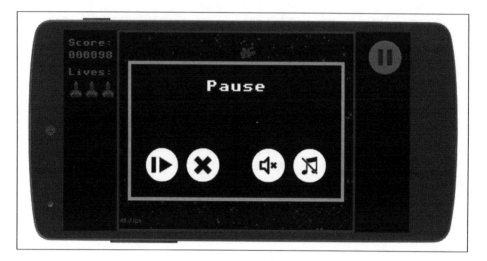

The code for the **Pause** dialog itself is a little more complex than the one for QuitDialog, mainly because it has four different actions; it also needs to check the sound and music status to decide which image to use.

Let's dig into the code:

```
public class PauseDialog extends BaseCustomDialog
  implements View.OnClickListener {
  private PauseDialogListener mListener;

  public PauseDialog(YassActivity activity) {
    super(activity);
    setContentView(R.layout.dialog_pause);
    findViewById(R.id.btn_music).setOnClickListener(this);
```

```
    findViewById(R.id.btn_sound).setOnClickListener(this);
    findViewById(R.id.btn_exit).setOnClickListener(this);
    findViewById(R.id.btn_resume).setOnClickListener(this);
    updateSoundAndMusicButtons();
  }

  public void setListener(PauseDialogListener listener) {
    mListener = listener;
  }

  @Override
  public void onClick(View v) {
    if (v.getId() == R.id.btn_sound) {
      mParent.getSoundManager().toggleSoundStatus();
      updateSoundAndMusicButtons();
    }
    else if (v.getId() == R.id.btn_music) {
      mParent.getSoundManager().toggleMusicStatus();
      updateSoundAndMusicButtons();
    }
    else if (v.getId() == R.id.btn_exit) {
      super.dismiss();
      mListener.exitGame();
    }
    else if (v.getId() == R.id.btn_resume) {
      dismiss();
    }
  }

  @Override
  public void dismiss() {
    super.dismiss();
    mListener.resumeGame();
  }

  public void updateSoundAndMusicButtons() {
    [...]
  }

  public interface PauseDialogListener {
    void exitGame();
    void resumeGame();
  }
}
```

The structure is the same as before. We set the class to be the click listener for each button, and react accordingly inside onClick. We have hidden the code of updateSoundAndMusicButtons because it is very similar to the one in MainFragment.

Note that PauseDialogListener only cares about exiting and resuming the game. Modifications to the sound status are done directly through the SoundManager, which is accessed via the parent activity.

The last part is the modifications in GameFragment; this is basically replacing the old AlertDialog.Builder with the new class, since the other functionality was already there:

```java
@Override
public boolean onBackPressed() {
  if (mGameEngine.isRunning() && !mGameEngine.isPaused()){
    pauseGameAndShowPauseDialog();
    return true;
  }
  return super.onBackPressed();
}

private void pauseGameAndShowPauseDialog() {
  if (mGameEngine.isPaused()) {
    return;
  }
  mGameEngine.pauseGame();
  PauseDialog dialog = new PauseDialog(getYassActivity());
  dialog.setListener(this);
  showDialog(dialog);
}

public void resumeGame() {
  mGameEngine.resumeGame();
}

public void exitGame() {
  mGameEngine.stopGame();
  getYassActivity().navigateBack();
}
```

Game Over dialog

Let's go for one more dialog, the **Game Over** one that will ask us to choose between playing again or exiting to the main menu. To handle the GameOverDialog, we need to add some code to the GameFragment to start a new game. We will extract the code we already have for that into a method that can be called from the fragment.

We also need access to the fragment from "somewhere" inside the GameEngine to be able to display the dialog when the event happens. We are going to do that by passing the fragment to the GameController.

The dialog itself is very similar to PauseDialog, so we will not include the layout or the code here, just the interface we have defined for it that we called GameOverDialogListener.

```
public interface GameOverDialogListener {
    void exitGame();

    void startNewGame();
}
```

Let's start with the modifications to GameFragment. This class will be the one implementing GameOverDialogListener.

As it happens, GameFragment already has a method called exitGame, which we were invoking from the PauseDialog, so the only one to implement is startNewGame.

For that we are going to extract all the logic for creating the GameEngine to a method and then we will call it from the two places where a game can start:

- The onGlobalLayout method when the fragment is created and measured

- startNewGame when the "**Play Again?**" button is clicked on the GameOver dialog

The code is like this:

```
@Override
public void startNewGame() {
  // Exit the current game
  mGameEngine.stopGame();
  // Start a new one
  prepareAndStartGame();
}


private void prepareAndStartGame() {
  GameView gameView = (GameView)
    getView().findViewById(R.id.gameView);
  mGameEngine = new GameEngine(getActivity(), gameView, 4);
  mGameEngine.setInputController(new
    CompositeInputController(getView(), getYassActivity()));
  mGameEngine.setSoundManager(
    getYassActivity().getSoundManager());
  new ParallaxBackground(mGameEngine, 20,
    R.drawable.seamless_space_0).addToGameEngine(mGameEngine, 0);
  new GameController(mGameEngine,
    GameFragment.this).addToGameEngine(mGameEngine, 2);
  new FPSCounter(mGameEngine).addToGameEngine(mGameEngine, 2);
  new ScoreGameObject(getView(),
    R.id.score_value).addToGameEngine(mGameEngine, 0);
  new LivesCounter(getView(),
    R.id.lives_value).addToGameEngine(mGameEngine, 0);
  mGameEngine.startGame();
  if (Build.VERSION.SDK_INT >= Build.VERSION_CODES.JELLY_BEAN) {
    InputManager inputManager = (InputManager)
    getActivity().getSystemService(Context.INPUT_SERVICE);
    inputManager.registerInputDeviceListener(GameFragment.this,
      null);
  }
}
```

When we start the game, we first have to stop the previous one. Even when the GameOverDialog is in front, the GameEngine is not paused or stopped. In fact we can see the parallax background moving behind the dialog. This is a nice effect and we want to keep it like that, but that means we need to stop the current game before starting a new one or we will have two engines running at the same time, which is terrible for performance and battery life.

Note that there is no creation of a Player in the initialization. This is something we removed when we made the GameController manage the lives, but it is worth highlighting this again.

On the other hand we need to be able to show a dialog from inside the GameController since the utility methods for showing dialogs are implemented on the base fragment. That is why we need to pass a parameter to the constructor and store it as a member variable.

```
public GameController(GameEngine gameEngine, GameFragment parent) {
  mParent = parent;
  [...]
}


@Override
public void onGameEvent(GameEvent gameEvent) {
  [...]
  else if (gameEvent == GameEvent.GameOver) {
    mState = GameControllerState.GameOver;
    showGameOverDialog();
  }
}

private void showGameOverDialog() {
  mParent.getActivity().runOnUiThread(new Runnable() {
    @Override
    public void run() {
      GameOverDialog quitDialog = new GameOverDialog(mParent);
      quitDialog.setListener(mParent);
      mParent.showDialog(quitDialog);
    }
  });
}
```

As part of the handling of the GameOver event, we create and show the GameOverDialog. Note that since game events arrive in the UpdateThread and the creation and display of the dialog must be run on the UIThread, we need to use a Runnable object.

Other dialogs

There are two more dialogs in the game that we have not worked with yet. Those dialogs are:

- The Notice dialog of a controller being connected.
- The Touch Control information dialog

Both dialogs are just an image, and tapping on them should dismiss them so there are neither complex layouts nor any need for custom listeners.

We will, however, work on the controller connected dialog in *Chapter 10, To the Big Screen* because we want to show it in different circumstances: on a TV rather than on a phone.

Designing for multiple screen sizes

While we have designed our GameView to scale equally in all screen sizes and aspect ratios by making use of the appropriate screen units, Android views do not work this way; however, we can follow the standard Android procedures for them.

For apps, it is recommended that you tweak the layout based on the screen size. For games it makes sense to keep the same layout across all screen sizes and only vary the size and margins of some items.

 Games should keep the same layout for all screen sizes.

As a rule of thumb, you should always use RelativeLayout to design your layouts, where every item on the screen is positioned relative to something else. This allows the layout to adapt smoothly to all screen sizes. This concept is at the core of responsive design.

To have a proper display in all screen sizes, we are going to qualify the dimensions; this is included on the Android SDK and is recommended practice.

 Qualifying dimensions is a best practice for apps and games.

Qualifying resources works by selecting different dimension specifications based on the screen sizes and applying them dynamically. Note that since Android 3.2 qualifying resources using the normal, large, and xlarge keywords has been considered obsolete (although it is the first thing you find when looking at the documentation).

There are three ways to qualify resources based on screen size:

- **Smallest width**: this takes the smallest width of the device regardless of whether it is in landscape or in portrait. This is useful when you need to guarantee the minimum size of any dimension. It does not change on screen rotation.

- **Available screen width**: the current screen width. Note that this changes when the orientation changes, and other resources, such as layouts, may change as well.

- **Available screen height**: complementary to the previous one.

The way to use these is to create a `resources` directory appending the qualifier, such as `values-sw720dp` or `values-w820dp`. Note that these qualifiers are defined in dips.

- A normal phone will have values between 320x480dp and 480x800dp since they can vary from 3.2 to over 5 inches.

- A 7" tablet will start at around 600x960dp.

- A 10" tablet will typically have at least 720x1280dp.

We are going to qualify some dimensions based on the available screen width and we are going to separate phones, small tablets, and large tablets. We will use the directories `values-w820dp` (which is already created by the wizard) and `values-w1024dp`.

Let's look at the dimensions we have defined for our game so far:

```
<resources>
  <dimen name="square_button_padding">18dp</dimen>
  <dimen name="square_button_border">6dp</dimen>
  <dimen name="round_button_padding">6dp</dimen>
  <dimen name="btn_round_size">60dp</dimen>

  <dimen name="menu_margin">8dp</dimen>
  <dimen name="game_frame_width">6dp</dimen>
  <dimen name="game_menu_width">100dp</dimen>

  <dimen name="life_size">30dp</dimen>

  <dimen name="activity_horizontal_margin">16dp</dimen>
  <dimen name="activity_vertical_margin">16dp</dimen>

  <dimen name="dialog_width">400dp</dimen>
  <dimen name="dialog_height">250dp</dimen>
</resources>
```

Note that since our `TextViews` are using the standard android styles, we have no dimensions for text sizes. If you are using your own styles for text, qualifying the text size is also advisable.

We will not modify the size of the touch targets. Because of that, we are keeping the square and round button dimensions for all sizes.

 The size of touch targets should not change in line with screen sizes.

The margins were defined by Android Studio for `w820dp` when we created the default project so we do not need to touch these either.

The margins of the game and the size of the dialogs are the dimensions we do need to update. This alone will make it look much better on 7" and 10" tablets.

Our worst case for phones is the narrowest one, when it has 480 dp width, because it leaves us with only 280 dp of game area. Even then though, this is more than 50 percent of the screen and looks OK.

On the other hand, the layout starts looking bad when the aspect ratio of the game is too wide. So for `w820dp` we will take 150 dp for the margin instead, and for `w1280dp` we will take 200 dp. You can easily play with the preview tool on Android Studio and tweak these values until you like the result. Life size should also be larger, since the space for three of them is also larger on those screens.

We will make the dialogs slightly larger on larger screens as well.

All in all, `values-w820dp` will have the following `dimens.xml`:

```
<dimen name="activity_horizontal_margin">64dp</dimen>
<dimen name="menu_margin">12dp</dimen>

<dimen name="game_menu_width">150dp</dimen>
<dimen name="life_size">45dp</dimen>

<dimen name="dialog_width">500dp</dimen>
<dimen name="dialog_height">300dp</dimen>
```

While for `values-w1080dp` we will have these:

```
<dimen name="menu_margin">16dp</dimen>

<dimen name="game_menu_width">200dp</dimen>
<dimen name="life_size">60dp</dimen>

<dimen name="dialog_width">600dp</dimen>
<dimen name="dialog_height">400dp</dimen>
```

This technique allows us to modify the UI to adapt to larger screens without touching the layout at all.

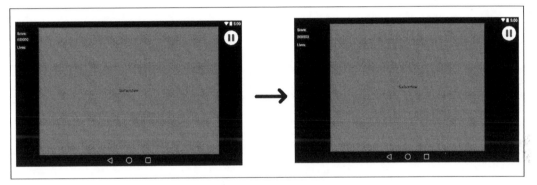

Before and after qualifying the layouts for w820dp

Summary

We have learned how to customize the UI of our game using the standard tools, drawables, and views that Android provides. This includes custom fonts, state lists drawables, shape drawables and, especially, custom dialogs that replace the default ones in a way that matches the look and feel of our game.

We also modified the game to include a score and multiple lives. We modified the UI of the GameFragment to display both of them. For that functionality. we extended the game event system to work as an event bus for all the GameObjects.

While the game is starting to look complete, it still feels a bit clunky at times and that is because we are not using any animations. In the next chapter we will learn the different techniques for animations that Android provides and will apply them.

8

The Animation Framework

Android provides a variety of powerful APIs to apply animation to UI elements. This chapter aims at providing an overview of the options available to help you decide which approach is best for your needs.

Before we start adding animations, we will refactor our code a bit to make the usage of animations easier by creating a callback on our base fragment once the layout has been completed.

Then, we will see how to define a traditional frame-by-frame animations that can be used in an `ImageView`. We will also see how to incorporate them in our `GameEngine` in the form of `AnimatedSprite`.

The core of the chapter is about the different ways to animate views. We will start talking about interpolators and their role in the Android Animation Framework. Then, we will learn about the old method called view animation and we will use it to animate some areas of the game, including how to show and hide our custom dialogs.

Then, we will talk about `ValueAnimator`, `PropertyAnimator`, and finally, `ViewPropertyAnimator`, explaining how they are different, more versatile, and complex than view animations and in which cases each of them are preferred. We will also do some examples of them.

Finally, we will animate the TextViews of the main screen using different approaches so you can check their differences and similarities.

Updating BaseFragment

Usually animations (especially `ViewPropertyAnimator`) require the layout of the views to be completed before they can be applied. We already have a method for this in the `GameFragment`, so we are going to generalize it and make it a part of the `BaseFragment`.

The method uses `ViewTreeObserver` to check when the layout of the view has been completed. The code we will add to the `BaseFragment` is like this:

```
@Override
public void onViewCreated(View view, Bundle savedInstanceState) {
  super.onViewCreated(view, savedInstanceState);
  getYassActivity().applyTypeface(view);
  final ViewTreeObserver obs = view.getViewTreeObserver();
  obs.addOnGlobalLayoutListener(new ViewTreeObserver.
OnGlobalLayoutListener() {
    @Override
    public synchronized void onGlobalLayout() {
      ViewTreeObserver viewTreeObserver =
        getView().getViewTreeObserver();
      if (viewTreeObserver.isAlive()) {
        if (Build.VERSION.SDK_INT <
          Build.VERSION_CODES.JELLY_BEAN) {
          viewTreeObserver.removeGlobalOnLayoutListener(this);
        } else {
          viewTreeObserver.removeOnGlobalLayoutListener(this);
        }
        onLayoutCompleted();
      }
    }
  });
}
```

Since we have removed a lot of code from `GameFragment`, the new version is much simpler:

```
@Override
public void onViewCreated(View view, Bundle savedInstanceState) {
  super.onViewCreated(view, savedInstanceState);
  view.findViewById(R.id.btn_play_pause).setOnClickListener(this);
}
```

```
@Override
protected void onLayoutCompleted() {
  prepareAndStartGame();
}
```

With these modifications, we can use `onLayoutCompleted` in the `MainMenuFragment` later in the chapter when we start adding animations.

AnimationDrawable

The `AnimationDrawable` is how you define a frame-by-frame animation in Android. It describes a drawable as a list of other drawable resources that are played sequentially to create an animation. This is an animation in the most traditional sense: a sequence of independent images, played one after another.

We can define the frames of an animation in code using the `AnimationDrawable` class, but it is much easier to use XML. This file lists the frames that compose the animation and their duration. The XML is composed by a root node of the `<animation-list>` type and a series of child nodes of the `<item>` type that define a frame using a drawable resource and the frame duration:

```
<?xml version="1.0" encoding="utf-8"?>
<animation-list xmlns:android="http://schemas.android.com/apk/res/
android"
  android:oneshot=["true" | "false"] >
  <item
    android:drawable="@[package:]drawable/drawable_resource_name"
    android:duration="integer" />
</animation-list>
```

This XML file belongs to the `res/drawable/` directory of your Android project, because it is considered a drawable.

 The `AnimationDrawable` resources are placed in the `drawable` directory.

Let's see this with an example. We are going to make a simple animation that makes the lights of our spaceship blink. For this, we will use four frames:

- Lights off (normal spaceship)
- Left light on
- Lights off (again)
- Right light on

Note that we can reuse the same drawable for different frames, allowing us to save some space.

The four frames of our spaceship animation

The definition of the spaceship with blinking lights is like this:

```xml
<?xml version="1.0" encoding="utf-8"?>
<animation-list xmlns:android="http://schemas.android.com/apk/res/
android"
  android:oneshot="false">
  <item android:drawable="@drawable/ship_2"
    android:duration="600" />
  <item android:drawable="@drawable/ship_1"
    android:duration="400" />
  <item android:drawable="@drawable/ship_2"
    android:duration="600" />
  <item android:drawable="@drawable/ship_3"
    android:duration="400" />
</animation-list>
```

We make the light stay on only for 400 milliseconds and then no lights for 600 milliseconds. Then, we go for the other light.

We have defined `oneShot` to `false`. This makes the animation repeat from the beginning once the last frame has finished. If you want to have animations that are played only once, you should set `oneShot` to `true`.

To test this, we can add an `ImageView` to the layout of the main menu and set the `AnimationDrawable` for it:

```xml
<ImageView
  android:id="@+id/ship_animated"
  android:layout_width="50dp"
  android:layout_height="50dp"
  android:layout_centerHorizontal="true"
  android:src="@drawable/ship_animated"
  android:layout_below="@+id/btn_start"
/>
```

If we try this, we will see that the animation does not work. `AnimationDrawable` is not auto played. Also, it's important to note that the `start` method of the `AnimationDrawable` cannot be called inside the activity's `onCreate` method, because the `AnimationDrawable` is not yet fully attached to the window. We will have to wait until the window is fully created, which will be notified by the `onWindowFocusChanged` method in the activity.

 AnimationDrawables are not played automatically, we have to start them in code.

However, the animation can be started from the `onViewCreated` method of the fragment. Since we already have the `onLayoutCompleted` method that is called a bit later, we will use this one instead for consistency:

```
@Override
protected void onLayoutCompleted() {
    ImageView iv = (ImageView)
        getView().findViewById(R.id.ship_animated);
    ((AnimationDrawable)iv.getDrawable()).start();
}
```

But this is not enough for us: `AnimationDrawable` defines a frame-by-frame animation that can be used in `ImageView`. What is really interesting is to be able to use this same XML definition to describe animated sprites. For this, we are going to create a new class that extends from `Sprite` and takes care of the animation.

Animated sprites

To create animated sprites, we need to take care of the specifics of `AnimationDrawable`. Since we already have all the code that draws a `Sprite` on the screen, the new `AnimatedSprite` class will only have to take care of counting the time to select which bitmap should be drawn.

Note that this will only work for `AnimationDrawable` when all the frames are defined as bitmaps, other XML resources such as shapes are not supported by our `Sprite` base class.

Let's look at the code of `AnimatedSprite`:

```java
public abstract class AnimatedSprite extends Sprite {

  private final AnimationDrawable mAnimationDrawable;
  private int mTotalTime;
  private long mCurrentTime;

  public AnimatedSprite(GameEngine gameEngine,
    int drawableRes, BodyType bodyType) {
    super(gameEngine, drawableRes, bodyType);
    // Now, the drawable must be an animation drawable
    mAnimationDrawable = (AnimationDrawable) mSpriteDrawable;
    // Calculate the total time of the animation
    mTotalTime = 0;
    for (int i=0; i<mAnimationDrawable.getNumberOfFrames(); i++) {
      mTotalTime += mAnimationDrawable.getDuration(i);
    }
  }

  @Override
  protected Bitmap obtainDefaultBitmap() {
    AnimationDrawable ad = (AnimationDrawable) mSpriteDrawable;
    return ((BitmapDrawable) ad.getFrame(0)).getBitmap();
  }

  @Override
  public void onUpdate(long elapsedMillis,
    GameEngine gameEngine) {
    mCurrentTime += elapsedMillis;
    if (mCurrentTime > mTotalTime) {
      if (mAnimationDrawable.isOneShot()) {
        return;
      }
      else {
        mCurrentTime = mCurrentTime % mTotalTime;
      }
    }
    long animationElapsedTime = 0;
    for (int i=0; i<mAnimationDrawable.getNumberOfFrames(); i++) {
      animationElapsedTime += mAnimationDrawable.getDuration(i);
      if (animationElapsedTime > mCurrentTime) {
        mBitmap = ((BitmapDrawable)
          mAnimationDrawable.getFrame(i)).getBitmap();
        break;
```

```
                }
            }
        }
    }
```

We have created a new method named `obtainDefaultBitmap` that is called from the constructor. For normal sprites, this method just returns the bitmap. In the case of `AnimatedDrawable`, we initialize it to the first frame.

The constructor has the same parameters as the normal sprite, but if the drawable resource is not an `AnimationDrawable`, a `ClassCastException` will be thrown. Error handling was not included to make the code easier to follow.

Another thing that is done in the constructor is the calculation of the total time of the `AnimationDrawable` by adding the duration of all the frames. We will need this value each time we run `onUpdate`, so we should get it in advance.

During `onUpdate`, we add the elapsed milliseconds to the total time, then we check whether the total time the `AnimatedSprite` has been running is longer than the total time of the animation. If this is the case, we check whether `AnimationDrawable` is set to `oneShot` or not. If it is `oneShot`, we do nothing, since the last image has already been set. If the animation is to be repeated, we just make `mCurrentTime` get back into the interval by applying the module operator.

Once we know that the current time will be in the animation time range, we iterate over the frames, checking which one is the current frame and setting the bitmap in this frame to the `mImage` member variable, which is the one used by the base class to draw on the canvas.

Drawing the bitmap on the canvas is already done by the parent `Sprite` class.

Note that all the classes that extend from `AnimatedSprite` must call the super method while overriding `onUpdate`. Otherwise, the code that updates the image will not be executed.

 When extending `AnimatedSprite`, don't forget to call super while overriding `onUpdate`.

Now, let's animate our in-game spaceship.

We just need to update `Player` to extend from `AnimatedSprite`, change the image resource we pass to the constructor, and remember to call the super method in `onUpdate`:

```
public class Player extends AnimatedSprite {

  public Player(GameEngine gameEngine) {
    super(gameEngine, R.drawable.ship_animated,
      BodyType.Circular);
    [...]
  }

  @Override
  public void onUpdate(long elapsedMillis, GameEngine gameEngine)
    {
    super.onUpdate(elapsedMillis, gameEngine);
    [...]
  }
}
```

We have a spaceship with blinking lights!

Animating views

The Android framework provides two animation systems:

- View animation
- Property animation

View animation has been present since the first version of Android, while property animation was introduced in Android 3.0. The latter is recommended, because it is more consistent and offers more features.

The view animation system can only be used to animate views. It is also constrained in that it only exposes a few aspects of a `View` object to animate, such as the scaling and rotation of a view but not the background color for instance.

Another disadvantage of the view animation system is that it only modifies where the view is drawn and not the actual view itself. For example, if you animate a button to move across the screen, the button will draw correctly, but the actual location considered for a click on the button does not change and this can be problematic.

View animation modifies the place where the view is drawn, not the view itself.

On the other hand, the property animation system allows us to animate any property of any object (views and nonviews) and the object itself is actually modified.

The view animation system, however, is easier to use and requires less code. If view animation accomplishes everything you need to do, there is no need to use the property animation system.

 View animation is simpler. Property animation is more advanced.

While using `ViewPropertyAnimation`, the animation only receives a parameter of the final value, because it is animated from the current one. This may require some initialization.

All in all, it is good to know both the animation systems and apply the one that fits best for each case.

Regardless of the system, animations are usually easy to implement in Android, but it takes a lot of work to tweak the parameters to make the animation feel right. An animation that does not feel good is worse than no animation at all, but an animation that is right makes the game feel much nicer and smoother. Be prepared to pay a lot of attention to the detail while working on them.

 Tweaking animations requires a lot of time.

As a rule of thumb, animations should be long enough to be noticeable (otherwise, adding them will be pointless), but not so long that they make the game feel slow. This means that a transition animation should have a duration between 300 and 400 milliseconds.

XML versus code

Both view animation and property animation (as almost any resource) can be defined in code or XML. Unless you require some value that could only be obtained in runtime it is better to use XML because all the files are external to the code and the animation can be modified without touching the Java source.

Having the animations defined as a resource also allows us to use them at different places in the code and be sure that any change in the animation will affect all the places where it is used. If we define the animations in code we will have to check each place where the animation is built or rely on utility classes, which are not nice to handle.

There is a middle ground where you can define the animation in XML and then read it and modify some of the parameters using code. This approach is quite powerful; it gives us control over the animation while keeping most of its definition outside the code.

Interpolators

The animation system plays an animation between a start time and end time. Every frame of the animation is displayed at a specific time between the start and end. By default it follows a linear function, but this can be changed. In games, this technique is usually known as **tweening**, but in Android it is called **interpolation**. Let's see how it works.

[Interpolators are the equivalent of tweening animations in general game jargon.]

Animations use a time index to calculate the values. This time index is basically a normalized time, a value between 0.0 and 1.0.

In the simplest case, the value of the time index is taken to calculate the transformation of the object. In the case of a transformation, 0.0 corresponds to the start position, 1.0 to the end position, and 0.5 to halfway between the start and the end. This is exactly what the linear interpolator does.

In general, we can transform the time index into another value by using a mathematical function. This is exactly what an interpolator does.

A time interpolator is essentially a function that takes a value between 0.0 and 1.0 and transforms it into another value that is used to calculate the animation as the time index.

Android provides a set of default interpolators that cover the basic configurations and should be enough for most cases. In case you need something very special, you can create your own interpolator that just needs to implement a one-method interface.

We are not going to enter the detail of the mathematical functions, but just an overview of what they look like. The interpolators defined in Android are:

- **Linear**: a simple linear function.
- **Cycle**: the animation follows a sinusoidal curve using time index 1 as a full circumference.
- **Bounce**: the animation bounces back a few times when it reaches the end.
- **Decelerate**: the animation slows towards the end.
- **Accelerate**: the animation goes faster towards the end.
- **AccelerateDecelerate**: The animation accelerates in the beginning and slows down at the end.
- **Overshoot**: The animation goes over the end and then goes back.
- **Anticipate**: Before starting, the animation goes back to get an impulse. This is the opposite of overshoot.
- **AnticipateOvershoot**: This combines both overshoot and anticipate.

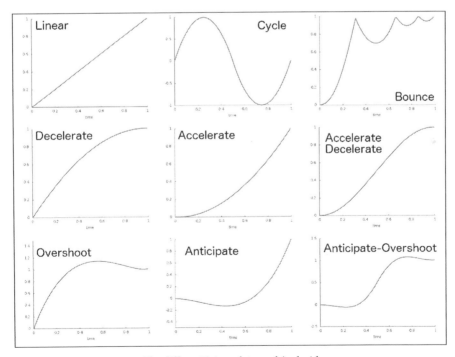

The different interpolators of Android

There are a few more interpolators added to API level 21 for the animations that follow the Material Design guidelines. We do not really need them for a game. We want funny, good looking animations; we do not care if they do not look real, which is a core characteristic of Material Design.

Interpolators are a common concept that can be applied to all the ways of animating views we are going to work with.

View animation

The original and simpler way of animating views in Android is to use view animation. This creates an `Animation` object either by loading it from XML or programmatically, which is then applied to the view. They are relatively easy to set up and offer enough capabilities to meet most needs.

There are some important details about view animations. They are as follows:

- When we animate a view, all the children of the view are affected as well.

- Regardless of how your animation may move or resize, the bounds of the view that is animated will not automatically adjust to accommodate it. Even so, the animation will still be drawn beyond the bounds of its view and will not be clipped. However, clipping will occur if the animation exceeds the bounds of the parent view. This can be fixed by setting `clipChildren` to false in the parent view.

- The views will return to their original state once the animation is completed. If you plan to use this type of animations to reveal or hide a view, you must be sure of setting its visibility to the desired state before the animation starts and after the animation ends. This can be easily achieved using a listener.

- The bounds of the view are not changed during animation. This implies that the touch area is the same regardless of the place where the view is drawn. This is one of the most relevant reasons why we would want to use property animations instead.

The files that define the animations must be placed under the `res/animation` folder and their definition is as follows:

```xml
<?xml version="1.0" encoding="utf-8"?>
<set xmlns:android="http://schemas.android.com/apk/res/android"
  android:interpolator="@[package:]anim/interpolator_resource"
  android:shareInterpolator=["true" | "false"] >
  <alpha
    android:fromAlpha="float"
```

```
        android:toAlpha="float" />
    <scale
        android:fromXScale="float"
        android:toXScale="float"
        android:fromYScale="float"
        android:toYScale="float"
        android:pivotX="float"
        android:pivotY="float" />
    <translate
        android:fromXDelta="float"
        android:toXDelta="float"
        android:fromYDelta="float"
        android:toYDelta="float" />
    <rotate
        android:fromDegrees="float"
        android:toDegrees="float"
        android:pivotX="float"
        android:pivotY="float" />
    <set>
        ...
    </set>
</set>
```

Some of the attributes defined in the format are positions. They can be defined in three different ways:

- Pixels relative to the default position (for example 50)
- Percentage relative to the View itself (for example 50%)
- Percentage relative to the parent View (for example 50%p)

The usage of pixels is discouraged, the percentage relative to the view or the parent view is normally the way to go.

A set is nothing more than a way to group other properties. Most of the times, you'll use only one, but they can be nested to define more complex animations.

The set can have an interpolator, which will be applied to all the children if the `shareInterpolator` attribute is set to true. This allows all the animations to flow together smoothly. This is how it is used most of the time, but it is possible for each component to have its own interpolator.

The concepts are pretty much the same ones we already used when we used the transformation matrix on the `DrawThread`. We can scale, translate, rotate, and modify the alpha.

Alpha is the simplest one; it just has initial and final values.

Scale receives the initial and final scale on both axes and also the pivot point. This pivot point is the position from where the scale will be applied. It is usually provided as a percentage. The most common configuration is to put 50 percent on both axes, so it grows from the center of the view. But other configurations can work nicely like 0 percent on both, which will make it grow from the top left.

Translate receives the deltas of origin and the destination on both axes. They are also positions, and can be defined with references of the percentage to the parent view.

Rotate receives the from and to degrees and also the pivot point from which the rotation is applied. Note that this allows you to rotate a view from a position relative to the parent view or even outside the view itself, which may come in handy.

There are a few attributes that are common to all the tags. They are as follows:

- `startOffset`: allows us to define an offset so the animation does not start straight away.
- `duration`: defines how long the animation is going to last.
- `repeatCount`: allows us to make the animation repeat, either infinitely or a specific number of times.
- `repeatMode`: only used while repeating. It allows us to reverse the animation instead of repeating it from the beginning.
- `interpolator`: The interpolator to use (in case `shareInterpolator` is set to false).

There is a known issue of `repeatCount` not working for sets when defined in XML, although it does work for individual animations. You can, however, set the `repeatCount` in code after loading the animation and this works too.

 `repeatCount` will not work when defined for sets in XML.

The way a repeating animation interacts with `startOffset` could be counter intuitive. The offset is considered a part of the animation and it is therefore repeated. We will see an example of that later in this chapter.

Again, as happened with the transformation matrix, the order of the definition in the animation is very important. The result of first translate and then rotate is not the same as when we first rotate and then translate. This should be clear to everyone by now.

Animating dialogs

We are going to animate the show and hide of dialogs in the game using view animations.

Although we are not using the platform's default animations for the dialogs, it is advised to be consistent in our game and to ensure all the dialogs have the same animations. This is why the changes are to be made in a single place, so all the dialogs will use the same animations.

Let's see the modifications we have to make to `BaseCustomDialog` to add animations:

```
public void show() {
  if (mIsShowing) {
    return;
  }
  mIsHiding = true;
  [...]
  startShowAnimation();
}

private void startShowAnimation() {
  Animation dialogIn = AnimationUtils.loadAnimation(mParent,
    R.animator.dialog_in);
  mRootView.startAnimation(dialogIn);
}

public void dismiss() {
  if (!mIsShowing) {
    return;
  }

  if (mIsHiding) {
    return;
  }
  mIsHiding = true;
  startHideAnimation();
}

private void startHideAnimation() {
  Animation dialogOut = AnimationUtils.loadAnimation(mParent,
    R.animator.dialog_out);
  dialogOut.setAnimationListener(this);
  mRootView.startAnimation(dialogOut);
```

```
    }

    @Override
    public void onAnimationEnd(Animation paramAnimation) {
      hideViews();
      mIsShowing = false;
      onDismissed();
    }

    protected void onDismissed() {
    }
```

We have a `startShowAnimation` method that is called at the end of `show`, and a `startHideAnimation` method that is called at the end of `dismiss`.

Both methods are quite simple; they load an `Animation` using `AnimationUtils` and then apply it to `mRootView` using the `startAnimation` method.

However, there are some details that need comments:

- We are adding views to the content just before starting the animation and removing them when the animation is done, so there is no need to change their visibility. In other cases (when the views remain in the hierarchy after the animation finishes), you may need to update the visibility of the view in the `AnimationListener`.

- The `BaseCustomDialog` implements `AnimationListener`, and we use it to detect when the hiding animation has finished to remove the views at that moment.

- We have a new method named `onDismissed`. This is called once the animation has ended. Until now, the dismissal of the dialog was an instantaneous operation. This is no longer the case. The actions that were done when dismissing should be moved to `onDismiss`.

- We are using two variables to determine the status of the dialog: `mIsShowing` and `mIsHiding`. The dialog is considered to be showing from the moment the show animation begins till the dismiss animation is completed. However we should not dismiss a dialog that is already being dismissed, so there is a need for `mIsHiding` to prevent this case.

The animations themselves are defined in XML, so they are independent of the fact that the dialogs are animated. We are going to see several animations for dialogs to get a deeper understanding of the framework and its possibilities. We will work with pairs of animations that are complementary:

- Grow from center / shrink to center
- Enter from top / exit through top

To make the dialog grow and shrink from and to the center, we just need to use scale.

The code to grow from the center is like this:

```xml
<?xml version="1.0" encoding="UTF-8"?>
<set xmlns:android="http://schemas.android.com/apk/res/android"
  android:interpolator="@android:anim/decelerate_interpolator"
  >
  <scale
    android:fromXScale="0.5"
    android:toXScale="1.0"
    android:fromYScale="0.5"
    android:toYScale="1.0"
    android:pivotX="50%"
    android:pivotY="50%"
    android:duration="400"
  />
</set>
```

The definition to shrink to the center is as follows:

```xml
<?xml version="1.0" encoding="UTF-8"?>
<set xmlns:android="http://schemas.android.com/apk/res/android"
  android:interpolator="@android:anim/accelerate_interpolator">
  <scale
    android:fromXScale="1.0"
    android:toXScale="0.5"
    android:fromYScale="1.0"
    android:toYScale="0.5"
    android:pivotX="50%"
    android:pivotY="50%"
    android:duration="400"
  />
</set>
```

As you can see, both animations are similar but the parameters of `from` and `to` are reversed.

Note that we start on a scale of 0.5 instead of 0. The animation of a smaller size is not really visible, mostly because of the decelerate interpolator, but you can set it to 0 if you want.

We also have the pivot point set to 50% on both axes. This is what makes it scale from the center.

An interesting variant is to apply the scale only on one axis. It feels like the view is unfolded from the middle of the screen. This is left as an exercise for the reader.

The other pair of animations use translation instead of scale. We will make the dialog enter and exit from the top, but it is really easy to change the code to make it use any side of the screen.

This is the animation's definition to enter from the top:

```xml
<?xml version="1.0" encoding="utf-8"?>
<set xmlns:android="http://schemas.android.com/apk/res/android"
  android:interpolator="@android:anim/overshoot_interpolator">
  <translate
    android:fromYDelta="-100%p"
    android:toYDelta="0%p"
    android:duration="500" />
</set>
```

This the code to exit through the top:

```xml
<?xml version="1.0" encoding="utf-8"?>
<set xmlns:android="http://schemas.android.com/apk/res/android"
    android:interpolator="@android:anim/anticipate_interpolator">
  <translate
    android:fromYDelta="0%p"
    android:toYDelta="-100%p"
    android:duration="500" />
</set>
```

Note that the y delta is using the percentage relative to the parent view. The entering animation starts at -100 percent of the size of the parent from the top (one whole screen up). For the exiting animation, we only have to reverse the deltas.

Finally, there is another important decision to make about these animations, that is which interpolators to use. The most common configurations are:

- Linear on both: simple, but a bit boring
- Decelerate to show / accelerate to hide: this feels smoother than the linear, and gives a more professional look
- Overshoot to show / anticipate to hide: since the view goes over the end position and then goes back, it makes the animation feel more playful

You can use any combination of the animations and interpolators or create your own look and feel. Modify the code and try it until you are happy with the result. Just by changing the interpolator the animation feels different.

Delaying the action in the dialogs to onDismissed

Because the animations take some time, the actions that were performed on the dialog when the user clicked on a button should be delayed until the animation is finished.

To do this, we are going to store the id of the view that was clicked, and then check on it in the `onDismissed` method to trigger the appropriate action. This is a change we have to make to each dialog.

Let's start by looking at the changes we have to make to `GameOverDialog`:

```
@Override
public void onClick(View v) {
  mSelectedId = v.getId();
  dismiss();
}

@Override
protected void onDismissed() {
  if (mSelectedId == R.id.btn_exit) {
    mListener.exitGame();
  }
  else if (mSelectedId == R.id.btn_resume) {
    mListener.startNewGame();
  }
}
```

Simple, right? The code is almost the same as before but moved from `onClick` to `onDismiss`, so it is executed later.

Next, `PauseDialog` is similar:

```java
@Override
public void onClick(View v) {
  [...]
  else if (v.getId() == R.id.btn_exit) {
    mSelectedId = v.getId();
    super.dismiss();
  }
  else if (v.getId() == R.id.btn_resume) {
    mSelectedId = v.getId();
    super.dismiss();
  }
}

@Override
protected void onDismissed () {
  if (mSelectedId == R.id.btn_exit) {
    mListener.exitGame();
  }
  else if (mSelectedId == R.id.btn_resume) {
    mListener.resumeGame();
  }
}

@Override
public void dismiss() {
  super.dismiss();
  mSelectedId = R.id.btn_resume;
}
```

This case is a bit more complex, since there are buttons that still initiate some action (music and sound), but do not dismiss the dialog. We also add a default selected action (resume in this case) to be used when the user dismisses the dialog.

Note that both actions inside `onClick` call the `super.dismiss()` method explicitly to avoid being overwritten by the default action.

Finally, for `QuitDialog`, we have the same idea again:

```
@Override
public void onClick(View v) {
  mSelectedId = v.getId();
  dismiss();
}

@Override
protected void onDismissed() {
  if (mSelectedId == R.id.btn_exit) {
    mListener.exit();
  }
}
```

This is it. The dialogs are animated and the actions are performed after the dialog is dismissed.

Pulsating buttons

Let's add one more animation using animated views. We will animate the button to start the game, making it grow and shrink in both axes in a loop, simulating the button pulsating. The idea is that it is a button that "wants to be clicked".

For this, we are going to use a composite animation. The animation will scale the button on the X and Y axis, but the animations will be different. The X will grow for the complete duration of the animation, while the Y will only do it in the second part. Then we make the animations repeat indefinitely in reverse mode.

The code for the animation in XML is like this:

```
<?xml version="1.0" encoding="utf-8"?>
<set xmlns:android="http://schemas.android.com/apk/res/android"
  android:interpolator=
    "@android:anim/accelerate_decelerate_interpolator">
  <scale
    android:fromXScale="1.0"
    android:toXScale="1.2"
    android:fromYScale="1.0"
    android:toYScale="1.0"
    android:pivotX="50%"
    android:pivotY="50%"
    android:duration="800"
    android:repeatMode="reverse"
```

```
        android:repeatCount="infinite"
    />
    <scale
        android:fromXScale="1.0"
        android:toXScale="1.0"
        android:fromYScale="1.0"
        android:toYScale="1.1"
        android:pivotX="50%"
        android:pivotY="50%"
        android:startOffset="300"
        android:duration="500"
        android:repeatMode="reverse"
        android:repeatCount="infinite"
    />
</set>
```

As we mentioned in a previous section, the `repeatCount` attribute does not work for the `<set>` tag. We could do it in code, but it is simpler to just add it to each of the animations since we only have two. This is why `repeatCount` and `repeatMode` are set on both `<scale>` tags.

Note that the `infinite` keyword is accepted as `repeatCount`. We do not need to use awkward constants for it.

The way repeat interacts with `startOffset` is sometimes counter-intuitive. The value of `startOffset` will be applied to each iteration. In this particular case, this behavior comes in handy because we want the animation on the *y* axis to start later than the one on *x* during every iteration. But if we were to make a repeating animation that has a delayed start, it would not work as expected.

 The `startOffset` is part of the animation and it will be included in each repetition.

For a repeating animation with a delayed start, the best solution is to use a different method to add an initial delay. Android provides us with `Timer`/`TimerTask` and the possibility to post a `Runnable` with a delay for this.

Setting the animation to the view is very simple, just a couple lines of code in
`MainMenuFragment`; one to load the `Animation` and one to start it:

```
@Override
public void onViewCreated(View view, Bundle savedInstanceState) {
  super.onViewCreated(view, savedInstanceState);
  […]
  Animation pulseAnimation = AnimationUtils.
loadAnimation(getActivity(), R.animator.button_pulse);
  view.findViewById(R.id.btn_start).startAnimation(
    pulseAnimation);
}
```

Feel free to play with the parameters, even make the two components have different
times, so they offset each other. The values we have in the example are chosen to
make it very noticeable; you can make it more subtle using a smaller final scale and/
or a longer period, which I recommend.

Property animation

The second way to manage animations in Android was introduced in Android 3.0
(API level 11). It is designed in a very generic way, so it can handle animations on
any property of any object. The system is extensible and lets you animate properties
of custom types as well.

There are many ways to use property animations. The simplest one is to use
`ValueAnimator`. This is as easy as defining an animation that goes from one value to
another, has a duration, and optionally an interpolator. Then you add a listener that
is invoked each time there is a new value, and finally you start the animation.

This code will create a `ValueAnimator` that animates a float from 0 to 42 along
1,000 milliseconds:

```
ValueAnimator animation = ValueAnimator.ofFloat(0f, 42f);
animation.setDuration(1000);
animation.addUpdateListener(new ValueAnimator.AnimatorUpdateListener()
{
  @Override
  public void onAnimationUpdate(ValueAnimator animation) {
    Float currentValue = (Float) animation.getAnimatedValue();
    // Do something with the value
  }
});
animation.start();
```

Value animators do not modify values per se, but you have control over what you want to do with the animated value inside the `onAnimationUpdate` method of the listener.

We are not going to use any `ValueAnimator` in YASS, but they can be really useful for other types of games. We can use them whenever we want a smooth transition of a variable from one value to the next. Some cases where value animators are interesting for games are:

- Adding bonus scores after finishing a level
- Adding XP points after finishing a quest / defeating an opponent
- Decreasing HP points after a hit / increasing after a recovery potion

In general, value animators can be used any time we have a value that we want to animate smoothly. You can even use a custom progress bar to display the value and just update it on the callback of the `ValueAnimator`.

You can use a `PropertyAnimator` instead of a `ValueAnimator` if you want Android to modify the value of the property in the object directly. For this particular case of views, we have a special class called `ViewPropertyAnimator` that is easier to use and read than `PropertyAnimator` and is designed specially to animate views.

ViewPropertyAnimator

This animation technique provides a simple way to animate several properties of a view in parallel using a single underlying `Animator` object. It also modifies the actual values of the view's properties.

One drawback of using `ViewPropertyAnimator` is that it is more limited. We can only animate the basic attributes of the view (position, scale, alpha, and rotation), while with `PropertyAnimation` we can animate virtually anything.

It is worth mentioning in advance that this animation technique only requires final values for an animation. It is meant to start the animation from the current values of the view. This means that sometimes, you may need to initialize the view to an initial position.

Because this type of animation works as a modification of the values of the view, animated views stay in their final state once the animation is completed. This makes them very useful for puzzle-like or board games.

Views animated with `ViewPropertyAnimator` stay at the end position after the animation has ended.

`ViewPropertyAnimator` uses two concepts to obtain the coordinates where the view is drawn: position and translation. You can animate the position or you can animate the translation. If you are going to use only one of them, it does not make much of a difference. Just remember that `translateX` will have the origin (also known as [0,0]) at the current position of the view and that a view will be drawn at the vectorial sum of its position and translation.

Moving a spaceship around

To see the power of `ViewPropertyAnimator`, we are going to add another animation to the main menu. We are going to take the spaceship we used to display the frame-by-frame animation and then make it move around the screen randomly.

I believe this animation is too much and makes the main menu feel too crowded, so I recommend removing it in the final game, but it is nevertheless a great example of how the framework works.

Because each animation starts from the previous position of the view, the resulting effect is something you cannot achieve with the old framework.

Let's look at the code:

```
@Override
protected void onLayoutCompleted() {
  [...]
  animateShip();
}

private void animateShip() {
  View iv = getView().findViewById(R.id.ship_animated);
  // Get a random position on the screen
  Random r = new Random();
  int targetX = r.nextInt(getView().getWidth());
  int targetY = r.nextInt(getView().getHeight());
  // Animate
  iv.animate()
    .x(targetX)
    .y(targetY)
    .setDuration(500)
    .setInterpolator(new AccelerateDecelerateInterpolator())
```

```
        .setListener(new Animator.AnimatorListener() {
          @Override
          public void onAnimationEnd(Animator animation) {
            animateShip();
          }

          @Override
          public void onAnimationStart(Animator animation) {}

          @Override
          public void onAnimationCancel(Animator animation) {}

          @Override
          public void onAnimationRepeat(Animator animation) {}
        });
    }
```

We are invoking `animateShip` once the layout is completed and then we will do it again each time the animation is completed.

To animate the ship, we get the view we want to animate and then select a random position on the screen using `Random` and the dimensions of the root view of the fragment.

We call `animate` on the view. This returns an object of `ViewPropertyAnimator` type. We can configure the animation using different methods on this object and each of them will return the object again, so they can be chained in a very easy to read code.

We are configuring the animation by setting the target *x* and *y* positions (we are not touching the translation at all), selecting the duration, and setting an interpolator of `AccelerateDecelerateInterpolator` type. We are also setting a listener, so we are notified when the animation ends and we can call `animateShip` to create another one. Note that `AnimationListener` is an interface and we must implement all its methods even if we don't use them.

Finally, we could call `start` to make the animation start immediately, but it is not necessary.

We are always using the same animation duration, so sometimes the ship will move much faster than others. We could make it have a constant speed by using the distance between the origin and the destination points to calculate the duration of the animation.

It is important to check at which position in the layout the `ImageView` was added, since the z-index is provided by the order. I recommend you place the ship straight after the background image, so it goes behind the titles and buttons.

Animating the main menu

To complete the chapter, we are going to animate the game title and subtitle. To give a comparison of the different possibilities Android offers to make animations, we will create each of them in three different ways: view animation in XML, `ViewPropertyAnimation` in code, and object animator in XML.

First, we will animate the main title to make it enter from the left of the screen to its normal position at the center. We will use a bounce interpolator to make it look fun.

As good practice, we will externalize the start offset and the duration of the animation as integers using a file named `integers.xml` under the `res/values` folder:

```
<integer name="tittle_start_offset">400</integer>
<integer name="tittle_duration">1600</integer>
```

The animation will not start straight away to give the player some time to actually notice the screen. We have a long duration, because the bounce interpolator does not look good otherwise.

The first version using view animation in XML is defined like this:

```
<?xml version="1.0" encoding="utf-8"?>
<set xmlns:android="http://schemas.android.com/apk/res/android"
  android:interpolator="@android:anim/bounce_interpolator">
  <translate
    android:startOffset="@integer/tittle_start_offset"
    android:fromXDelta="-100%p"
    android:toXDelta="0%p"
    android:repeatCount="0"
    android:duration="@integer/tittle_duration" />
</set>
```

We use percentage related to the parent view as the original delta to put the view completely out of the screen. The -100%p means 100 percent of the parent width to the left.

The code to load the animation and start it is to be placed inside onLayoutCompleted and it is very simple:

```
Animation titleAnimation =
  AnimationUtils.loadAnimation(getActivity(),
  R.animator.title_enter);
title.startAnimation(titleAnimation);
```

Note that the animation is considered to be started as soon as we call startAnimation. This means that the translation is also animated during the start offset and is set to the initial value of the animation.

 The start offset is considered a part of the animation for view animators and the value is set to the initial one while the animation is waiting to start.

Let's compare this definition with the one for ViewPropertyAnimator in code:

```
View title = getView().findViewById(R.id.main_title);
title.setTranslationX(-getView().getWidth());

int duration =
  getResources().getInteger(R.integer.tittle_duration);
int startOffset =
  getResources().getInteger(R.integer.subtitle_start_offset);

title.animate()
  .translationX(0)
  .setStartDelay(startOffset)
  .setDuration(duration)
  .setInterpolator(new BounceInterpolator())
  .start();
```

Because the duration and offset are defined as integers, we need to obtain them before running the animation.

Since the view is initially placed at the location we want it to finish, we are going to animate the translation and keep the position as it is.

Note that since ViewPropertyAnimator only receives the final value as a parameter, we need to set it to a default initial position outside the screen. To do this, we use the setTranslationX method of the view. By doing this, the final value of the translation is 0.

Finally, we set the interpolator and call `start`. The result is the same as with the previous method but, as you have seen, there are a few significant differences in the procedure.

The third approach is to define this same animation as an object animator in XML and then load and use it in code. The XML definition is as follows:

```
<set xmlns:android="http://schemas.android.com/apk/res/android"
    android:interpolator="@android:anim/bounce_interpolator">
    <objectAnimator
        android:interpolator="@android:anim/bounce_interpolator"
        android:propertyName="translationX"
        android:valueTo="0"
        android:startOffset="@integer/tittle_start_offset"
        android:duration="@integer/tittle_duration" />
</set>
```

The `<objectAnimator>` tag is generic in itself and uses `propertyName` as the name of the property to modify using reflection.

Once the animation is defined, we have to load and start it:

```
title.setTranslationX(-title.getX()-title.getWidth());

AnimatorSet set = (AnimatorSet)
    AnimatorInflater.loadAnimator(getActivity(),
    R.animator.title_enter_property);
set.setTarget(title);
set.start();
```

As happened in the previous example, we need to make an initialization of the translation. Although we could set a `valueFrom` in XML, we do not know the size of the screen when we define XML and we cannot use the values referenced to the parent view, so we have to initialize it in code.

All in all, the three versions perform the same animation conceptually, but the way they are defined is slightly different.

Let's see another example. For the subtitle, we are going to animate the alpha to make it appear after the animation of the title is finished. To make this animation run after the previous one, we can use start delay or we can set a listener to the previous animation and start it when this animation finishes.

Using a listener is more precise, but adding delay is way simpler so we will go for this. As we did for the title animation, we will define some integers for the duration and the start offset, which in this case is the sum of the duration and the start offset of the title animation:

```
<integer name="subtitle_start_offset">2000</integer>
<integer name="subtitle_duration">600</integer>
```

The XML for doing it using view animation is like this:

```
<set xmlns:android="http://schemas.android.com/apk/res/android">
  <alpha android:fromAlpha="0.0"
    android:toAlpha="1.0"
    android:startOffset="@integer/subtitle_start_offset"
    android:duration="@integer/subtitle_duration"/>
</set>
```

The code to run it is also very similar to what we just saw for the title:

```
Animation subtitleAnimation =
  AnimationUtils.loadAnimation(context,
  R.animator.subtitle_enter);
subtitle.startAnimation(subtitleAnimation);
```

Again, the fact that `startOffset` is considered a part of the animation is very convenient, because it allows us to set the alpha to 0 for the first 2,000 milliseconds without touching the view.

Let's compare it with `ViewPropertyAnimation`:

```
View subtitle = getView().findViewById(R.id.main_subtitle);
subtitle.setAlpha(0);

int subtitleDuration =
  getResources().getInteger(R.integer.subtitle_duration);
int subtitleStartOffset =
  getResources().getInteger(R.integer.subtitle_start_offset);

subtitle.animate()
  .alpha(1)
  .setDuration(subtitleDuration)
  .setStartDelay(subtitleStartOffset)
  .setInterpolator(new DecelerateInterpolator())
  .start();
```

Also, very similarly to the previous one, we need to initialize the value of alpha in the view. We also need to load the integer values to use them in the configuration.

Lastly, the same animation is defined as a `PropertyAnimation` in XML:

```
<set xmlns:android="http://schemas.android.com/apk/res/android">
<objectAnimator
  android:interpolator="@android:anim/decelerate_interpolator"
  android:propertyName="alpha"
  android:valueFrom="0"
  android:valueTo="1"
  android:startOffset="@integer/subtitle_start_offset"
  android:duration="@integer/subtitle_duration" />
</set>
```

Then, it is loaded and assigned to the subtitle view:

```
subtitle.setAlpha(0);
AnimatorSet set = (AnimatorSet)
  AnimatorInflater.loadAnimator(context,
  R.animator.fade_in_property);
set.setTarget(subtitle);
set.start();
```

In this case, we also need to preset the alpha to 0, because the start offset is not considered a part of the animation for `PropertyAnimator`. If we do not set it, it will stay set to 1 until the animation starts running.

In general, there is no silver bullet and each type of animation is better for different cases. While using simple visual effects to make a game look nicer, view animators are usually enough and also easier to set up. If the view is going to be interactive and you use animation to translate the elements of the game, then `PropertyAnimation` (or any of its variants) is the only way to go.

Summary

We have learned how to do frame-by-frame animations and how to animate views using the two different frameworks that Android provides, view animation and `PropertyAnimation`.

We have studied the differences between and limitations of each of them and learned when to use one or the other.

We have animated the dialogs and also the main menu. For the titles, we have seen how we could achieve the same result with different approaches.

All in all, the game looks much smoother since a lot of the content is animated now.

We could say that the game is finished, but we will add some more features to make it more interesting. Google provides us with an API to manage achievements and leaderboards. Both features are a part of Google Play services and this is what we will do next!

9
Integrating Google
Play Services

Google provides Google Play Services as a way to use special features in apps. Being the game services subset the one that interests us the most. Note that Google Play Services are updated as an app that is independent from the operating system. This allows us to assume that most of the players will have the latest version of Google Play Services installed.

More and more features are being moved from the Android SDK to the Play Services because of this.

Play Services offer much more than just services for games, but there is a whole section dedicated exclusively to games, **Google Play Game Services** (**GPGS**). These features include achievements, leaderboards, quests, save games, gifts, and even multiplayer support.

GPGS also comes with a standalone app called "Play Games" that shows the user the games he or she has been playing, the latest achievements, and the games his or her friends play. It is a very interesting way to get exposure for your game.

Even as a standalone feature, achievements and leaderboards are two concepts that most games use nowadays, so why make your own custom ones when you can rely on the ones made by Google?

GPGS can be used on many platforms: Android, iOS and web among others. It is more used on Android, since it is included as a part of Google apps.

There is extensive step-by-step documentation online, but the details are scattered over different places. We will put them together here and link you to the official documentation for more detailed information.

For this chapter, you are supposed to have a developer account and have access to the Google Play Developer Console. It is also advisable for you to know the process of signing and releasing an app. If you are not familiar with it, there is very detailed official documentation at `http://developer.android.com/distribute/googleplay/start.html`.

There are two sides of GPGS: the developer console and the code. We will alternate from one to the other while talking about the different features.

Setting up the developer console

Now that we are approaching the release state, we have to start working with the developer console.

The first thing we need to do is to get into the **Game services** section of the console to create and configure a new game. In the left menu, we have an option labeled **Game services**. This is where you have to click. Once in the **Game services** section, click on **Add new game**:

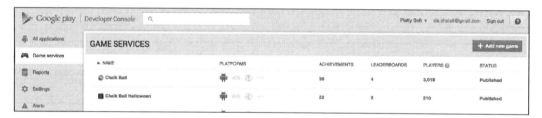

This bring us to the set up dialog. If you are using other Google services like **Google Maps** or **Google Cloud Messaging (GCM)** in your game, you should select the second option and move forward. Otherwise, you can just fill in the fields for **I don't use any Google APIs on my game yet** and continue. If you don't know whether you are already using them, you probably aren't.

Now, it is time to link a game to it. I recommend you publish your game beforehand as an alpha release. This will let you select it from the list when you start typing the package name.

 Publishing the game to the alpha channel before adding it to Game services makes it much easier to configure.

If you are not familiar with signing and releasing your app, check out the official documentation at `http://developer.android.com/tools/publishing/app-signing.html`.

Finally, there are only two steps that we have to take when we link the first app. We need to authorize it and provide branding information. The authorization will generate an OAuth key—that we don't need to use since it is required for other platforms—and also a game ID. This ID is unique to all the linked apps and we will need it to log in. But there is no need to write it down now, it can be found easily in the console at anytime.

 Authorizing the app will generate the game ID, which is unique to all linked apps.

Note that the app we have added is configured with the release key. If you continue and try the login integration, you will get an error telling you that the app was signed with the wrong certificate:

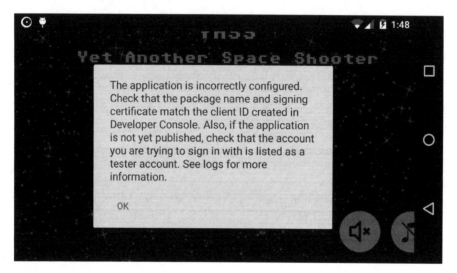

You have two ways to work with this limitation:

- Always make a release build to test GPGS integration
- Add your debug-signed game as a linked app

I recommend that you add the debug signed app as a linked app. To do this, we just need to link another app and configure it with the SHA1 fingerprint of the debug key. To obtain it, we have to open a terminal and run the keytool utility:

```
keytool -exportcert -alias androiddebugkey -keystore <path-to-debug-
keystore> -list -v
```

Note that in Windows, the debug `keystore` can be found at `C:\Users\<USERNAME>\.android\debug.keystore`. On Mac and Linux, the debug `keystore` is typically located at `~/.android/debug.keystore`.

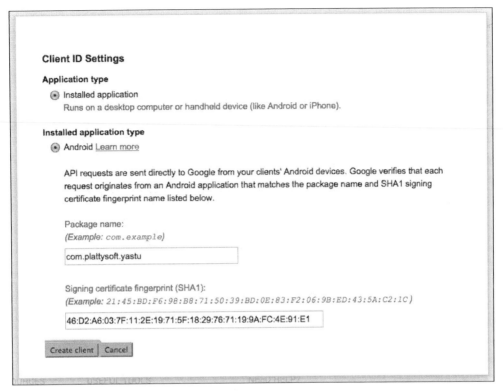

Dialog to link the debug application on the Game Services console

Now, we have the game configured. We could continue creating achievements and leaderboards in the console, but we will put it aside and make sure that we can sign in and connect with GPGS.

The only users who can sign in to GPGS while a game is not published are the testers. You can make the alpha and/or beta testers of a linked app become testers of the game services, and you can also add e-mail addresses by hand for this. You can modify this in the Testing tab.

 Only test accounts can access a game that is not published.

The e-mail of the owner of the developer console is prefilled as a tester. Just in case you have problems logging in, double-check the list of testers.

A game service that is not published will not appear in the feed of the Play Services app, but it will be possible to test and modify it. This is why it is a good idea to keep it in draft mode until the game itself is ready and publish both the game and the game services at the same time.

Setting up the code

The first thing we need to do is to add the Google Play Services library to our project. This should already have been done by the wizard when we created the project, but I recommend you to double-check it now.

The library needs to be added to the `build.gradle` file of the main module. Note that Android Studio projects contain a top-level `build.gradle` and a module-level `build.gradle` for each module. We will modify the one that is under the `mobile` module.

Make sure that the play services' library is listed under dependencies:

```
apply plugin: 'com.android.application'


dependencies {
  compile 'com.android.support:appcompat-v7:22.1.1'
  compile 'com.google.android.gms:play-services:7.3.0'
}
```

At the point of writing, the latest version is 7.3.0. The basic features have not changed much and they are unlikely to change. You could force Gradle to use a specific version of the library, but in general I recommend you use the latest version.

Once you have it, save the changes and click on **Sync Project with Gradle Files**.

To be able to connect with GPGS, we need to let the game know what the game ID is. This is done through the `<meta-data>` tag on `AndroidManifest.xml`. You could hardcode the value here, but it is highly recommended that you set it as a resource in your Android project.

We are going to create a new file for this under `res/values`, which we will name `play_services.xml`. In this file we will put the game ID, but later we will also have the achievements and leaderboard IDs in it. Using a separate file for these values is recommended because they are constants that do not need to be translated:

```
<application>
  <meta-data android:name="com.google.android.gms.games.APP_ID"
    android:value="@string/app_id" />
  <meta-data android:name="com.google.android.gms.version"
    android:value="@integer/google_play_services_version"/>
  [...]
</application>
```

Adding this metadata is extremely important. If you forget to update the `AndroidManifest.xml`, the app will crash when you try to sign in to Google Play services. Note that the integer for the gms version is defined in the library and we do not need to add it to our file.

 If you forget to add the game ID to the strings the app will crash.

Now, it is time to proceed to sign in. The process is quite tedious and requires many checks, so Google has released an open source project named BaseGameUtils, which makes it easier. Unfortunately this project is not a part of the play services' library and it is not even available as a library. So, we have to get it from GitHub (either check it out or download the source as a ZIP file).

 BaseGameUtils abstracts us from the complexity of handling the connection with Play Services.

Even more cumbersome, BaseGameUtils is not available as a standalone download and has to be downloaded together with another project. The fact that this significant piece of code is not a part of the official library makes it quite tedious to set up. Why it has been done like this is something that I do not comprehend myself.

The project that contains BaseGameUtils is called `android-basic-samples` and it can be downloaded from `https://github.com/playgameservices/android-basic-samples`.

 Adding BaseGameUtils is not as straightforward as we would like it to be.

Once `android-basic-samples` is downloaded, open your game project in Android Studio. Click on **File** > **Import Module** and navigate to the directory where you downloaded `android-basic-samples`. Select the `BaseGameUtils` module in the `BasicSamples/libraries` directory and click on **OK**.

Finally, update the dependencies in the `build.gradle` file for the `mobile` module and sync gradle again:

```
dependencies {
  compile project(':BaseGameUtils')
  [...]
}
```

After all these steps to set up the project, we are finally ready to begin the sign in.

We will make our main `Activity` extend from `BaseGamesActivity`, which takes care of all the handling of the connections, and sign in with Google Play Services.

One more detail: until now, we were using `Activity` and not `FragmentActivity` as the base class for `YassActivity` (`BaseGameActivity` extends from `FragmentActivity`) and this change will mess with the behavior of our dialogs while calling `navigateBack`. We can change the base class of `BaseGameActivity` or modify `navigateBack` to perform a pop-on fragment navigation hierarchy. I recommend the second approach:

```
public void navigateBack() {
  // Do a pop on the navigation history
  getFragmentManager().popBackStack();
}
```

This util class has been designed to work with single-activity games. It can be used in multiple activities, but it is not straightforward. This is another good reason to keep the game in a single activity.

 The BaseGameUtils is designed to be used in single-activity games.

The default behavior of `BaseGameActivity` is to try to log in each time the `Activity` is started. If the user agrees to sign in, the sign in will happen automatically. But if the user rejects doing so, he or she will be asked again several times.

I personally find this intrusive and annoying, and I recommend you to only prompt to log in to Google Play services once (and again, if the user logs out). We can always provide a login entry point in the app.

This is very easy to change. The default number of attempts is set to 3 and it is a part of the code of `GameHelper`:

```
// Should we start the flow to sign the user in automatically on
   startup? If
// so, up to
// how many times in the life of the application?
static final int DEFAULT_MAX_SIGN_IN_ATTEMPTS = 3;
int mMaxAutoSignInAttempts = DEFAULT_MAX_SIGN_IN_ATTEMPTS;
```

So, we just have to configure it for our activity, adding one line of code during `onCreate` to change the default behavior with the one we want: just try it once:

```
getGameHelper().setMaxAutoSignInAttempts(1);
```

Finally, there are two methods that we can override to act when the user successfully logs in and when there is a problem: `onSignInSucceeded` and `onSignInFailed`. We will use them when we update the main menu at the end of the chapter.

Further use of GPGS is to be made via the `GameHelper` and/or the `GoogleApiClient`, which is a part of the `GameHelper`. We can obtain a reference to the `GameHelper` using the `getGameHelper` method of `BaseGameActivity`.

Now that the user can sign into Google Play services we can continue with achievements and leaderboards. Let's go back to the developer console.

Achievements

We will first define a few achievements in the developer console and then see how to unlock them in the game. Note that to publish any game with GPGS, you need to define at least five achievements. No other feature is mandatory, but achievements are.

 We need to define at least five achievements to publish a game with Google Play Game services.

If you want to use GPGS with a game that has no achievements, I recommend you to add five dummy secret achievements and let them be.

To add an achievement, we just need to navigate to the **Achievements** tab on the left and click on **Add achievement**:

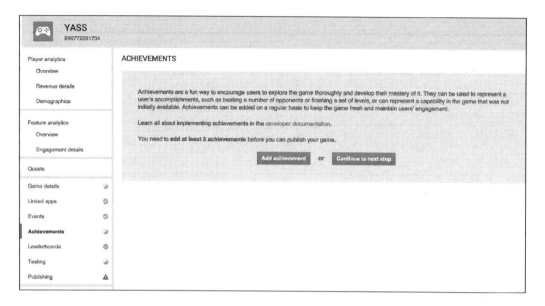

The menu to add a new achievement has a few fields that are mostly self-explanatory. They are as follows:

- **Name**: the name that will be shown (can be localized to different languages).

- **Description**: the description of the achievement to be shown (can also be localized to different languages).

- **Icon**: the icon of the achievement as a 512x512 px PNG image. This will be used to show the achievement in the list and also to generate the locked image and the in-game popup when it is unlocked.

- **Incremental achievements**: if the achievement requires a set of steps to be completed, it is called an incremental achievement and can be shown with a progress bar. We will have an incremental achievement to illustrate this.

- **Initial state**: **Revealed/Hidden** depending on whether we want the achievement to be shown or not. When an achievement is shown, the name and description are visible, players know what they have to do to unlock it. A hidden achievement, on the other hand, is a secret and can be a funny surprise when unlocked. We will have two secret achievements.

- **Points**: GPGS allows each game to have 1,000 points to give for unlocking achievements. This gets converted to XP in the player profile on Google Play games. This can be used to highlight that some achievements are harder than others, and therefore grant a bigger reward. You cannot change these once they are published, so if you plan to have more achievements in the future, plan ahead with the points.

- **List order**: The order of the achievements is shown. It is not followed all the time, since on the Play Games app the unlocked ones are shown before the locked ones. It is still handy to rearrange them.

Dialog to add an achievement on the developer console

As we already decided, we will have five achievements in our game and they will be as follows:

- **Big Score**: score over 100,000 points in one game. This is to be granted while playing.

- **Asteroid killer**: destroy 100 asteroids. This will count them across different games and is an incremental achievement.

- **Survivor**: survive for 60 seconds.

- **Target acquired**: a hidden achievement. Hit 20 asteroids in a row without missing a hit. This is meant to reward players that only shoot when they should.

- **Target lost**: this is supposed to be a funny achievement, granted when you miss with 10 bullets in a row. It is also hidden, because otherwise it would be too easy to unlock.

So, we created some images for them and added them to the console.

The developer console with all the configured achievements

Each achievement has a string ID. We will need these ids to unlock the achievements in our game, but Google has made it easy for us. We have a link at the bottom named **Get resources** that pops up a dialog with the string resources we need. We can just copy them from there and paste them in our project in the `play_services.xml` file we have already created.

Architecture

For our game, given that we only have five achievements, we are going to add the code for achievements directly into the `ScoreObject`. This will make it less code for you to read so we can focus on how it is done. However, for a real production code I recommend you define a dedicated architecture for achievements.

The recommended architecture is to have an `AchievementsManager` class that loads all the achievements when the game starts and stores them in three lists:

- All achievements
- Locked achievements
- Unlocked achievements

Then, we have an `Achievement` base class with an abstract `check` method that we implement for each one of them:

```
public boolean check (GameEngine gameEngine, GameEvent gameEvent)
{
}
```

This base class takes care of loading the achievement state from local storage (I recommend using `SharedPreferences` for this) and modify it as per the result of `check`.

The achievements check is done at `AchievementManager` level using a `checkLockedAchievements` method that iterates over the list of achievements that can be unlocked. This method should be called as a part of `onEventReceived` of `GameEngine`.

This architecture allows you to check only the achievements that are yet to be unlocked and also all the achievements included in the game in a specific dedicated place.

In our case, since we are keeping the score inside the `ScoreGameObject`, we are going to add all achievements code there.

Note that making the `GameEngine` take care of the score and having it as a variable that other objects can read are also recommended design patterns, but it was simpler to do this as a part of `ScoreGameObject`.

Unlocking achievements

To handle achievements, we need to have access to an object of the class `GoogleApiClient`. We can get a reference to it in the constructor of `ScoreGameObject`:

```
private final GoogleApiClient mApiClient;

public ScoreGameObject(YassBaseFragment parent, View view,
  int viewResId) {
  [...]
```

```
    mApiClient =
        parent.getYassActivity().getGameHelper().getApiClient();
}
```

The parent `Fragment` has a reference to the `Activity`, which has a reference to the `GameHelper`, which has a reference to the `GoogleApiClient`.

Unlocking an achievement requires just a single line of code, but we also need to check whether the user is connected to Google Play services or not before trying to unlock an achievement. This is necessary because if the user has not signed it, an exception is thrown and the game crashes.

 Unlocking an achievement requires just a single line of code.

But this check is not enough. In the edge case, when the user logs out manually from Google Play services (which can be done in the achievements screen), the connection will not be closed and there is no way to know whether he or she has logged out.

We are going to create a utility method to unlock the achievements that does all the checks and also wraps the unlock method into a `try/catch` block and make the API client disconnect if an exception is raised:

```
private void unlockSafe(int resId) {
    if (mApiClient.isConnecting() || mApiClient.isConnected()) {
        try {
            Games.Achievements.unlock(mApiClient, getString(resId));
        } catch (Exception e) {
            mApiClient.disconnect();
        }
    }
}
```

Even with all the checks, the code is still very simple.

Let's work on the particular achievements we have defined for the game. Even though they are very specific, the methodology to track game events and variables and then check for achievements to unlock is in itself generic, and serves as a real-life example of how to deal with achievements.

The achievements we have designed require us to count some game events and also the running time. For the last two achievements, we need to make a new GameEvent for the case when a bullet misses, which we have not created until now. The code in the Bullet object to trigger this new GameEvent is as follows:

```
@Override
public void onUpdate(long elapsedMillis, GameEngine gameEngine) {
  mY += mSpeedFactor * elapsedMillis;
  if (mY < -mHeight) {
    removeFromGameEngine(gameEngine);
    gameEngine.onGameEvent(GameEvent.BulletMissed);
  }
}
```

Now, let's work inside ScoreGameObject. We are going to have a method that checks achievements each time an asteroid is hit. There are three achievements that can be unlocked when that event happens:

- **Big score**, because hitting an asteroid gives us points
- **Target acquired**, because it requires consecutive asteroid hits
- **Asteroid killer**, because it counts the total number of asteroids that have been destroyed

The code is like this:

```
private void checkAsteroidHitRelatedAchievements() {
  if (mPoints > 100000) {
    // Unlock achievement
    unlockSafe(R.string.achievement_big_score);
  }
  if (mConsecutiveHits >= 20) {
    unlockSafe(R.string.achievement_target_acquired);
  }
  // Increment achievement of asteroids hit
  if (mApiClient.isConnecting() || mApiClient.isConnected()) {
    try {
      Games.Achievements.increment(mApiClient,
        getString(R.string.achievement_asteroid_killer), 1);
    } catch (Exception e) {
      mApiClient.disconnect();
    }
  }
}
```

We check the total points and the number of consecutive hits to unlock the corresponding achievements.

The "Asteroid killer" achievement is a bit of a different case, because it is an incremental achievement. These type of achievements do not have an `unlock` method, but rather an `increment` method. Each time we increment the value, progress on the achievement is updated. Once the progress is 100 percent, it is unlocked automatically.

 Incremental achievements are automatically unlocked, we just have to increment their value.

This makes incremental achievements much easier to use than tracking the progress locally. But we still need to do all the checks as we did for `unlockSafe`.

We are using a variable named `mConsecutiveHits`, which we have not initialized yet. This is done inside `onGameEvent`, which is the place where the other hidden achievement target lost is checked. Some initialization for the "Survivor" achievement is also done here:

```
public void onGameEvent(GameEvent gameEvent) {
  if (gameEvent == GameEvent.AsteroidHit) {
    mPoints += POINTS_GAINED_PER_ASTEROID_HIT;
    mPointsHaveChanged = true;
    mConsecutiveMisses = 0;
    mConsecutiveHits++;
    checkAsteroidHitRelatedAchievements();
  }
  else if (gameEvent == GameEvent.BulletMissed) {
    mConsecutiveMisses++;
    mConsecutiveHits = 0;
    if (mConsecutiveMisses >= 20) {
      unlockSafe(R.string.achievement_target_lost);
    }
  }
  else if (gameEvent == GameEvent.SpaceshipHit) {
    mTimeWithoutDie = 0;
  }
  [...]
}
```

Each time we hit an asteroid, we increment the number of consecutive asteroid hits and reset the number of consecutive misses. Similarly, each time we miss a bullet, we increment the number of consecutive misses and reset the number of consecutive hits.

As a side note, each time the spaceship is destroyed we reset the time without dying, which is used for "Survivor", but this is not the only time when the time without dying should be updated. We have to reset it when the game starts, and modify it inside onUpdate by just adding the elapsed milliseconds that have passed:

```
@Override
public void startGame(GameEngine gameEngine) {
  mTimeWithoutDie = 0;
  [...]
}

@Override
public void onUpdate(long elapsedMillis, GameEngine gameEngine) {
  mTimeWithoutDie += elapsedMillis;
  if (mTimeWithoutDie > 60000) {
    unlockSafe(R.string.achievement_survivor);
  }
}
```

So, once the game has been running for 60,000 milliseconds since it started or since a spaceship was destroyed, we unlock the "Survivor" achievement.

With this, we have all the code we need to unlock the achievements we have created for the game. Let's finish this section with some comments on the system and the developer console:

- As a rule of thumb, you can edit most of the details of an achievement until you publish it to production.

- Once your achievement has been published, it cannot be deleted. You can only delete an achievement in its prepublished state. There is a button labeled Delete at the bottom of the achievement screen for this.

- You can also reset the progress for achievements while they are in draft. This reset happens for all players at once. There is a button labeled **Reset achievement progress** at the bottom of the achievement screen for this.

Also note that GameBaseActivity does a lot of logging. So, if your device is connected to your computer and you run a debug build, you may see that it lags sometimes. This does not happen in a release build for which the log is removed.

Leaderboards

Since YASS has only one game mode and one score in the game, it makes sense to have only one leaderboard on Google Play Game Services. Leaderboards are managed from their own tab inside the Game services area of the developer console.

Unlike achievements, it is not mandatory to have any leaderboard to be able to publish your game.

If your game has different levels of difficulty, you can have a leaderboard for each of them. This also applies if the game has several values that measure player progress, you can have a leaderboard for each of them.

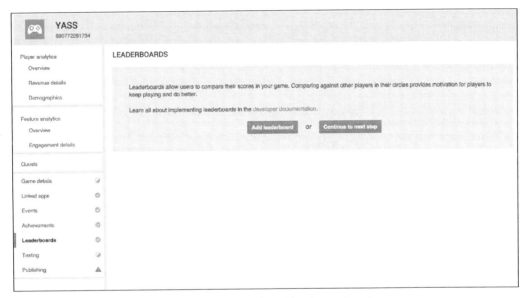

Managing leaderboards on Play Games console

Leaderboards can be created and managed in the **Leaderboards** tag. When we click on Add leaderboard, we are presented with a form that has several fields to be filled. They are as follows:

- **Name**: the display name of the leaderboard, which can be localized. We will simply call it `High Scores`.
- **Score formatting**: this can be **Numeric**, **Currency**, or **Time**. We will use **Numeric** for YASS.
- **Icon**: a 512x512 px icon to identify the leaderboard.
- **Ordering**: **Larger is better** / **Smaller is better**. We are going to use **Larger is better**, but other score types may be **Smaller is better** as in a racing game.

- **Enable tamper protection**: this automatically filters out suspicious scores. You should keep this on.

- **Limits**: if you want to limit the score range that is shown on the leaderboard, you can do it here. We are not going to use this

- **List order**: the order of the leaderboards. Since we only have one, it is not really important for us.

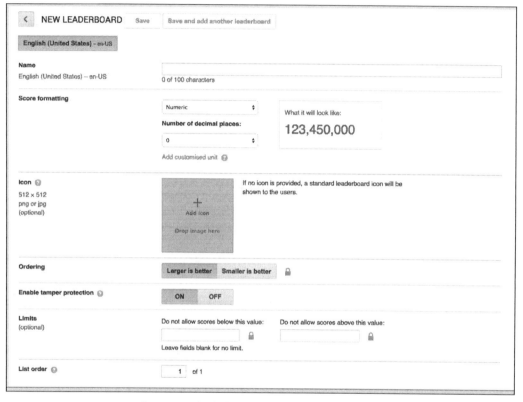

Setting up a leaderboard on the Play Games console

Now that we have defined the leaderboard, it is time to use it in the game. As happens with achievements, we have a link where we can get all the resources for the game in XML. So, we proceed to get the ID of the leaderboard and add it to the strings defined in the `play_services.xml` file.

We have to submit the scores at the end of the game (that is, a `GameOver` event), but also when the user exits a game via the pause button. To unify this, we will create a new `GameEvent` called `GameFinished` that is triggered after a `GameOver` event and after the user exits the game.

We will update the `stopGame` method of `GameEngine`, which is called in both cases to trigger the event:

```
public void stopGame() {
  if (mUpdateThread != null) {
    synchronized (mLayers) {
      onGameEvent(GameEvent.GameFinished);
    }
    mUpdateThread.stopGame();
    mUpdateThread = null;
  }
  [...]
}
```

We have to set the `updateThread` to null after sending the event, to prevent this code being run twice. Otherwise, we could send each score more than once.

Similarly, as happens for achievements, submitting a score is very simple, just a single line of code. But we also need to check that the `GoogleApiClient` is connected and we still have the same edge case when an Exception is thrown. So, we need to wrap it in a `try`/`catch` block.

To keep everything in the same place, we will put this code inside `ScoreGameObject`:

```
@Override
public void onGameEvent(GameEvent gameEvent) {
  [...]
  else if (gameEvent == GameEvent.GameFinished) {
    // Submit the score
    if (mApiClient.isConnecting() || mApiClient.isConnected()) {
      try {
        Games.Leaderboards.submitScore(mApiClient,
          getLeaderboardId(), mPoints);
      }
      catch (Exception e){
        mApiClient.disconnect();
      }
    }
  }
}

private String getLeaderboardId() {
  return mParent.getString(R.string.leaderboard_high_scores);
}
```

This is really straightforward. GPGS is now receiving our scores and it takes care of the timestamp of the score to create daily, weekly, and all time leaderboards. It also uses your Google+ circles to show the social score of your friends. All this is done automatically for you.

The final missing piece is to let the player open the leaderboards and achievements UI from the main menu as well as trigger a sign in if they are signed out.

Opening the Play Games UI

To complete the integration of achievements and leaderboards, we are going to add buttons to open the native UI provided by GPGS to our main menu.

For this, we are going to place two buttons in the bottom-left corner of the screen, opposite the music and sound buttons. We will also check whether we are connected or not; if not, we will show a single sign-in button.

For these buttons we will use the official images of GPGS, which are available for developers to use. Note that you must follow the brand guidelines while using the icons and they must be displayed as they are and not modified. This also provides a consistent look and feel across all the games that support Play Games.

Since we have seen a lot of layouts already, we are not going to include another one that is almost the same as something we already have.

The main menu with the buttons to view achievements and leaderboards.

To handle these new buttons we will, as usual, set the `MainMenuFragment` as `OnClickListener` for the views. We do this in the same place as the other buttons, that is, inside `onViewCreated`:

```
@Override
public void onViewCreated(View view, Bundle savedInstanceState) {
  super.onViewCreated(view, savedInstanceState);
  [...]
  view.findViewById(
    R.id.btn_achievements).setOnClickListener(this);
  view.findViewById(
    R.id.btn_leaderboards).setOnClickListener(this);
  view.findViewById(R.id.btn_sign_in).setOnClickListener(this);
}
```

As happened with achievements and leaderboards, the work is done using static methods that receive a `GoogleApiClient` object. We can get this object from the `GameHelper` that is a part of the `BaseGameActivity`, like this:

```
GoogleApiClient apiClient =
  getYassActivity().getGameHelper().getApiClient();
```

To open the native UI, we have to obtain an `Intent` and then start an `Activity` with it. It is important that you use `startActivityForResult`, since some data is passed back and forth.

To open the achievements UI, the code is like this:

```
Intent achievementsIntent =
  Games.Achievements.getAchievementsIntent(apiClient);
startActivityForResult(achievementsIntent, REQUEST_ACHIEVEMENTS);
```

This works out of the box. It automatically grays out the icons for the unlocked achievements, adds a counter and progress bar to the one that is in progress, and a padlock to the hidden ones.

Similarly, to open the leaderboards UI we obtain an intent from the Games. Leaderboards class instead:

```
Intent leaderboardsIntent =
  Games.Leaderboards.getLeaderboardIntent(
  apiClient,
  getString(R.string.leaderboard_high_scores));
startActivityForResult(leaderboardsIntent, REQUEST_LEADERBOARDS);
```

In this case, we are asking for a specific leaderboard, since we only have one. We could use getLeaderboardsIntent instead, which will open the Play Games UI for the list of all the leaderboards.

 We can have an intent to open the list of leaderboards or a specific one.

What remains to be done is to replace the buttons for the login one when the user is not connected. For this, we will create a method that reads the state and shows and hides the views accordingly:

```
private void updatePlayButtons() {
  GameHelper gameHelper = getYassActivity().getGameHelper();
  if (gameHelper.isConnecting() || gameHelper.isSignedIn()) {
    getView().findViewById(
      R.id.btn_achievements).setVisibility(View.VISIBLE);
    getView().findViewById(
      R.id.btn_leaderboards).setVisibility(View.VISIBLE);
    getView().findViewById(
      R.id.btn_sign_in).setVisibility(View.GONE);
  }
  else {
    getView().findViewById(
     R.id.btn_achievements).setVisibility(View.GONE);
    getView().findViewById(
     R.id.btn_leaderboards).setVisibility(View.GONE);
    getView().findViewById(
      R.id.btn_sign_in).setVisibility(View.VISIBLE);
  }
}
```

This method decides whether to remove or make visible the views based on the state. We will call it inside the important state-changing methods:

- `onLayoutCompleted`: the first time we open the game to initialize the UI.

- `onSignInSucceeded`: when the user successfully signs in to GPGS.

- `onSignInFailed`: this can be triggered when we auto sign in and there is no connection. It is important to handle it.

- `onActivityResult`: when we come back from the Play Games UI, in case the user has logged out.

But nothing is as easy as it looks. In fact, when the user signs out and does not exit the game, `GoogleApiClient` keeps the connection open. Therefore the value of `isSignedIn` from `GameHelper` still returns true. This is the edge case we have been talking about all through the chapter.

As a result of this edge case, there is an inconsistency in the UI that shows the achievements and leaderboards buttons when it should show the login one.

 When the user logs out from Play Games, `GoogleApiClient` keeps the connection open. This can lead to confusion.

Unfortunately, this has been marked as work as expected by Google. The reason is that the connection is still active and it is our responsibility to parse the result in the `onActivityResult` method to determine the new state. But this is not very convenient.

Since it is a rare case we will just go for the easiest solution, which is to wrap it in a `try/catch` block and make the user sign in if he or she taps on leaderboards or achievements while not logged in. This is the code we have to handle the click on the achievements button, but the one for leaderboards is equivalent:

```
else if (v.getId() == R.id.btn_achievements) {
  try {
    GoogleApiClient apiClient =
      getYassActivity().getGameHelper().getApiClient();
    Intent achievementsIntent =
      Games.Achievements.getAchievementsIntent(apiClient);
    startActivityForResult(achievementsIntent,
      REQUEST_ACHIEVEMENTS);
  }
  catch (Exception e) {
    GameHelper gameHelper = getYassActivity().getGameHelper();
```

```
        gameHelper.disconnect();
        gameHelper.beginUserInitiatedSignIn();
    }
}
```

Basically, we have the old code to open the achievements activity, but we wrap it in a `try/catch` block. If an exception is raised, we disconnect the game helper and begin a new login using the `beginUserInitiatedSignIn` method.

It is very important to disconnect the `gameHelper` before we try to log in again. Otherwise, the login will not work.

 We must disconnect from GPGS before we can log in using the method from the `GameHelper`.

Finally, there is the case when the user clicks on the login button, which just triggers the login using the `beginUserInitiatedSignIn` method from the `GameHelper`:

```
if (v.getId() == R.id.btn_sign_in) {
    getYassActivity().getGameHelper().beginUserInitiatedSignIn();
}
```

Once you have published your game and the game services, achievements and leaderboards will not appear in the game description on Google Play straight away. It is required that "a fair amount of users" have used them. You have done nothing wrong, you just have to wait.

Other features of Google Play services

Google Play Game Services provides more features for game developers than achievements and leaderboards. None of them really fit the game we are building, but it is useful to know they exist just in case your game needs them. You can save yourself lots of time and effort by using them and not reinventing the wheel.

The other features of Google Play Games Services are:

- **Events and quests**: these allow you to monitor game usage and progression. Also, they add the possibility of creating time-limited events with rewards for the players.
- **Gifts**: as simple as it sounds, you can send a gift to other players or request one to be sent to you. Yes, this is seen in the very mechanical Facebook games popularized a while ago.

- **Saved games**: the standard concept of a saved game. If your game has progression or can unlock content based on user actions, you may want to use this feature. Since it is saved in the cloud, saved games can be accessed across multiple devices.

- **Turn-based and real-time multiplayer**: Google Play Game Services provides an API to implement turn-based and real-time multiplayer features without you needing to write any server code.

If your game is multiplayer and has an online economy, it may be worth making your own server and granting virtual currency only on the server to prevent cheating. Otherwise, it is fairly easy to crack the gifts/reward system and a single person can ruin the complete game economy.

However, if there is no online game economy, the benefits of gifts and quests may be more important than the fact that someone can hack them.

Let's take a look at each of these features.

Events

The event's APIs provides us with a way to define and collect gameplay metrics and upload them to Google Play Game Services.

This is very similar to the `GameEvents` we are already using in our game. Events should be a subset of the game events of our game. Many of the game events we have are used internally as a signal between objects or as a synchronization mechanism. These events are not really relevant outside the engine, but others could be. Those are the events we should send to GPGS.

To be able to send an event from the game to GPGS, we have to create it in the developer console first.

To create an event, we have to go to the **Events** tab in the developer console, click on **Add new event**, and fill in the following fields:

- **Name**: a short name of the event. The name can be up to 100 characters. This value can be localized.

- **Description**: a longer description of the event. The description can be up to 500 characters. This value can also be localized.

- **Icon**: the icon for the event of the standard 512x512 px size.

- **Visibility**: as for achievements, this can be revealed or hidden.

- **Format**: as for leaderboards, this can be **Numeric**, **Currency**, or **Time**.

- **Event type**: this is used to mark events that create or spend premium currency. This can be **Premium currency sink**, **Premium currency source**, or **None**.

While in the game, events work pretty much as incremental achievements. You can increment the event counter using the following line of code:

```
Games.Events.increment(mGoogleApiClient, myEventId, 1);
```

You can delete events that are in the draft state or that have been published as long as the event is not in use by a quest. You can also reset the player progress data for the testers of your events as you can do for achievements.

While the events can be used as an analytics system, their real usefulness appears when they are combined with quests.

Quests

A quest is a challenge that asks players to complete an event a number of times during a specific time frame to receive a reward.

Because a quest is linked to an event, to use quests you need to have created at least one event.

You can create a quest from the quests tab in the developer console. A quest has the following fields to be filled:

- **Name**: the short name of the quest. This can be up to 100 characters and can be localized.

- **Description**: a longer description of the quest. Your quest description should let players know what they need to do to complete the quest. The description can be up to 500 characters. The first 150 characters will be visible to players on cards such as those shown in the Google Play Games app.

- **Icon**: a square icon that will be associated with the quest.

- **Banner**: a rectangular image that will be used to promote the quest.

- **Completion Criteria**: this is the configuration of the quest itself. It consists of an event and the number of times the event must occur.

- **Schedule**: the start and end date and time for the quest. GPGS uses your local time zone, but stores the values as UTC. Players will see these values appear in their local time zone. You can mark a checkbox to notify users when the quest is about to end.

- **Reward Data**: this is specific to each game. It can be a JSON object, specifying the reward. This is sent to the client when the quest is completed.

Once configured in the developer console, you can do two things with the quests:

- Display the list of quests
- Process a quest completion

To get the list of quests, we start an activity with an intent that is provided to us via a static method as usual:

```
Intent questsIntent =
    Games.Quests.getQuestsIntent(mGoogleApiClient,
    Quests.SELECT_ALL_QUESTS);
startActivityForResult(questsIntent, QUESTS_INTENT);
```

To be notified when a quest is completed, all we have to do is register a listener:

```
Games.Quests.registerQuestUpdateListener(mGoogleApiClient, this);
```

Once we have set the listener, the onQuestCompleted method will be called once the quest is completed. After completing the processing of the reward, the game should call claim to inform Play Game services that the player has claimed the reward.

The following code snippet shows how you might override the onQuestCompleted callback:

```
@Override
public void onQuestCompleted(Quest quest) {
  // Claim the quest reward.
  Games.Quests.claim(mGoogleApiClient, quest.getQuestId(),
    quest.getCurrentMilestone().getMilestoneId());
  // Process the RewardData to provision a specific reward.
  String reward = new
    String(quest.getCurrentMilestone().getCompletionRewardData(),
    Charset.forName("UTF-8"));
}
```

The rewards themselves are defined by the client. As we mentioned before, this will make the game quite easy to crack and get rewards. But usually, avoiding the hassle of writing your own server is worth it.

Gifts

The gifts feature of GPGS allows us to send gifts to other players and to request them to send us one as well. This is intended to make the gameplay more collaborative and to improve the social aspect of the game.

As for other GPGS features, we have a built-in UI provided by the library that can be used. In this case, to send and request gifts for in-game items and resources to and from friends in their Google+ circles. The request system can make use of notifications.

There are two types of requests that players can send using the game gifts feature in Google Play Game Services:

- A wish request to ask for in-game items or some other form of assistance from their friends
- A gift request to send in-game items or some other form of assistance to their friends

A player can specify one or more target request recipients from the default request-sending UI. A gift or wish can be consumed (accepted) or dismissed by a recipient.

To see the gifts API in detail, you can visit `https://developers.google.com/games/services/android/giftRequests`.

Again, as for quest rewards, this is done entirely by the client, which makes the game susceptible to piracy.

Saved games

The saved games service offers cloud game saving slots. Your game can retrieve the saved game data to allow returning players to continue a game at their last save point from any device.

This service makes it possible to synchronize a player's game data across multiple devices. For example, if you have a game that runs on Android, you can use the saved games service to allow a player to start a game on their Android phone and then continue playing the game on a tablet without losing any of their progress. This service can also be used to ensure that a player's game play continues from where it was left off even if their device is lost, destroyed, or traded in for a newer model or if the game was reinstalled

The saved games service does not know about the game internals, so it provides a field that is an unstructured binary blob where you can read and write the game data. A game can write an arbitrary number of saved games for a single player subjected to user quota, so there is no hard requirement to restrict players to a single save file.

Saved games are done in an unstructured binary blob.

The API for saved games also receives some metadata that is used by Google Play Games to populate the UI and to present useful information in the Google Play Game app (for example, last updated timestamp).

Saved games has several entry points and actions, including how to deal with conflicts in the saved games. To know more about these check out the official documentation at `https://developers.google.com/games/services/android/savedgames`.

Multiplayer games

If you are going to implement multiplayer, GPGS can save you a lot of work. You may or may not use it for the final product, but it will remove the need to think about the server-side until the game concept is validated.

You can use GPGS for turn-based and real-time multiplayer games. Although each one is completely different and uses a different API, there is always an initial step where the game is set up and the opponents are selected or invited.

In a turn-based multiplayer game, a single shared state is passed among the players and only the player that owns the turn has permission to modify it. Players take turns asynchronously according to an order of play determined by the game.

A turn is finished explicitly by the player using an API call. Then the game state is passed to the other players, together with the turn.

There are many cases: selecting opponents, creating a match, leaving a match, canceling, and so on. The official documentation at `https://developers.google.com/games/services/android/turnbasedMultiplayer` is quite exhaustive and you should read through it if you plan to use this feature.

In a real-time multiplayer there is no concept of turn. Instead, the server uses the concept of room: a virtual construct that enables network communication between multiple players in the same game session and lets players send data directly to one another, a common concept for game servers.

 Real-time multiplayer service is based on the concept of Room.

The API of real-time multiplayer allows us to easily:

- Manage network connections to create and maintain a real-time multiplayer room

- Provide a player-selection user interface to invite players to join a room, look for random players for auto-matching, or a combination of both

- Store participant and room-state information on the Play Game services' servers while the game is running

- Send room invitations and updates to players

To check the complete documentation for real-time games, please visit the official web at `https://developers.google.com/games/services/android/realtimeMultiplayer`.

Summary

We have added Google Play services to YASS, including setting up the game in the developer console and adding the required libraries to the project.

Then, we defined a set of achievements and added the code to unlock them. We have used normal, incremental, and hidden achievement types to showcase the different options available.

We have also configured a leaderboard and submitted the scores, both when the game is finished and when it is exited via the pause dialog.

Finally, we have added links to the native UI for leaderboards and achievements to the main menu.

We have also introduced the concepts of events, quests, and gifts and the features of saved games and multiplayer that Google Play Game services offers.

The game is ready to publish now. In the next chapter, we will see how to make it work on Android TV.

10
To the Big Screen

We have a game that runs properly on phones and tablets. So what about Android TV?

I believe Android TV has the potential to become a big gaming platform in the near future. Although other systems have tried to bring Android games to the big screen—namely OUYA, GameStick, and Amazon FireTV—there is a major difference: Android TV is not designed to be a box you plug into your TV but rather the Operating System in your SmartTV.

That makes a lot of difference because people will have it by default. I was skeptical about OUYA until I tried it. It was a great experience, but if I hadn't been an Android game developer I probably would not have tried it. Android TV can break that barrier.

In addition to that, adding support to Android TV is fairly simple and it may allow you to get more reach, so, why not do it anyway?

TVs are different from phones, they are bigger and they do not have a touch screen. They are also usually watched from a larger distance. Because of that Android TV has a different UI and some extra requirements for apps to run on it.

The main requirements when it comes to porting a game to Android TV are to support landscape orientation and be usable with a controller. We already do that. If your game does not support landscape or is not designed to work with a gamepad, then porting to Android TV will require a lot more work and may not be the best investment for your time; however, if you have landscape and controller support, go for it!

Project configuration

There are two different approaches to adding Android TV to your project. They are conceptually different but the code you have to write is almost the same for both of them, although in different places. According to the characteristics of your project, you may prefer one or another. These options are:

- Building a separate APK for Android TV
- Using the same APK for phones, tablets, and TVs

The default option of Android Studio is to create a build variant for Android TV. It did that when we used the wizard to set up our project and we added TV support. That is why we have the `mobile` and `tv` directories. The main project is `mobile` and `tv` is configured to be a build variant or "flavor".

Flavors are a powerful way to build different APKs from the same code base, allowing us to modify parts, be it code or resources. It is particularly useful when you have to publish the same game in different markets. On the other hand, if you have a single APK, it has to be able to adapt to the different configurations on its own.

Each approach has advantages and disadvantages.

Some reasons why you would want to have a separate APK for Android TV are:

- Using a lower target API for the mobile version (Android TV requires target SDK 21 – Lollipop)
- Using higher-resolution assets for TV without including them into the mobile package
- Having separated special features for mobile/TV

On the other hand, the main advantages of having a single APK are:

- Easier to publish (only one file to upload)
- Easier to maintain

Given that we will not have any special features built in for Android TV, we are going to use the single-APK approach. Note that, if you want to do a build variant, the modifications are almost the same, but done in the `tv` directory instead.

 Publishing on Android TV requires target SDK 21.

The official documentation suggests that we include the `Leanback` library, which requires `minSDK` version 17. Since we are not building an app, but a game, and the library is about UIs, we can ignore it and keep the `minSDK` to 15.

Testing for Android TV

There are several ways to test the builds for Android TV. The obvious and simplest one is to use an emulator.

Emulators for Android TV—as for phones—are virtual machines that run exactly the same version of the operating system as the real device. Therefore they are very reliable but also quite slow.

Of course, ideally you should be able to test your game on a real device. At the time of writing, there are several smart TVs announced with Android TV, but the best devices to test are the ADT-1 (Developer Kit) and the Nexus Player.

ADT-1 however is in short supply and is hard to get. The Nexus Player on the other hand is a fairly cheap device.

However, unless you require to test gameplay, navigation can be easily tested with an emulator.

 Unless you require to test gameplay, an emulator should be enough to test the game.

Note that emulators do not include Google Play Services but a real device will have them.

I also noticed that the theme on the ADT-1 is slightly different than the one on the emulator and the text on the Start button was of a different color. Nothing major, and also easy to fix.

Declaring a TV Activity

Android TV uses the Leanback interface, which is designed for big screens controlled by a remote. This UI displays apps and games in a different way from phones. The launcher is also different. Because of this, apps and games need to declare an Activity with a particular intent filter so the Leanback launcher can find them and make them available to the user.

This intent filter will declare the app to be available for launch on a Leanback interface.

The easiest way to proceed is to create a new `Activity` that extends from our normal activity and then override some methods if necessary to adapt to the TV interface. For now, we will create `YassTvActivity` that just extends `YassActivity`:

```
public class YassTvActivity extends YassActivity {
}
```

We will then declare it on `AndroidManifest.xml` with the proper intent filter:

```
<activity
  android:name=".YassTvActivity"
  android:label="@string/app_name"
  >
  <intent-filter>
    <action android:name="android.intent.action.MAIN" />
    <category
      android:name="android.intent.category.LEANBACK_LAUNCHER" />
  </intent-filter>
</activity>
```

As you can see, the intent filter is almost the same as the one for the normal launch activity except that the category has a different name (LEANBACK_LAUNCHER instead of LAUNCHER).

Note that on Android you cannot declare the same activity twice on the manifest, but you can declare multiple intent filters for the same activity. You can use the same activity for both mobile and TV, like this:

```
<activity
  android:screenOrientation="sensorLandscape"
  android:name=".YassActivity"
  android:hardwareAccelerated="false"
  android:label="@string/title_activity_main" >
  <intent-filter>
    <action android:name="android.intent.action.MAIN" />
    <category android:name="android.intent.category.LAUNCHER" />
  </intent-filter>
  <intent-filter>
    <action android:name="android.intent.action.MAIN" />
    <category
      android:name="android.intent.category.LEANBACK_LAUNCHER" />
  </intent-filter>
</activity>
```

We are going to use a separate activity to allow minor tweaks in the code, but keep the possibility of having the same activity with two intent filters in mind, although I advise using it only if you are sure that you will not need to override anything.

There is no way to define qualifiers for TV, and that has been done purposefully by the Android team to enforce responsive layout design. The only way to know we are running on a TV is to programmatically check for the Leanback feature or to use a specific activity for TVs and override some methods on it.

Providing a home screen banner

Android TV apps must declare a banner in the manifest. This is another requirement that does not exist for mobile apps.

The banner is used by the Leanback UI to navigate among apps and games. It has a different aspect ratio than the icon. In particular, the banner is an image of 320x180 px that we have to put under the `drawable-xhdpi` directory.

The banner is a 320x180 px image

This image is as important for TV as the icon is for mobile, it is the entry point to your game on the TV. While we—as developers—can install and run apps on a TV without providing this, there is no easy entry point to launch the app from the Leanback UI without providing the banner.

To define which image is to be used as the banner, we need to add it as one of the attributes of the `<appication>` tag in the `AndroidManifest.xml`.

```
<application
   [...]
   android:banner="@drawable/banner_small" >
```

This attribute was introduced on Lollipop and it is one of the reasons why we need to compile with target SDK 21 to be able to publish for Android TV.

Our game in the Leanback UI of an emulator

Declaring it as a game

As you can see in the previous screenshot, the Leanback UI separates apps from games, and our game is listed among the apps. We are building a game and we want to be classified as such.

This is another property of the `<application>` tag that was also introduced in Lollipop for Android TV; we can declare the app to be a game.

```
<application
   [...]
   android:isGame="true">
```

This will show the banner in the **Games** category.

YASS listed in the Games category on an ADT-1

Declaring Leanback support

To allow Google Play to list our game when searching from an Android TV, we need to specifically declare that we support the Leanback UI. To do that, we have to declare that we use the Leanback feature:

```
<uses-feature android:name="android.software.leanback"
    android:required="false" />
```

Note that we declare that we use it but we mark it as not required. This is important because otherwise the game will not appear for devices that do not have the Leanback feature. If we were to have two separate APKs, we should mark this feature as required on the TV build variant only.

Declaring a uses-feature means that your app makes use of it. Marking it as not required means that it can do without it, but it will make use of it if present.

 Declaring a uses-feature means that your app makes use of it. Marking it as not required means that it can do without it.

If you are using separate APKs for mobile and TV, you should declare the uses-feature for Leanback only on the TV build variant and do nothing on the mobile one. By doing that, the TV APK will appear only on devices with Leanback UI and the mobile APK will appear only on devices without Leanback support.

The default state for the Leanback feature is to not be required.

Declaring touchscreen capability as not required

Because of how the uses-feature system works, we need to fix the requested features to make our game available on Android TV. Essentially this means that we cannot ask for features that the TV does not have, otherwise the game will not appear as available for it.

This is not as simple as it looks since some features get automatically included without doing anything.

Because of the nature of Android, touchscreen capability is required by default but, if we don't mark it as not required, the game will not be listed on Google Play for Android TV, since the device does not have a touchscreen.

 The touchscreen feature is required by default on Android apps.

This is really easy to fix, we just need to declare touchscreen capability as not required on the AndroidManifest.xml.

```
<uses-feature android:name="android.hardware.touchscreen"
    android:required="false" />
```

Note that this also means that the game should be completely usable without a touchscreen. For that we have a special section about handling menus with a controller later in this chapter.

There are other features that are not available on Android TV and you must make sure to mark them as not required (and handle cases when they are not available) if you use them. The features are:

- Touchscreen: android.hardware.touchscreen
- Touchscreen emulator: android.hardware.faketouch
- Telephony: android.hardware.telephony
- Camera: android.hardware.camera

- Bluetooth: `android.hardware.bluetooth`
- Near Field Communications (NFC): `android.hardware.nfc`
- GPS: `android.hardware.location.gps`
- Microphone: `android.hardware.microphone`
- Sensors: `android.hardware.sensor`

For games only, the touchscreen and sensor aspect may be worrying, but there are games that use location and/or the camera as an integral part of the game. This may be a deal-breaker when it comes to bringing the game to the TV.

 If your game relies on GPS or the Camera, it's probably not a good fit for a TV.

In addition to this, some `uses-permission` declarations imply a requirement for hardware features. The permissions that implicitly require features are:

- `RECORD_AUDIO` requires the use of `android.hardware.microphone`.
- `CAMERA` requires:
    - `android.hardware.camera`
    - `android.hardware.camera.autofocus`
- `ACCESS_COARSE_LOCATION` requires:
    - `android.hardware.location`
    - `android.hardware.location.network`
- `ACCESS_FINE_LOCATION` requires:
    - `android.hardware.location`
    - `android.hardware.location.gps`

If you use any of these permissions, you should ensure to mark the appropriate feature as not required and act accordingly when not present.

To detect if a feature is present or not to enable or disable some parts of the game on runtime, you can use the `hasSystemFeature` method of `PackageManager`. Like this:

```
getPackageManager().hasSystemFeature(
    "android.hardware.touchscreen")
```

Note that `getPackageManager` is available at the `Context` level, so you can access it from the `Activity`.

Reviewing the manifest

Once we have added the activity for the TV to the Leanback launcher, made sure that the Leanback and touchscreen features are requested but not required, configured the banner, and marked it as a game, we are done modifying `AndroidManifest.xml`.

The updated version of the manifest is as follows:

```xml
<?xml version="1.0" encoding="utf-8"?>
<manifest xmlns:android="http://schemas.android.com/apk/res/android"
  package="com.plattysoft.yass" >

  <application
    android:icon="@mipmap/ic_launcher"
    android:label="@string/app_name"
    android:isGame="true"
    android:banner="@drawable/banner_small"
    android:theme="@style/AppTheme" >

    <uses-feature android:name="android.software.leanback"
      android:required="false" />

    <uses-feature android:name="android.hardware.touchscreen"
      android:required="false" />

    <meta-data android:name="com.google.android.gms.games.APP_ID"
      android:value="@string/app_id" />
    <meta-data android:name="com.google.android.gms.version"
      android:value="@integer/google_play_services_version"/>

    <activity
      android:screenOrientation="sensorLandscape"
      android:name=".YassActivity"
      android:hardwareAccelerated="false"
      android:label="@string/title_activity_main" >
      <intent-filter>
        <action android:name="android.intent.action.MAIN" />
        <category android:name="android.intent.category.LAUNCHER"
          />
      </intent-filter>
    </activity>
```

```
    <activity
       android:name=".YassTvActivity"
       android:label="@string/app_name" >
       <intent-filter>
          <action android:name="android.intent.action.MAIN" />
          <category
             android:name="android.intent.category.LEANBACK_LAUNCHER"
                />
       </intent-filter>
    </activity>
  </application>
</manifest>
```

Showing controller instructions

One of the special requirements for an app to be approved for Android TV is to provide a dialog indicating how the controller is mapped. For this Google provides us with a template that we can use and it is available online: (`http://developer.android.com/training/tv/games/index.html`).

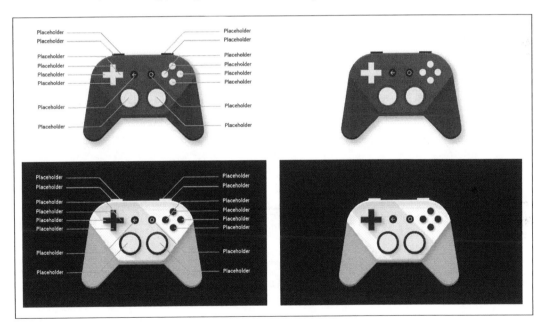

Template for controller mapping

We already have a dialog that is displayed when a controller is connected, but we never updated it from being just an `AlertDialog`. It is time we made it a custom dialog.

The logic for phones was to show the dialog only the first time the main menu was loaded and a controller was connected. For Android TV, we want a different behavior: we want to show the dialog every time the game is opened.

To do this, we are going to overwrite the method `showControllerHelp` on `MainMenuFragment` to use a custom dialog with the template image modified to include the controls of our game.

As for other custom dialogs we have already made, we have to create a layout and a class. The layout is extremely simple, just an image:

```xml
<?xml version="1.0" encoding="utf-8"?>
<RelativeLayout xmlns:android="http://schemas.android.com/apk/res/android"
  android:layout_gravity="center"
  android:background="@drawable/dialog_bg"
  android:layout_width="@dimen/dialog_width"
  android:layout_height="@dimen/dialog_height">

  <ImageView
    android:id="@+id/controller_help_image"
    android:layout_width="wrap_content"
    android:layout_height="wrap_content"
    android:layout_centerInParent="true"
    android:src="@drawable/controller_help"/>

</RelativeLayout>
```

And the class is also very simple thanks to `BaseCustomDialog`:

```java
public class ControllerHelpDialog extends BaseCustomDialog implements
View.OnClickListener {
  public ControllerHelpDialog(YassActivity a) {
    super(a);
    setContentView(R.layout.dialog_controller_help);
    findViewById(
      R.id.controller_help_image).setOnClickListener(this);
  }

  @Override
  public void onClick(View v) {
    dismiss();
  }
}
```

We are setting the layout and then handling the click on the image as a dismiss. When using a controller, the dialog will only be dismissed when using the keys *B* or back; we will take care of proper key handling on dialogs later in the chapter and make it also dismiss when clicking on the *A* button.

Finally, we need to do some changes on `MainMenuFragment` to show this newly created dialog and also to modify the logic of when to show it:

```
private void displayGamepadHelp() {
    showDialog(new ControllerHelpDialog(getYassActivity()));
}

private boolean shouldDisplayGamepadHelp() {
    PackageManager pm = getYassActivity().getPackageManager();
    boolean isLeanback =
        pm.hasSystemFeature("android.software.leanback");
    if (isLeanback) {
        boolean shownAlready = YassActivity.sGamepadHelpShown;
        YassActivity.sGamepadHelpShown = true;
        return !shownAlready;
    }
    if (isGameControllerConnected()) {
        return
            PreferenceManager.getDefaultSharedPreferences(getActivity())
            .getBoolean(PREF_SHOULD_DISPLAY_GAMEPAD_HELP, true);
    }
    return false;
}
```

In the method `shouldDisplayGamePadHelp` we will check if we use the Leanback feature to know if we are on a TV or not.

If the Leanback feature is not present, we use the same code as before: we display the dialog if a controller is connected and we have not displayed it before.

As mentioned before, we will keep the logic we had for phones, but for TVs we will always display the dialog.

In the case of an Android TV, we want to show it when the app is opened. Since `shouldDisplayGamepadHelp` is executed during the `onResume` method of the fragment, we will store the fact that it has been shown already in a static variable, so the dialog is not shown again when we come back to the fragment after a game over. Then we return true if the dialog has not been shown yet.

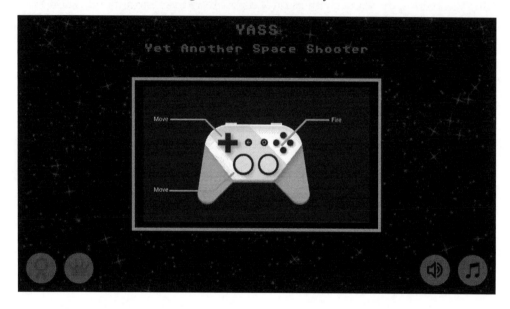

If you plan to support other controllers or consoles such as the MOGA, OUYA, or Nvidia Shield, you should have a different image for each of the controllers and detect which one is connected by using the device descriptor. In the particular case of OUYA, since it is a different marketplace, you can just have another build variant with a special graphic.

Dealing with overscan

Layouts for TV have some special requirements due to the evolution of TV standards and the desire to always present a full screen picture to viewers. For this reason, TV devices may clip the outside edge of an app layout in order to ensure that the entire display is filled. This behavior is generally referred to as **overscan**.

To avoid screen elements being clipped due to overscan, it is recommended to add a 10% margin on all sides of layouts. When talking about dips, this translates into a 48dp margin on the left and right edges and a 27dp margin on the top and bottom.

While we could just add that padding on the layout for all the devices, we will create special layouts for Android TV as a practical example of how to do it. As we mentioned before, there is no resource qualifier for TV; we have to rely on the Leanback feature being present or not.

We already have a special activity that is launched on the Leanback interface. We will also create special fragments for TV where the only difference will be the layout. To put the two pieces together, we will override the methods that create the fragments and replace them on the TV activity.

This means that we need to first extract the creation of the fragments to a method we can override. This is already the case for the GameFragment, which is created when we start a game, but not for MainMenuFragment. That fragment is only created during onCreate of the activity, so we will refactor the code by extracting the creation of the MainMenuFragment to a new method.

```
@Override
protected void onCreate(Bundle savedInstanceState) {
  super.onCreate(savedInstanceState);
  setContentView(R.layout.activity_yass);
  if (savedInstanceState == null) {
    getFragmentManager().beginTransaction()
      .add(R.id.container, createMenuFragment(), TAG_FRAGMENT)
      .commit();
  }
  [...]
}

protected Fragment createMenuFragment() {
  return new MainMenuFragment();
}

public void startGame() {
  navigateToFragment(new GameFragment());
}
```

To add the margins to the game itself, we will create a file fragment_game_tv.xml as the layout for the GameTvFragment with the following declaration:

```
<?xml version="1.0" encoding="utf-8"?>
<FrameLayout
  xmlns:android="http://schemas.android.com/apk/res/android"
  android:layout_width="match_parent"
  android:layout_gravity="center"
  android:paddingTop="27dp"
```

```
            android:paddingLeft="48dp"
            android:paddingRight="48dp"
            android:paddingBottom="27dp"
            android:background="@color/background"
            android:layout_height="match_parent">

        <include layout="@layout/fragment_game" />

    </FrameLayout>
```

We just put a `FrameLayout` at the top level with the padding required to deal with overscan and then include the layout that is normally used for the game.

Note that we use padding and not margin because we want to make the background to be a child of the `FrameLayout` so it fills the rest of the layout.

On the code side, the class for `GameTvFragment` is also quite simple:

```
    public class GameTvFragment extends GameFragment {
      @Override
      public View onCreateView(LayoutInflater inflater,
        ViewGroup container, Bundle savedInstanceState) {
        return inflater.inflate(R.layout.fragment_game_tv,
          container, false);
      }
    }
```

We extend `GameFragment` and override the method `onCreateView` to use the alternative layout we just created. Since the normal layout is imported, all the views keep their ids and nothing else is necessary for the `GameTvFragment` to work.

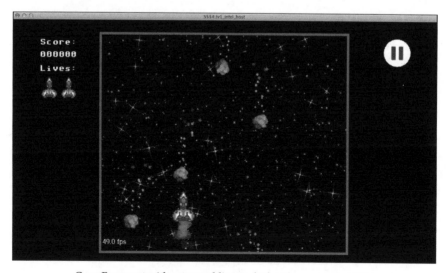

GameFragment with extra padding to deal with overscan on TVs

The case of the main menu is a bit more complicated because of the background image being an `ImageView` inside the layout. We have two possible solutions:

- Import the layout as before and set the visibility of the background image to GONE

- Extract all the common layout to a new file and import it on both the mobile and the TV layouts

The last option is easier to read and maintain, so we will do it that way.

We'll move all the layout information to a new file named `fragment_main_menu_common.xml`, which is essentially all the layout except the background image, which will go on each of the other layouts.

Then we create two files for the different layouts; the one for mobiles looks like this:

```xml
<?xml version="1.0" encoding="utf-8"?>
<FrameLayout
  xmlns:android="http://schemas.android.com/apk/res/android"
  android:layout_width="match_parent"
  android:layout_height="match_parent" >
  <ImageView
    android:id="@+id/main_menu_bg"
    android:layout_width="match_parent"
    android:layout_height="match_parent"
    android:scaleType="centerCrop"
    android:src="@drawable/seamless_space_0"/>

  <include layout="@layout/fragment_main_menu_common" />
</FrameLayout>
```

Simple enough—we have replaced the top level view with a `FrameLayout`, added the background, and included the common elements.

The layout for Android TV is essentially the same, but we add margins to the imported layout:

```xml
<?xml version="1.0" encoding="utf-8"?>
<FrameLayout
  xmlns:android="http://schemas.android.com/apk/res/android"
  android:layout_width="match_parent"
  android:layout_gravity="center"
  android:layout_height="match_parent">
  <ImageView
    android:layout_width="match_parent"
    android:layout_height="match_parent"
```

```
        android:scaleType="centerCrop"
        android:src="@drawable/seamless_space_0"/>

    <include layout="@layout/fragment_main_menu_common"
        android:layout_width="match_parent"
        android:layout_height="match_parent"
        android:layout_marginTop="27dp"
        android:layout_marginLeft="48dp"
        android:layout_marginRight="48dp"
        android:layout_marginBottom="27dp"/>
</FrameLayout>
```

Note that, to make the margins work with an `include` tag, you also need to set the `width` and the `height` but, thankfully, Android Studio gives us a warning on that.

Going into the code, we will implement a different way of doing the layout replacement on the TV fragment. We will extract the layout resource id to a method that can be overridden on the extended class. We will do it like this for the `MainMenuFragment`. This technique is especially useful when your fragment does some work during `onCreateView`.

The code on `MainMenuFragment` will be slightly modified to extract the layout resource to a method:

```
@Override
public final View onCreateView(LayoutInflater inflater, ViewGroup
container,
  Bundle savedInstanceState) {
  return inflater.inflate(getLayoutResId(), container, false);
}


protected int getLayoutResId() {
  return R.layout.fragment_main_menu;
}
```

Since we are extracting the layout because we do not want to override `onCreateView`, we are also declaring it final.

Now the `MainMenuTvFragment` class is just like this:

```
public class MainMenuTvFragment extends MainMenuFragment {
  @Override
  protected int getLayoutResId() {
    return R.layout.fragment_main_menu_tv;
  }
}
```

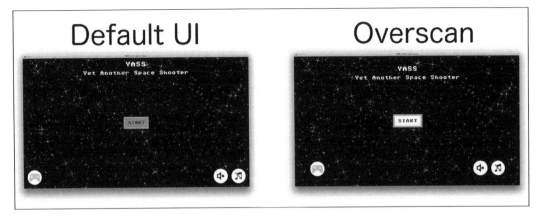

The main menu before and after applying margins for overscan

Finally, we have to override the specific methods that create the fragments in
`YassTvActivity`. At last some code is added into that class:

```
public class YassTvActivity extends YassActivity {

  public void startGame() {
    // Navigate the the game fragment, which makes the start
automatically
    navigateToFragment( new GameTvFragment());
  }

  protected Fragment createMenuFragment() {
    return new MainMenuTvFragment();
  }
}
```

Now that we have illustrated how to solve the problem of overscan in a few different
ways, let's move on to the last aspect: navigating the game with a controller.

Controller-based navigation

The most complex requirement for Android TV is that all the options of the game
must be accessible using a controller. If you are planning to release on console, you
should think about it in advance and not make overly complicated menus or dialogs.

 For Android TV, all the options in the game must be accessible using
a gamepad.

This is where the use of the native Android UI comes in handy. The Android framework handles directional navigation between layout elements automatically, so in principle you do not need to make any extra effort. However, you should still test the navigation with a controller to see if there are any navigation problems.

Users can also navigate your app using the arrow keys on a keyboard (the behavior is the same as when navigating with a D-Pad or trackball). Android provides a best-guess as to which view should be given focus in a given direction based on the layout of the views on screen. Sometimes, however, Android might guess wrong.

If the system does not pass focus to the view we want when navigating, we can override it by specifying which view should receive focus with the following attributes:

- `android:nextFocusUp`
- `android:nextFocusDown`
- `android:nextFocusLeft`
- `android:nextFocusRight`

Generally speaking, you should always have the A button provide the positive action and the B button provide the back action. Some controllers (such as the one on the ADT-1) provide dedicated back and home buttons, which should also work as such. All this is already handled by Android for you.

> The A button should always be a positive action and the B button should act as cancel/back.

In our case, there are a few problems with YASS that we have to address to provide full navigation. These problems are interesting because they are also common pitfalls.

If we run the game now we can see that the only focusable control on the main menu is the start button. It is not possible to navigate to any other view. This is a non-obvious particularity of the Android framework: `ImageView` is not focusable by default.

> ImageViews are not focusable by default.

Luckily we have defined a style for the round buttons. We can set `focusable` to true on the style and it will apply to all round buttons in the application:

```
<style name="iconButton" >
  <item name="android:background">@drawable/icon_button_bg</item>
  <item name="android:layout_width">@dimen/btn_round_size</item>
  <item name="android:layout_height">@dimen/btn_round_size</item>
  <item name="android:padding">@dimen/round_button_padding</item>
  <item name="android:focusable">true</item>
</style>
```

We could also use `ImageButton` instead of `ImageView`, which is focusable by default, but I think making the `ImageView` focusable is clearer.

Now we can navigate around the menu with the controller and we can see that the default navigation Android provides is good. The next step is to check the dialogs.

There are a couple of side effects when we interact with dialogs. Since they are not the standard Android dialogs, focus can be moved out of the dialog. Also the `GameFragment` uses a game input controller that is taking care of all the events. We need to do some fixes.

Dialogs and controllers

We are going to solve the problems one at a time. The first one is that focus can go to views outside the dialog.

This can be easily replicated by opening the game and moving the focus over the buttons on the background while the controller help dialog is present. The same issue is present on the quit dialog. In both cases, we can start a game with the dialog on top, which is wrong.

For touch, we solved that with the background view that acts as a click screen getting all the clicks and not letting the event pass to the other views behind it. For the controller navigation, however, we need something else.

There are several ways to fix this. One is to override the navigation on the layout; another is to ignore `onClick` events on the fragment if a dialog is being shown. We are going for yet another approach: passing the key events to the dialogs and filtering them there.

This approach also solves the second problem: while in a game, the input controller collects and consumes the controller presses.

Since all the `KeyEvent` and `MotionEvent` handling is done at activity level, we are going to do a small refactoring and move the logic of showing a dialog from the fragment to the activity.

We will move the method `showDialog` and the variable `mCurrentDialog` from `YassBaseFragment` to `YassActivity`.

In the base fragment we just have to replace the code of the `showDialog` method with this:

```
public void showDialog (BaseCustomDialog newDialog,
    boolean dismissOtherDialog) {
    getYassActivity().showDialog(newDialog, dismissOtherDialog);
}
```

The next step is to refactor the `dispatchKeyEvent` and `dispatchGenericMotionEvent` methods of `YassActivity` by making the dialog have preference over the input controller.

The updated version of `dispatchKeyEvent` is as follows:

```
@Override
public boolean dispatchKeyEvent (KeyEvent event) {
    if (mCurrentDialog != null && mCurrentDialog.isShowing()) {
        if (mCurrentDialog.dispatchKeyEvent(event)) {
            return true;
        }
    }
    else if (mGamepadControllerListener != null) {
        if (mGamepadControllerListener.dispatchKeyEvent(event)) {
            return true;
        }
    }
    return super.dispatchKeyEvent(event);
}
```

If the current dialog is not null and it is showing, then we call a method on it also called `dispatchKeyEvent`. If the key event was consumed (the method returned true) we return true.

Similarly we proceed with the gamepad controller listener if no dialog is being shown. We also return true if the event was consumed by the gamepad controller.

Finally, if the event was not consumed yet, we call the super method, which will take care of the event normally. This includes moving the focus around the views.

Similarly, we will modify dispatchGenericMotionEvent. Although we are not going to override any of those events on our dialogs, if you plan to customize navigation with the directional keys you also have to take care of the analog joysticks and you will need this method for that:

```
@Override
public boolean dispatchGenericMotionEvent(MotionEvent event) {
  if (mCurrentDialog != null && mCurrentDialog.isShowing()) {
    if (mCurrentDialog.dispatchGenericMotionEvent(event)) {
      return true;
    }
  }
  else if (mGamepadControllerListener != null) {
    if (mGamepadControllerListener.dispatchGenericMotionEvent(event)
) {
      return true;
    }
  }
  return super.dispatchGenericMotionEvent(event);
}
```

Finally, we have to update the handling of the back key:

```
@Override
public void onBackPressed() {
  if (mCurrentDialog != null && mCurrentDialog.isShowing()) {
    mCurrentDialog.dismiss();
    return;
  }
  final YassBaseFragment fragment = (YassBaseFragment)
    getFragmentManager().findFragmentByTag(TAG_FRAGMENT);
  if (fragment == null || !fragment.onBackPressed()) {
    super.onBackPressed();
  }
}
```

If we are showing a dialog, we just dismiss it. Otherwise we keep the code we had before: we ask the current fragment to handle the back key press and, if the event was not consumed, we pass it to the parent class.

Note that passing the back key event to the current fragment is important. In our game a back press while in the GameFragment means that we want to pause the game.

To complete this, we have to make the dialogs handle the keys. The default implementation on `BaseCustomDialog` is to just return false, meaning that the event was not consumed:

```
public boolean dispatchKeyEvent(KeyEvent event) {
  return false;
}

public boolean dispatchGenericMotionEvent(MotionEvent event) {
  return false;
}
```

We are going to do a very simple handling where we will only process the OK click when one of the buttons on the dialog is selected, but you could also prevent the focus from going to views outside the dialog with a more elaborate handling.

For `ControllerHelpDialog`, we will just dismiss it whenever an **OK** is pressed, regardless of which view is in focus:

```
public boolean dispatchKeyEvent(KeyEvent event) {
  if (event.getKeyCode() == KeyEvent.KEYCODE_BUTTON_A ||
      event.getKeyCode() == KeyEvent.KEYCODE_ENTER ||
      event.getKeyCode() == KeyEvent.KEYCODE_DPAD_CENTER) {
    dismiss();
    return true;
  }
  return false;
}
```

Note that, from the controller point of view, the **A** button is the **OK** button, but certain controllers also have the D-Pad center button and sometimes the *Enter* key, so we accept any of those key events as an **OK**.

In the case of the Quit dialog, the code is slightly different:

```
public boolean dispatchKeyEvent(KeyEvent event) {
  if (event.getKeyCode() == KeyEvent.KEYCODE_BUTTON_A ||
      event.getKeyCode() == KeyEvent.KEYCODE_ENTER ||
      event.getKeyCode() == KeyEvent.KEYCODE_DPAD_CENTER) {
    if (findViewById(R.id.btn_resume).isFocused() ||
        findViewById(R.id.btn_exit).isFocused()) {
      // Return false, so a proper click is sent
      return false;
    }
    return true;
  }
  return false;
}
```

In this dialog, whenever we get an OK event, we check if one of our buttons is focused. If that is the case, we return false, meaning that we let the upper level process it. That will pass the event to the activity, when it will be processed and sent back as a click.

If none of our actions are focused, we return true, meaning that we are consuming the event and nothing else should be done with it.

In any other case, we return false (again, not consuming the event) to let the activity handle the key event normally.

Finally, in the case of the pause and game over dialogs that are shown in the GameFragment, we do not need to do anything because the only item that is focusable on that UI is the pause button.

What we will do is set the pause button to not focusable and then let the system handle the keys:

```
< ImageView
  style="@style/iconButton"
  android:focusable="false"
  android:layout_gravity="top|right"
  android:id="@+id/btn_play_pause"
  android:layout_marginTop="@dimen/menu_margin"
  android:layout_marginRight="@dimen/menu_margin"
  android:src="@drawable/pause" />
```

Note that, while ImageView is not focusable by default, we have set that property at the style level, and we can always overwrite the value of the style in the definition of the layout.

With all this changes all the UI of our game is usable with a gamepad and we are finally ready to publish on Android TV.

Beyond this book

We made it! We have built a game from scratch using the Android SDK. We have built a game engine that has a separate UpdateThread and DrawThread, we have sprites that can move around, we have handled touch and gamepad controllers, and added collision detection, sound, and even particles.

We have also used the components of the Android framework to build our menus and dialogs and made use of the animation tools to make it more dynamic.

YASS also has achievements and leaderboards using Google Play Game Services and now it is ready to be played on Android TV as well.

At this point, there are a few things that can be done to improve the game and that can be a good exercise to help you move forward, if you feel like it. Some ideas are:

- Spawn multiple waves with increasing difficulty
- Include bigger asteroids that break in smaller parts when hit
- Add ship selection: provide several ships with different characteristics (speed, fire ratio, and so on)
- Implement power-ups like shields or improved lasers

While this book focuses on the development of a game, there are other aspects of making a game that have been overlooked but are also very important. The most relevant of them are game design and monetization.

 Game design and monetization are key aspects of making a game.

Game design is a discipline-independent from platform and code and it requires high-level considerations about the game itself. Game design is about making a game that is fun and engages the user. There are many books that are dedicated solely to this concept and it is beyond the scope of this book.

Monetization is also a big topic nowadays. If you plan to release a game just for fun you do not need to worry about it, but if you mean to make some money out of it, it is something to be evaluated.

The main options to monetize a game are:

- **Premium**: Make it a paid game
- **Ads**: Monetize the game by showing ads to the user, either banners or interstitials
- **In-App Purchases**: Offer the user the chance to purchase items inside the game

The advantage of making a paid game is that it is much simpler to build and it will give you fewer headaches.

Some examples of premium games that have done well on mobile are Monument Valley, Threes, and The Room (1 and 2).

The advantage of a free game, either with ads or In-App Purchases, is that the install barrier is the lowest there is. If someone is interested in the game, installing it is free. Paying for a game requires a conscious decision and many people will opt out, regardless of the price.

If you are planning to go the Free2Play road, be ready to worry about retention and conversion of the players. You will get familiar with terms like DAU, MAU, ARPU, and ARPPU, to name a few.

Some examples of successful free games with different monetization schemes are Candy Crush Saga, Clash of Clans, and Angry Birds.

Most studies will tell you that people make more money with In-App Purchases than with paid apps. While that it is true, creating a Free2Play game that monetizes well requires time and effort to tune it right; so does designing compelling In-App Purchases.

In my experience, making a good monetization design for a Free2Play game takes about as much time as making the game itself. If you do not design it carefully, you can get really low conversion rates, which turns into little or no revenue.

As a rule of thumb, do not push a monetization model in a game that does not feel right and invest your efforts into making the game fun.

Summary

We have our game ready for Android TV. We have updated the manifest to provide an activity to launch from the Leanback interface as well as a banner to show on the UI, and we have marked it as a game. We also reviewed the permissions to be sure that the game will be available on Google Play for Android TV, mainly marking touchscreen capability and Leanback as requested but not required.

From the code point of view, we added some extra padding to all the screens when running on the TV, to make sure the important content is never cut off because of overscan, and we tweaked the code on the dialogs to make them work nicely with controllers.

Finally we mentioned some pointers about how to improve the game further and talked briefly about game design and monetization.

It is time to start making your own game. Good luck and have fun!

API Levels for Android Versions

The following table shows the API levels of different Android platform versions, along with the version code:

Platform Version	API Level	VERSION_CODE
Android 5.1	22	`LOLLIPOP_MR1`
Android 5.0	21	`LOLLIPOP`
Android 4.4W	20	`KITKAT_WATCH`
Android 4.4	19	`KITKAT`
Android 4.3	18	`JELLY_BEAN_MR2`
Android 4.2, 4.2.2	17	`JELLY_BEAN_MR1`
Android 4.1, 4.1.1	16	`JELLY_BEAN`
Android 4.0.3, 4.0.4	15	`ICE_CREAM_SANDWICH_MR1`
Android 4.0, 4.0.1, 4.0.2	14	`ICE_CREAM_SANDWICH`
Android 3.2	13	`HONEYCOMB_MR2`
Android 3.1.x	12	`HONEYCOMB_MR1`
Android 3.0.x	11	`HONEYCOMB`
Android 2.3.4 Android 2.3.3	10	`GINGERBREAD_MR1`

Platform Version	API Level	VERSION_CODE
Android 2.3.2 Android 2.3.1 Android 2.3	9	GINGERBREAD
Android 2.2.x	8	FROYO
Android 2.1.x	7	ECLAIR_MR1
Android 2.0.1	6	ECLAIR_0_1
Android 2.0	5	ECLAIR
Android 1.6	4	DONUT
Android 1.5	3	CUPCAKE
Android 1.1	2	BASE_1_1
Android 1.0	1	BASE

Index

Thank you for buying
Mastering Android Game Development

About Packt Publishing

Packt, pronounced 'packed', published its first book, *Mastering phpMyAdmin for Effective MySQL Management*, in April 2004, and subsequently continued to specialize in publishing highly focused books on specific technologies and solutions.

Our books and publications share the experiences of your fellow IT professionals in adapting and customizing today's systems, applications, and frameworks. Our solution-based books give you the knowledge and power to customize the software and technologies you're using to get the job done. Packt books are more specific and less general than the IT books you have seen in the past. Our unique business model allows us to bring you more focused information, giving you more of what you need to know, and less of what you don't.

Packt is a modern yet unique publishing company that focuses on producing quality, cutting-edge books for communities of developers, administrators, and newbies alike. For more information, please visit our website at www.packtpub.com.

About Packt Open Source

In 2010, Packt launched two new brands, Packt Open Source and Packt Enterprise, in order to continue its focus on specialization. This book is part of the Packt Open Source brand, home to books published on software built around open source licenses, and offering information to anybody from advanced developers to budding web designers. The Open Source brand also runs Packt's Open Source Royalty Scheme, by which Packt gives a royalty to each open source project about whose software a book is sold.

Writing for Packt

We welcome all inquiries from people who are interested in authoring. Book proposals should be sent to author@packtpub.com. If your book idea is still at an early stage and you would like to discuss it first before writing a formal book proposal, then please contact us; one of our commissioning editors will get in touch with you.

We're not just looking for published authors; if you have strong technical skills but no writing experience, our experienced editors can help you develop a writing career, or simply get some additional reward for your expertise.

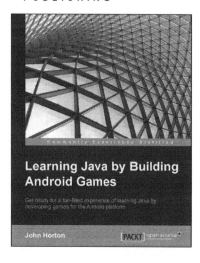

Learning Java by Building Android Games

ISBN: 978-1-78439-885-9   Paperback: 392 pages

Get ready for a fun-filled experience of learning Java by developing games for the Android platform

1. Acquaint yourself with Java and object-oriented programming, from zero previous experience.

2. Build four cool games for your phone and tablet, from retro arcade-style games to memory and education games, and gain the knowledge to design and create your own games too.

3. Walk through the fundamentals of building games and use that experience as a springboard to study advanced game development or just have fun.

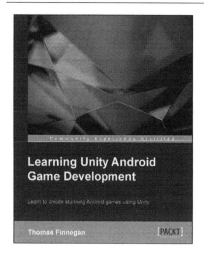

Learning Unity Android Game Development

ISBN: 978-1-78439-469-1   Paperback: 338 pages

Learn to create stunning Android games using Unity

1. Leverage the new features of Unity 5 for the Android mobile market with hands-on projects and real-world examples.

2. Create comprehensive and robust games using various customizations and additions available in Unity such as camera, lighting, and sound effects.

3. Precise instructions to use Unity to create an Android-based mobile game.

Please check **www.PacktPub.com** for information on our titles

Unity Android Game Development by Example Beginner's Guide

ISBN: 978-1-84969-201-4   Paperback: 320 pages

Learn how to create exciting games using Unity 3D for Android with the help of hands-on examples

1. Enter the increasingly popular mobile market and create games using Unity 3D and Android.

2. Learn optimization techniques for efficient mobile games.

3. Clear, step-by-step instructions for creating a complete mobile game experience.

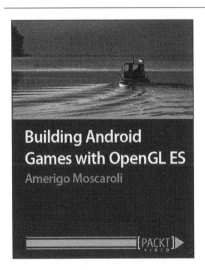

Building Android Games with OpenGL ES [Video]

ISBN: 978-1-78328-613-3   Duration: 01:42 hours

A comprehensive course exploring the creation of beautiful games with OpenGL ES

1. Create captivating games through creating simple and effective codes in Java.

2. Develop a version of the classic game Breakout and see how to monetize it.

3. Step-by-step instructions and theoretical concepts describe each activity before you implement them.

Please check **www.PacktPub.com** for information on our titles

Made in the USA
Lexington, KY
06 April 2016